D0098819

ATLANTIC
FEVER

Also by Edward Jablonski

ATLANTIC
FEVER

by
Edward
Jablonski

THE MACMILLAN COMPANY
New York, New York

Copyright © 1972 by Edward Jablonski

All rights reserved. No part of this book may be reproduced or transmitted in any form or by any means, electronic or mechanical, including photocopying, recording or by any information storage and retrieval system, without permission in writing from the Publisher.

The Macmillan Company

866 Third Avenue, New York, N.Y. 10022

Collier-Macmillan Canada Ltd., Toronto, Ontario

Library of Congress Catalog Card Number: 78-160375

First Printing

Printed in the United States of America

*For
Emily*

Contents

Prelude

Among the several motivations for crossing the Atlantic Ocean—fame, fortune, linking the commercial communities on either side—perhaps as powerful as any is a simple one, to paraphrase a mountaineer: the fact that it is there. Its watery vastness, its shifting surface and skies, its very unpredictability, fulfill any number of the requirements of the man searching for adventure, who hopes to accomplish what no other has done before: to be The First. To pit one's intelligence, skill and strength against an indifferent and inexorable Nature was the highest form of enterprise; should renown and affluence follow, so much the better.

There was the other side of the coin, of course. If you should not make it, your passing would be duly noted and you would be accorded an obituary fit for a king. For a brief time, in death, you would live as never before. So the risks had their compensations and rewards, and loss was its own kind of glory.

The sea was challenge enough, but the air above was irresistible. Practically from the moment he had learned to lift himself by mechanical means off the surface of the earth, man's dreams turned to the crossing of watery obstacles by air. As early as 1785 the English Channel had been crossed by balloonists Jean-Pierre Blanchard and Dr. John Jeffries (the latter an American) for the first time.

The Atlantic was another proposition, of course. Crossing the Channel in a drifting and dipping balloon was its own form of adversity, but even so, the greater, mysterious stretch of water beckoned. It stirred the imagination, it caused the adrenalin to flow—it sang the siren's song.

What excitement, then, when the New York *Sun* appeared on April 13, 1844, with, to quote, ASTOUNDING NEWS! And it was, for what followed was a factual account of the first crossing of the Atlantic by air in three days by an up to that moment unknown aeronaut Monck Mason and seven other adventurers. In seventy-five hours, the *Sun* reported with a plethora of exclamation points, the intrepid crew of the "Steering Balloon" *Victoria* had crossed from Britain to the United States, landing at Sullivan's Island, South Carolina. "Full Particulars of the Voyage !!!" were offered, begining with: "The great problem is at length solved. The air, as well as the earth and ocean, has been subdued by science and will become a common and convenient highway for mankind. *The Atlantic has been crossed in a balloon* and this too without difficulty, without any great apparent danger, with thorough control of the machine, and in the inconceivably brief period of seventy-five hours from shore to shore."

O brave new world!

Except that, to the *Sun*'s later chagrin, it was learned that they had been victimized by a hoaxer—generally believed to be the feverishly inventive Edgar Allan Poe—and no such voyage had ever occurred, nor did the *Victoria* or "Mr. Monck Mason" exist. Even so, the hoax had its impact. Just as Poe had probably been inspired by an announcement four years earlier by English aeronaut Charles Green that he would try to cross the Atlantic from England, the *Victoria* tale stirred the minds of practical men.

One of these was the respected American balloonist John Wise, who even a year before Poe's story broke had begun seeking financial backing for just such a venture. There appears to have been scant interest in the idea, for it was sixteen years before Wise found the money and the balloon—rather hopefully named the *Atlantic*—with which he might

John Wise (LEFT) and Thaddeus Lowe, pioneer aeronauts who made the first two attempts at crossing the Atlantic by air in balloons; neither managed to reach the Atlantic Ocean, let alone set out to fly over it. (*National Air & Space Museum, Smithsonian Institution*)

attempt the flight. In July of 1859 he set out from St. Louis, Missouri, with three others, and set course for New York. All went smoothly for a time, and as they wafted over Lake Ontario, one of the men aboard—a Mr. Hyde, a newspaperman—gazed down with some disdain upon the ships slowly scuttering over the surface of the lake. "How foolish," he exclaimed, "when air travel is here!"

His prediction had come prematurely. A sudden lake storm swept up and the *Atlantic* and its hapless passengers were tossed around frightfully as they were threatened with a plunge into the lake. They fought to remain aloft by throwing over all possible equipment, including a lifeboat. As suddenly as it had come, the storm moved onward and the *Atlantic* eventually bounced against solid land, tore through trees and finally came to rest, impaled upon a spruce, sixty feet in the air. Miraculously, no one was seriously injured. They had come to earth near Henderson, New York, and, in fact, had succeeded in making the longest balloon voyage—809 miles—up to that time. But they were still distant from the Atlantic and, after the experience at journey's end, Wise decided the time had not yet come for the Atlantic crossing.

His rival American aeronaut, Thaddeus Lowe, appears to have had a similar hope around the same time and began experimenting with large balloons for a similar voyage. Finally, in April of 1861, he set out, in a giant balloon the *Enterprise*, from Cincinnati (supposedly to take advantage of the prevailing westerly winds which would carry him Atlanticward). The theory did not quite work in practice, although the *Enterprise* did proceed in the general direction of the Atlantic, but Lowe came down nine hours later near the town of Unionville, South Carolina. He was not received with open arms, many of the locals mistaking him for some sort of envoy of the devil.

Lowe eventually ended up in jail, but was released when he was recognized as a famed balloonist by a former passenger of his. But his woe seemed unending. Out of jail, Lowe took a train to Columbia, where he was arrested as a Yankee spy. He talked himself out of that problem, but the coming of the Civil War ended his dream of an aerial conquest of the Atlantic. In fact, both Lowe and Wise offered their services to the Union in the war.

After the war Wise revived his thirty-year-old dream and, in 1873, became involved again in a transatlantic adventure, this time with the backing of the New York *Daily Graphic*. Needless to say, the enterprise did not suffer from a paucity of publicity. There was even a banner stretched across a main Manhattan thoroughfare announcing that the balloon, appropriately named *Daily Graphic*, was "now in process of construction in the show room of the Domestic Sewing Machine Co., Second and Third Floor."

As his assistant, the sixty-five-year-old Wise was given one Washington H. Donaldson, a young balloonist best known for his trapeze work while suspended under a balloon. The sponsors of the flight, the Goodsell brothers, owners of the *Graphic*, claimed that "this voyage is one of scientific inquiry and not for private gain," and editorialized—on the front page, no less—that "as soon as the aerostat is ready the party will sail without unnecessary publicity."

O brave new world, indeed.

Soon they were announcing that the "*Daily Graphic* concedes to public pressure to allow witnessing of preliminary inflation of the balloon, which will depart between September first and twelfth, depending on the weather." Soon, over Wise's objections and threats, the balloon was moved from the Brooklyn Navy Yard to the Capitaline Grounds (an exhibition area for fairs and circuses), where tickets of admission—fifty cents each—were sold to a *Graphic*-inflamed public. Quickly the whole enterprise degenerated into a literal circus—including "a brilliant pyrotechnical display"—and the unhappy Wise decided to withdraw, feeling rightly that the Goodsells were devoted to splash—even his own into the ocean—and not science.

Their total ignorance of ballooning was appalling and even before the "aerostat" was properly ready, they ordered the balloon inflated in order to fulfill their promise of its ascension before their own arbitrary deadline. They also noted in their paper that "Mr. Wise's course from the outset is marked by incapacity, cowardice, and excessive demands for money."

Perhaps, but when he advised the Goodsells during the inflation process that a certain bulge in the middle was a sign of trouble, they dismissed him with a remark that what the balloon required was not advice but a balloonist without fear. Wise must have taken little comfort, as he sadly stalked from the scene, to hear the bubble pop and the sound of escaping gas. It was October before the balloon was repaired and the "fearless" but no doubt not very experienced Donaldson took off on the flight across the Atlantic. Not exactly, however—in fact, the balloon came down, after a flight of some 40 miles, near New Canaan, Connecticut.

No really significant Atlantic attempts were made by balloon. It simply was not the vehicle for the job. While it was a beautiful way to fly—weather and winds being kindly—it was wayward and quirky. The floating peacefulness of balloon flight had its charm and dignity, of course. It was the British aviation pioneer J. T. C. Moore-Brabazon (later Lord Brabazon) who expressed something of this when he declared, "I have always said, and I say it again, that to go up in a balloon is the only way to go into the air like a gentleman." And it was writer Alan Wykes who observed so aptly, "Ballooning may be a gentlemanly way of taking to the air but it is also a very imprecise one if you have any special destination in mind."

This fact, after the failures of Wise and Lowe, may have eventually dawned upon nineteenth-century aeronauts who, though unhappy, relinquished the Atlantic to the ships at sea.

The twentieth century brought those changes which the frustrated adventurers were certain would eliminate practically all the obstacles. One was the invention of the airship around the turn of the century by Ferdinand von Zeppelin, in Germany, and refined by the Lebaudy brothers—Paul and Pierre—although the design was actually the work of one Henri Julliot in France. The airship, which depended upon some gas (usually highly inflammable hydrogen) to keep it aloft as did the balloon, improved upon that object in that it was elongated—cigarlike in form—which made it possible to attach controls of a sort to it. Another innovation was the fitting of an engine, or engines, for power. Thus was it possible to fly in a given direction at no great speed.

Still, this was an advance over the balloon, which was eternally at the mercies of the wind.

The dirigibles (so called because unlike the limp, shapeless balloon —which was filled out by gas—the form of the airship was determined by a light fabric-covered structure which contained the gasbags) were soon followed by the first true aircraft when the Wright brothers flew off the sands of Kitty Hawk on Thursday, December 17, 1903. The Wrights, as had no one before them, seem to have grasped the importance of power and control. Theirs was, therefore, the first successful modern flying machine and the ancestor of every plane that followed. But in 1903, unlike the airship, their "Flyer" was not capable of covering any great distances or of remaining aloft for any extended time; it could barely cross a small pasture pond, let alone the Atlantic Ocean.

While the heavier-than-air craft suffered its teething problems, the airship enjoyed a resurgence of life. It seemed that its age had finally come and that man would be able to conquer great distances with ease and in comfort. One of its advantages was size, and the larger it was, the more—theoretically, at least—it could lift: crew, supplies and other necessities.

Once the airship existed it was only a matter of time before the adventurer would appear upon the scene announcing his impending crossing of the Atlantic. Such was Walter Wellman, who had begun his busy professional life as a fourteen-year-old newspaperman in Sutton, Nebraska, in 1872. He worked his way eastward, marrying at twenty, and a year later founding the Cincinnati *Evening Post*. His taste for adventure led him into various attempts to reach the North Pole, two by ship and overland and three by airship, none of them successful. The last had been tried in Wellman's airship, the *America*, in 1909 and ended in the crash of the ship—though without injury to Wellman or his crew.

Wellman's fame earned him the sponsorship by both *The New York Times* and the London *Daily Telegraph* the following year of "the first flight ever to be made across the Atlantic Ocean." It was decided that the vehicle for the venture would be an airship rather than the flying machine (which few in 1910 took very seriously except as an overgrown toy of nutty sportsmen) and that the man for the job was Walter Wellman—a newspaperman himself.

Wellman set to work putting his old *America* back together, but with major differences. The original was of French design, built by Godard et Surcouf of Paris, but Wellman had his chief mechanic and engineer Melvin Vaniman create "a completely new design." The new *America* was longer by 68 feet compared to the original and finally emerged from Vaniman's workshop as an airship of the rather spectacular length of 228 feet; it was 52 feet in diameter at its greatest cross section in the middle. It was powered by two 80 horsepower engines, which turned four propel-

lers, two on either side of the gondola in which Wellman and his crew
would travel.

Besides Wellman and Vaniman, the crew consisted of assistant engineer Louis Loud and navigator Murray Simon, an Englishman who
officiated at the wheel; there were also another assistant engineer, Fred
Aubert, a twenty-year-old replacement for an earlier adventurer who
had had second thoughts, and a telegraph operator, John Irwin.

Slung under the gondola of the *America* was a large lifeboat which
carried emergency equipment and supplies and, since it was connected
to the airship by a short ladder, doubled also as a "parlor, smoking room
and dormitory."

Wellman's own peculiar contribution to the design of the *America*
was a gadget he called an "equilibrator." This was a 300-foot-long steel
cable which dangled from the aft end of the *America*'s gondola and an
ingenious device it was. Not only did it carry part of its fuel supply in
cylindrical drums which made up part of the equilibrator, but the thing
itself, according to Wellman's thinking, served to keep the airship from
rising too high above the surface of the sea. The idea was that as soon as
the *America* developed too much lift (sometimes caused by temperature
changes), the equilibrator would rise out of the water, but the weight of
wooden floats at the end, no longer buoyed up by the water, would cause
it to descend again. This would free Wellman and his crew of the waste-
ful necessity of tossing out ballast or ejecting gas. It was not, in fact, one
of Wellman's more inspired conceptions.

As work progressed on the remodeled *America* the public was kept
well-informed by the *Times* and the *Daily Telegraph* in their respective
countries, and they jointly announced that around mid-September
(1910) the flight would begin because then the weather was "expected to
be favorable." The weather, as it would soon be learned of the Atlantic,
did not cooperate and September came and went. Luckily Wellman was
not badgered by the type of promotional mind that had so sorely
afflicted Wise in his attempt nearly four decades earlier.

September merged into October and it appeared that the weather
would never be right. By the eighth the high winds that had been the
most serious problem subsided. Wellman announced that the *America*
would launch forth on the fourteenth. His intentions were good, but he
hadn't counted on the fog which enveloped the eastern coastline as far
north as Newfoundland. By this time rival newspapers began suggesting
that Wellman had no intentions of flying the Atlantic and that the
enterprise was nothing more than a promotional stunt for the *Times*.

Wellman, after reasoning that there was nothing above the Atlantic
into which they could bump, decided that they would leave the very
next morning, whatever the visibility.

A crowd of several thousand gathered that morning—Saturday, October 15, 1910—to watch the takeoff of the *America* from the Ocean Shore marina near Atlantic City, New Jersey. The air was dead calm and a thick fog lay close to the ground.

The *America* was rolled out of its hangar, with hundreds of willing assistants clinging to the guide ropes and holding it at the proper alti-

Walter Wellman (LEFT) and Melvin Vaniman, leaders of the first attempt to cross the Atlantic in the airship *America*; they managed, where Wise and Lowe failed, at least to get under way. That Wellman and Vaniman did not succeed could be attributed to the fact that airship design and the design of engines had not caught up with their dream. (*National Air & Space Museum, Smithsonian Institution*)

tude. The airship was guided, under the direction of Vaniman, to the ocean's edge. This in itself was a little milestone—neither Wise nor Lowe had ever gotten close to the ocean. The ship's tail-like equilibrator trailed along the ground leaving a track in the sand. Peering suspiciously at the fog-enshrouded waters Vaniman suggested that the *America* follow a motorboat through the shoals to avoid striking a reef—or anything—with the equilibrator before they even got properly under way.

Two boats were procured, one to precede the other to which the towline of the *America* was attached. As the crowd cheered, the trio of vessels moved slowly through the fog, gingerly avoiding all water obstacles. A British reporter aboard the second boat later wrote, "Within a

The *America* as seen from the deck of the *Trent* before Wellman and his crew abandoned the airship. The men may be seen in the lifeboat beneath the *America*. The equilibrator slashes a deadly wake through the water. (*Bain Collection: Library of Congress*)

few seconds the big airship, which floated evenly aloft about fifty feet above the level of the sea, a weirdly picturesque and impressive spectacle, was swallowed up by the fog, but at all times, as we towed her seawards, we in the motor-boat, more favourably situated than those on shore, never lost sight of the dirigible until the goodbyes were waved and we cast off the tow-line."

Particularly surprising was the ease with which the two men—the anonymous reporter and a "Mr. Chamberlin" (who happened also to be the son-in-law of Wellman)—could move the massive airship. They were "both amazed to find that we could tow the *America*, despite her tons of burden, and her huge equilibrator weighing upwards of a ton and a quarter, dragging in the water, almost as easily as we might tow a toy boat. As a measure of precaution we first placed a line round the motor's stern post, but found very soon that we could get to sea just as easily by holding the rope in our hands, and that we required no other assistance. We went slowly, the *America* trailing behind just as gracefully as a swan, and looking, as we thought, very weirdly picturesque, as she came along, moving very smoothly and majestically, and responding easily but without a jerk to every movement of the hand which held her rope.

"The last glimpse of the airship caught by those on the motor-boat disclosed Mr. Vaniman in the lifeboat below the *America*'s underhung steel car shouting orders to engineers Loud and Aubert in the engine-room to start the motors, and the dim outlines of Mr. Wellman seated on a biscuit-box in the car, with the navigator, Mr. Simon, at the wheel, it being possible to identify him by the fact that he had not yet exchanged his suit of seaman's blue for the airman's khaki, which all the rest of the crew had donned."

It was 8:30 in the morning when the towline was cast off and Vaniman ordered the engines started. They sputtered away with an assuring sound, although together they barely came up to their advertised 80 horsepower. They built up a speed of about 20 miles an hour, hardly a comfortable pace at which to cross the Atlantic. There was sufficient fuel for a ten-day trip. Wellman was, of course, counting a good deal on the prevailing winds which blew toward Europe.

When he started the engines of the *America* Vaniman initiated the first true Atlantic aerial adventure.

The engines were turned off and on through the day as Vaniman conserved fuel and the *America* nosed through the fog. Murray Simon had been, by 8:30 in the evening, at the wheel for more than twelve hours. He was tired but no less alert when suddenly looming out of the fog directly in the *America*'s path was a four-masted schooner, the *Bullard*. At that moment the *America* was roughly 100 feet above the ocean; the topmasts of the *Bullard* rose up 110 feet.

The master of the *Bullard*, Captain Sawyer, later described the effect the sudden appearance of the *America* had upon him and his crew. "There came from out of the dusk and fog the sound of a motor buzzing and the rattle of machinery. We thought that some steamer was close upon us and tooted our foghorn to warn passing vessels."

When lights appeared above them, the crew of the *Bullard* were certain they were mastlights of the "steamer." There was much shouting and running aboard the ship as all hands turned to avoid collision. All was mysterious for, though the lights were visible, no ship under them was. This did not help.

"Then out of the darkness and mist shot a big aerial phantom . . . going east and heading directly for the *Bullard*. The thing was such a big surprise for all hands that we were knocked off our pins."

Simon, at the wheel of the *America*, suffered his own surprise, but reacted instinctively as he, in his own words, "put the helm hard to starboard and just cleared her, our bilge passing over her spanker and must have given the gang aboard the deuce of a fright—we up in the air, with the motor spouting fire, and going like blazes over her, equilibrator clanking down below. . . ."

Captain Sawyer added a little to the narrative of what might have been history's first quasi-midair collision. "A muttering of voices on the ship in the air indicated very plainly that there was some excitement above us. But the airship had a perfect steering arrangement. She came at us almost like the wind [Sawyer estimated at a speed of "fifteen miles an hour"], and when almost on us she turned suddenly like a motor-car shooting around a corner, and passed harmlessly out to sea." No doubt dragging its equilibrator behind it.

After twenty hours at the wheel Simon was relieved by Wellman, and because he did not like the sleeping shelves which had been set up in the gondola, nor particularly caring for "making my way with sleep-bleared eyes down the companionway to the lifeboat," he curled up near the wheel on the deck of the gondola. By eight o'clock—it was now Sunday—he was back at the wheel and noting in his log:

> A bad time. We know now that we can never get across the Atlantic and the experiment is over. The action of the equilibrator is something fierce. Dragging behind us, it tries to pull our nose into the water. It drives us forward on our nose till the waves splash over the lifeboat. Wind freshening, hauling out of the west and south-west.

Within hours it was obvious that the *America* and its crew were due for a lashing storm at sea. The heightened wind tossed the waves in giant swells below them and had its effect upon their equilibrator. "I thought the ship would go to pieces at any moment," Simon later noted, "The equilibrator drags and pulls, riding over the seas, jerking and shocking the ship and setting up a rolling motion which threatens our total destruction."

The coming of night brought no alleviation of the storm and Wellman realized that they would have to take desperate measures if they were to survive. Aubert, the youngest member of the crew, meanwhile made his way into the lifeboat where he prepared bacon and eggs (one might assume, scrambled) which Wellman pronounced, "The most delicious I have ever tasted."

He then set Aubert upon his next task: breaking up the aft engine and throwing it overboard in order to lighten the load. They were dangerously close to the whipping waves and they needed altitude. That proved to be little help, for as the night went on the wind became more savage—"a velocity of fifty miles an hour," in Wellman's estimation. Soon every possible object—from tools to personal belongings—was cast out of the *America*. Fuel, too, was ejected. With the remaining fuel and with only one engine Wellman hoped to struggle toward the Azores, in the South Atlantic off the northern coast of Africa. This was a vain hope, if only because they were being blown in the opposite direction in the general proximity of Bermuda. Their single engine could not possibly make any headway in a fifty-mile gale.

The engine was switched off to conserve fuel and the *America* became little more than a balloon. The crew meanwhile bent its efforts toward keeping the airship airborne and preventing the lifeboat from damage, either by smacking into the sea or being whipped to kindling by the equilibrator. As they were thus occupied, the sun appeared suddenly and did its part. The gas in the balloon, heated and expanded, lifted them—and the equilibrator—more than 3,000 feet into the air. Vaniman quickly released some of the gas and brought the *America* down closer to the ocean, but, as a precaution, with the equilibrator free of the water.

This provided only a brief interlude as the exhausted crew drifted in the airship, practically a derelict. With the coming of the cool of evening, their troubles began all over again. The ship settled down and they frenziedly began throwing out anything that could be torn free. The *America*, free of precious weight, remained barely above the water.

The next morning, Tuesday, their fourth day since setting out, Wellman decided that "we should never make Bermuda," and ordered the lifeboat launched; they would abandon ship.

The sea was still rough, in the wake of the storm, as Vaniman valved the gas, lowering the *America* near the water to enable Simon to release the boat. "This was so hazardous an operation," Wellman later revealed, "that much time elapsed before it could be completed; and, during it, the equilibrator struck Irwin, the wireless operator, and Louis Loud, the engineer, and also knocked a small hole in the lifeboat. But we accomplished it and released the airship."

Luckily for Wellman and his crew, they had come down about three miles from the H. M. S. *Trent* on its way from Bermuda to New York.

The lookout had spotted a strange, rather large object bobbing near the water and informed Capt. Claud Down. Ordering the *Trent* to make for the object—it could be a ship in distress—Down studied it through his glasses. It was no large fish, nor a ship, and it gleamed curiously when little rays of the early morning sun managed to break through the overcast.

Then to his surprise the object rose into the air and flew out of sight. "I was astonished at first, of course; seeing anything go *upward* doesn't seem in the natural order of things," Down later told newsmen. "But of course that in itself was the answer. It was an airship—couldn't be anything else. And there'd been enough hullabaloo about the *America*. I was not long in arriving at the conclusion that this was her, that she'd come down—I couldn't tell why, naturally—and had now ascended again. From observation, there was no reason to continue on to the scene of the occurrence. But I did. I couldn't *see* anything, but the sea doesn't always oblige in regard to revelations. One thinks of men, rescue. Naturally I continued on."

As the *Trent* made its way through the rather heavy seas, Down saw a distress signal arc up from the spot. There were, obviously, men there who needed rescue. Battling the waves the *Trent* pushed onward. Then Down observed something that appeared to be "of the peculiar shape of a sea-serpent," which of course was the now floating equilibrator (of which the Captain knew and which caused no superstitious fears in him). Finally—it was already nine in the morning—they sighted a boat bobbing around in the water. It took three hours of hard work before the five men and their mascot, a kitten, were taken aboard the *Trent*.

As Wellman stepped aboard he was greeted by the first mate, light-heartedly he had hoped, by the words, "Captain Wellman, I presume."

Frostily Wellman turned to the mate and informed him that Americans found English dialect as amusing as Englishmen found the American dialect. This rather puzzled the mate and ended all promise of any whimsy the occasion might have offered. The defeated crew of the now gone *America* were then tendered all the courtesies to those who have been fated to be rescued at sea. But the one thing that Wellman did realize was that they had failed; they had survived but they had failed. The Atlantic, beckoning and mocking, remained the domain of the ship. But it had been, as one news writer had indicated, "a glorious failure."

ATLANTIC FEVER

1

Not for the Money

It would be an indefensible omission to disregard a major factor in the promotion of the great transatlantic aerial adventures: namely money.

Prizes of cash had encouraged airmen for quite some time to perform feats of epochal derring-do. Blériot, for example, had crossed the English Channel to claim the London *Daily Mail* prize (which added up to a substantial $5000 in 1909). The *Daily Mail*, as well as the London *Times*, were owned by one Alfred Charles William Harmsworth—better known as Lord Northcliffe. An interest in aviation, and in increasing the circulation of the relatively young *Daily Mail*, prompted Northcliffe to offer a number of prizes in the early days of aviation. He put up money to give to the first pilot who would fly the 183 miles from London to Manchester; then for the first circuit of England and other such feats.

Then, not quite ten years after the Wrights had flown, Northcliffe announced in April, 1913 that the *Daily Mail* was offering a prize of £10,000 (roughly $50,000) "to the first person who crosses the Atlantic from any point in the United States, Canada, or Newfoundland to any point in Great Britain or Ireland in 72 continuous hours."

The first aircraft designer who had enough confidence in his plane to announce his decision to compete for the prize was the American, and bitter rival of the Wrights, Glenn Curtiss. An outstanding pioneer in the design of hydroplanes, Curtiss had, by early 1912, developed the first flying boat, equally at home in the air and on the water. With the backing of Rodman Wanamaker, heir to a department store fortune, Curtiss produced a large flying boat named *America*. This was not a tribute to Wellman's efforts of only three years before; it was Wanamaker's wish that the flight—for which he was putting up $25,000— would commemorate in 1914 the centenary of the peace between Britain and the United States.

To even out the enterprise a British pilot, Lt. John Cyril Porte, was selected to fly the plane. Work proceeded rapidly on the craft and by the summer the *America* was completed and being tested on Lake Keuka, near Hammondsport, New York. All boded well, for the plane performed not too badly, particularly after Curtiss added a third engine (power was always a problem with early aircraft). The plan was to fly to Newfoundland, take off officially on the flight from there, make a refueling stop at the Azores and then fly on to Britain.

As with the earlier *America* this dream did not materialize; hardly had the final test flight taken place when the news arrived from Europe that some archduke and his wife had been assassinated at a place called Sarajevo. That was on June 28, 1914. The deadline for the takeoff was August 15—otherwise weather conditions over the Atlantic were unpredictable and forbidding. On August 4 Britain declared war on Germany; shortly afterward John Porte returned to England and active duty with the Royal Navy. (He introduced many of Curtiss's ideas to British navy flying and contributed several of his own to the development of flying boats during the war.)

The coming of what came to be called the Great War canceled the flight of the *America*. However, the British bought the finished craft and ordered an additional sixty for use as patrol boats during the war.

The chief enemy of the patrol boat was the submarine. The German U-boat was hunted by the flying boats and attacked whenever found.

But there was still a problem. The U-boats often sank shiploads of flying boats as they were being transported to Britain across the Atlantic. The solution was, as Curtiss saw it, in the specially built *America* (the standard versions were not equipped for Atlantic crossings). He would build a flying boat capable of getting over the Atlantic under its own power and by wing, out of reach of the submarines.

With the cooperation of the U.S. Navy Curtiss set to work designing an entirely new plane. The events and developments of the war had made the once revolutionary *America* obsolete. The newer design would be larger, more powerful—and more deadly, for it would be a bomber. It was an ambitious project which, in December, 1917, officially got under way when Secretary of the Navy Josephus Daniels signed the papers which assigned Curtiss the job of turning out a large seaplane-bomber. Several Navy engineers were sent to the Curtiss plant in Buffalo to participate. Soon a tough winter caused Curtiss to move the whole project to Garden City, on Long Island, New York.

Designing the plane was an involved community effort with responsibilities and arguments shared by both Curtiss's engineers and the Navy. Navy man Holden Richardson was responsible for the hull design; involved in the work, besides Curtiss of course, were his two chief designers, W. L. Gilmore and Henry Kleckler. There were disagreements on several points from the hull design to the use of pontoons on the tips of the wings to keep them out of the water. British visitors were reportedly inclined, upon inspecting what had come to be called the "Navy Curtiss," to find the "machine impossible, and is not likely to be of any use whatever."

Despite this expert opinion—John Cyril Porte is supposed to have commented with a simple, "It is very interesting," which was ominous—the Navy pressed on. Behind this pressure was Adm. Douglas W. Taylor, who had initiated and sponsored the project.

Actual work began on the NCs—familiarity had bred brevity—in January, 1918 (they were also referred to, even more familiarly, as "Nancies," but the name did not sit too well with the Navy). An initial order had been placed for four. The hulls, curiously enough, were not all made by Curtiss; two were produced by Lawley & Sons in Neponset, Massachusetts, and one by the Herreschoff Manufacturing Company of Bristol, Rhode Island. To speed up production, Curtis did a great deal of subcontracting (although with a view in mind of making a 10 percent profit on the deal). The wings and tail surfaces were made by the Locke Body Company in Manhattan—some twenty-three miles from Garden City. There being no standard Navy truck big enough for their transportation (the wing panels were over 45 feet long and 12 feet wide), it

Christening of the Curtiss *America*, an early flying boat that designer Glenn Curtiss was sure could fly the Atlantic in 1914. Left to right: British pilot John Cyril Porte, George Hallett, his assistant, Curtiss, and Katherine Mossan, who did the honors. (*National Air & Space Museum, Smithsonian Institution*)

The *America* undergoing tests on Lake Keuka, New York; it was an advanced aircraft for its time. (*National Air & Space Museum, Smithsonian Institution*)

Closeup of the Curtiss *America* during the installation of a third engine on the upper wing. The between-the-wings engines proved inadequate. Note the enclosed cabin-cockpit and the headlight on the bow. (*National Air & Space Museum, Smithsonian Institution*)

was necessary to rent trucks from theatrical moving companies which were generally used to move theater sets. Producing the NCs had become quite a production. As it was, in order to remove the panels from the Locke factory it was necessary to knock out portions of the building.

Piece by piece the first plane, logically called the NC-1, was assembled at Garden City and then moved to the Naval Air Station at Rockaway Beach. A special hangar had been built there to house the four planes; to the embarrassment of all, it was learned that the single NC-1 filled half the hangar space. Once all planes were finished, two would have to stay out in the cold.

When finally assembled the NC-1 was an impressive aircraft; its wings stretched an amazing 126 feet from tip to tip. Its fuselage—or hull, for it was decidedly shipshape—measured 45 feet; its beam was 10 feet wide. The total length from nose to tip of tail was 68 feet 3½ inches. Originally it had been intended to power the plane with three Liberty engines, but these had not proved up to the job. A fourth engine was added behind the first three. Thus did three engines pull, and the fourth push, the plane through the air at a speed of around 80 miles an hour.

The first test of the NC-1 took place on October 4, 1918, and much to the surprise of a number of people, the odd-looking seaplane flew. After a series of tests, so certain were its designers of its airworthiness, it was decided to fly to Washington to "show her off to the brass."

In the morning of November 7, the plane took off and headed southward from Rockaway. A half hour later a radiator sprang a leak and could not be repaired while the plane was airborne. Hull designer Richardson, who shared the controls with copilot David McCulloch, decided they'd best set the NC down. Waves were running as high as ten feet when the big plane settled in the water. It was a real test, actually, although unintended, of the rough-water capability of Richardson's hull design. After the repairs were made, the NC-1 took off from the surging waves and flew on, without further incident, to the Navy's Anacostia Air Station.

It was here that Admiral Taylor could pronounce the design good

The *America* skimming the surface of Lake Keuka, before the installation of the third engine. An added passenger stands nonchalantly just forward of the port engine. (*National Air & Space Museum, Smithsonian Institution*)

and order the other planes to be hurried along "and put them into action."

Just as war had intervened to spoil Curtiss's first attempt to cross the Atlantic in 1914, the coming of the Armistice within a week after the NC-1 had flown to Washington canceled the need for the transatlantic delivery of the flying boats—and of the project itself. Work was stopped on the NC-2 and nothing further would be done on the NC-3 and NC-4.

The end of the war, however, brought a renewal of Lord North-cliffe's *Daily Mail* offer for the first transatlantic flight. While the U.S. Navy could not become involved in any international competition for mere gelt, there was the greater glory of the Navy to consider. Why not continue with the idea of crossing the Atlantic Ocean? It would certainly bring attention to the Navy, which like all other military services quickly receded from the minds of the general public, and a money-dispensing Congress, as soon as the war had ended.

At the same time, the Northcliffe prize stirred up the adventurers who were not above taking a bit of money. After all, there was a good deal of risk involved—no one had ever actually flown the Atlantic. In Britain, therefore, a number of airmen began making preparations (not knowing at the time that the U.S. Navy, too, was making its own; the project was still considered "Secret," for reasons obvious only to the military mind).

According to the original announcement in the *Daily Mail*, the rules stated: "The prize will be awarded to the aviator who shall first cross the Atlantic (either way) in an aeroplane from any point in the United States, Canada, or Newfoundland to any point in Great Britain or Ireland, in 72 consecutive hours. The competition is open to persons of any nationality holding an aviator's certificate issued by the International Aeronautical Federation and duly entered on the competitors' register of the Royal Aero Club." The motivation, the renewal announcement stated, was "to stimulate the production of more powerful engines and more suitable aircraft."

Notice of entry had to be given not less than fourteen days before the entrant hoped to make his flight. There was a fee of £100 (none of which went to the *Daily Mail*, but was used to defray the expenses of the Royal Aero Club in conducting the competition). "Only one aircraft may be used for each attempt," the rules continued. "It may be repaired *en route*. It will be so marked before starting that it can be identified on reaching the other side. Any intermediate stoppages may be made on water. Towing is not prohibited. The start may be made from land or water, but in the latter case the competitor must cross the coastline in flight. The finish may also be made on land or water, the time being taken at the moment of crossing the coastline in flight or touching land. If the pilot has at any time to leave the aircraft and board a ship, he must resume his flight from approximately the same point at which he went on board."

The rules appear to have taken about every possible contingency into consideration, even the unlikely one of having one's plane towed from shore to shore. The rule of intermediate stoppage, on water only, of course, placed a rather heavy burden on any airman who chose to fly in a landplane.

Almost at the moment that the renewal of the *Daily Mail* prize was announced, preparations in Britain for the transatlantic flight began with a flurry of activity. Pilots were encouraged, even assisted in this, by aircraft manufacturers whose postwar survival hinged upon a general popular interest and confidence in aviation. Several entries were filed with the Royal Aero Club (the intent of the U.S. Navy was filed with the British Government; the NCs, clearly, were not to be regarded as competitors); before long the serious contenders had dwindled down to about half a dozen planes.

Two were rather quickly, and prematurely, eliminated. One entrant, a Short *Shamrock*, piloted by Maj. J. C. P. Wood and Capt. C. C. Wylie, was en route, on April 8, to Ireland where it was to take off officially. Wood and Wylie had selected the most difficult route—the west to east crossing, bucking the winds—but even before they arrived in Ireland trouble with their plane forced them down into the Irish Sea. They were rescued but the *Shamrock* was definitely out of the running.

Another worthy contender, a twin-engined biplane, the Boulton Paul P-8, crewed by Maj. K. S. Savory, Capt. J. H. Woolner and Capt. A. L. Howarth, cracked up during a takeoff. A second P-8 being readied as a back-up craft was too far from completion at the time, so that trio withdrew from the race.

The four remaining British teams elected to fly west to east (that is, with the helpful prevailing winds pushing them toward Europe), so all planes were dismantled, packed up and shipped to Newfoundland. The first arrival was a Sopwith, the *Atlantic*, whose pilot was Harry Hawker, Sopwith's dashing test pilot, and whose navigator was Lt. Comdr. Kenneth Mackenzie-Grieve. The *Atlantic* was a new design with some rather interesting features: it dropped its landing gear after takeoff to lessen the load and wind resistance; also, just in the event of trouble, the top deck of the fuselage, between cockpit and rudder, was detachable and could serve as a lifeboat. Hawker and Mackenzie-Grieve arrived at St. John's, Newfoundland, on March 29, 1919.

They found that the best site for an airfield had already been reserved by the advance party of F. P. Raynham (pilot) and Capt. C. W. F. Morgan, whose Martinsyde was named *Raymor* in their honor. The *Raymor* arrived in April, followed by a Handley Page V/1500 (a four-engined bomber which had come a little late to have bombed Berlin in the war). Its crew consisted of Adm. Mark Kerr, who commanded, and Maj. H. G. Brackley (the pilot), Maj. Trygve Gran and F. Wyatt. It was by far the largest of the British planes assembling at St. John's with its wingspan of 126 feet (the same as that of the NCs).

The final arrival, on May 26, was a Vickers Vimy (which, like the Handley Page, had been designed as a World War I bomber) that would be flown by Captain John Alcock and navigated by Lt. Arthur Whitten Brown.

By this time, the Navy's NC-1, NC-3 and NC-4 had come and gone. The arrival of the American flying boats at Trepassey, Newfoundland, threw the British camp into consternation. Although not officially entered in the competition, the fact that the well-organized and outfitted Navy airmen stood a good chance of making the flight first would have taken all the edge off any that followed. Hawker, particularly, since he had been waiting around from the end of March, was given over to making remarks. He dismissed the effort as a "Cook's tour across the ocean" and offered further to "eat the seaplane" that actually made it.

Hawker, as no doubt did other "intrepid" airmen, did not consider the Navy project truly sporting. For one thing, so carefully planned was the flight that the Navy had strung a "bridge of ships"—no less than sixty—across the Atlantic along the path the NCs would take to the Azores, and from there on to Lisbon, Portugal. This kind of thing, some believed, eliminated all the adventure from the flight. The Navy insisted that it was not interested in a bold undertaking, but in science.

To contribute further to the tempest, a U.S. Navy blimp, the C-5, floated into St. John's and moored near Quidi Vidi Lake nearby. It had settled right in the middle of the English camp. The NCs, at least, had had the good taste to land at Trepassey Bay, about sixty miles to the south. The Navy was rather coy about the C-5, under command of Lt. Comdr. Emory W. Coil, at first denying that it was interested in making a cross-Atlantic try by nonrigid airship. Some word had filtered back from England that the British were preparing one of their own for just such an attempt. Eventually the Navy admitted that it just might take advantage of that "bridge of ships" that had been laid across the Atlantic for the NCs. There were those who agreed with Hawker and thought the Navy had the C-5 on hand to save the Naval face just in case the NCs never got off.

While the preparations for the flight of the NCs had been quite elaborate, the C-5's were not. The cruiser *Chicago* was on hand to serve as a floating base, but no hangar had been built, nor any real mooring equipment provided. So it was that on May 15 a strong wind roared across Quidi Vidi and, despite all the efforts of the crew, the airship was blown loose of its moorings. It was already twenty-five feet in the air before the last three men aboard jumped to safety (though one broke an ankle) and ruefully watched the C-5 blown out to sea. It was never seen again by its crew—which ended another lighter-than-air Atlantic venture. That left only the NCs as a threat to the sporting Britons.

The flight of the big Navy boats began officially on May 2, 1919, with the formation of "NC Seaplane Division 1" under the command of Comdr. John H. Towers. An experienced pilot, Towers had been flying since 1911, when he took lessons from Glenn Curtiss; he had been one of the three first U.S. Navy pilots. He had worked with Curtiss on the design of the *America* in 1914, so that the idea of a transatlantic flight was not new to Towers. He would command the Division from the NC-3, the flagship, which was to be piloted by Comdr. Holden Richardson, who had contributed so much to the hull design of the NC.

Other aircraft in the Division were the NC-1, under the command of Lt. Comdr. Patrick N. L. Bellinger and with Lt. Comdr. Marc A. Mitscher as Pilot, and the NC-4, commanded by Lt. Comdr. Albert C. Read, with First Lt. Elmer F. Stone of the Coast Guard as pilot. Crews of the planes numbered six: the commander, pilot, a second pilot, a pilot/engineer, a radio operator and an engineer. The fourth plane, the NC-2, would not make the trip, as it had not proved to be an especially good performer, and it was cannibalized for spare parts: such as wings for the NC-1 which had been damaged in a gale and other parts for the NC-1 and NC-4 which had been damaged in a hangar fire.

The NC-4 was regarded with some suspicion as a jinx ship; this appeared to be confirmed when, a few hours before the scheduled take-off, Chief Mechanic E. H. Howard stepped too close to the spinning propellers of the plane and lost his hand at the wrist. As he made his way to the first-aid station he called back to the horror-stricken crew, "I'll be all right . . . Don't go without me." His place aboard the NC-4 was taken by Chief Machinist Mate Eugene S. Rhoads.

The crew of the NC-4, besides Read, Stone and Rhoads, consisted of Lt. Walter Hinton, copilot, Lt. James L. Breese, pilot/engineer, and Ensign Herbert C. Rodd, radio operator.

The three planes took off from the Naval Air Station at Rockaway at 10:00 in the morning. It was a fine clear day and the first leg of the flight was planned to end at Halifax that evening. They maintained fine formation until around two in the afternoon when the jinxed NC-4 developed engine troubles and dropped behind. Towers and Bellinger continued on and arrived at Halifax at seven in the evening.

The NC-4, meanwhile, was having serious problems. Barely out of sight of Rockaway Read had to radio Towers that an engine had lost oil pressure. They continued on three engines and then one of them threw a connecting rod. While all this was happening, it might be noted, Chief Mechanic Rhoads, who had substituted for the injured Howard, was stretched out in the plane severely air-sick.

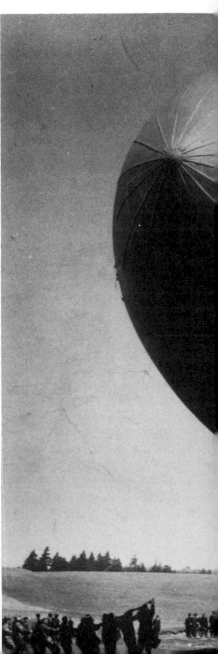

RIGHT The Navy C-5 which temporarily added a note of consternation to the various transatlantic preparations in Newfoundland in the spring of 1919. (*National Air & Space Museum, Smithsonian Institution*)

BELOW The C-5 getting away from its crew —which ended its part in the Atlantic race. (*Goodyear Tire & Rubber Company*)

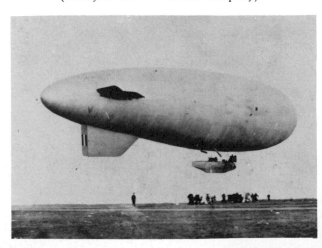

When the second engine went there was nothing else to do but set the plane down about eighty miles east of Cape Cod. Although Hinton had been able to land gently, there was a ten-foot sea which bounced the plane around roughly. The sturdy hull held, however—although Rhoads was unable to repair the engines. Read then decided to run on the two outer engines and taxi in to shore. He was still at sea when word came that the NC-1 and NC-3 had landed at Halifax.

The NC-4 continued plowing through the waves. Around midnight

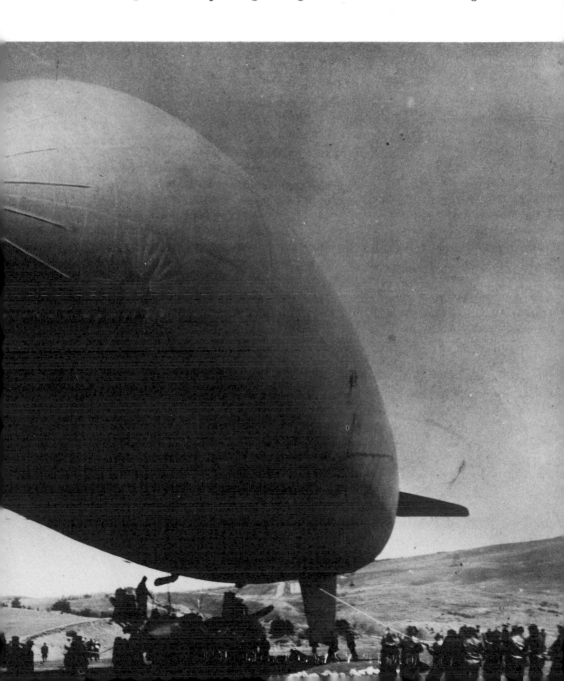

the water became smoother and the taxiing less hazardous, although Read kept his men on watch all night, spelling each other as the plane worked its way toward shore. Twice they spotted ships but they were not seen and they were unable to signal to them. It was frustrating to Read who, by then, was certain they were out of the flight. It was sunrise before the NC-4 puffed into the Naval Air Station at Chatham, Massachusetts. As soon as he could, Read wired Towers at Halifax informing him that they would require an engine change, rather plaintively asking, "Can you wait?"

Towers replied, "Navy Department orders earliest flight continuation. Sorry."

But then Towers was having his own problems. Upon arriving at Halifax he was disconcerted to find the propellers on both planes had begun cracking. They would have to be replaced, but no one had thought of shipping the special Olmstead propellers up to Halifax, for no one had anticipated that peculiar problem. In the flight to Halifax the NC-3 had carried a guest, young Lt. Comdr. Richard E. Byrd, aviation enthusiast and designer of some of the navigation instruments being used in the flight. Byrd was also deeply frustrated by the flight, as he had hoped to have commanded one of the planes, but had been eliminated on a technicality. He had already had a stint of overseas service—it had been right there at Halifax—and since part of the flight of the NCs was regarded by the Navy as overseas the opportunity to make it was given to men who had not had previous foreign service.

Byrd had hopped a ride in the NC-3 on the chance that he just might have been able to talk someone into letting him make the crossing in the C-5—but that hope was blown out to sea shortly after they had arrived.

But it was lucky for Towers that Byrd had come along. He recalled that while he had been stationed there during the war they had had a supply of Olmstead propellers. He was quickly dispatched to seek out the warehouse that held them. By late afternoon he had found a half dozen.

While the cracked propellers were being changed on the NCs at Halifax, the engine of the NC-4 was being replaced at Chatham. The disappointment was that, although it was a Liberty, it was 100 horsepower less than the other three. Read hoped it would get them to Trepassey, the stop beyond Halifax, where they could install a proper engine. The change, meanwhile, would put them behind two days—and Towers could not wait. Still, Read could not bring himself to withdraw from the flight, although officially it was all but accepted that the NC-4 was out of the running.

They were still waterbound when word had come that the other two planes, cracked props replaced, had left Halifax for Trepassey. Read by this time was in a quandary—should he simply throw in the towel, or should he skip Halifax and fly directly to Trepassey? He decided on the Trepassey try even though that meant staying up in the air for at least ten hours—and so far in the "epic flight" the NC-4 had been airborne all of 4 hours, 51 minutes, and grounded for five days.

It was Wednesday, May 14 (storms having kept them down for two days), before they managed to get away from Chatham. There was still a chance of catching the other two NCs at Trepassey before they set out for the Azores.

But, after a reasonably uneventful flight, one of the engines developed a loss of oil pressure and they had to set down at Halifax anyway. And there was trouble with the newly installed, untested engine. Rhoads spent a good deal of time checking and eventually the NC-4 headed for Trepassey. As they approached Trepassey Bay they were surprised to see a Navy blimp flying a rather wayward trajectory. Read studied it with his glasses—it was, of course, the C-5 off on a flight of its own. Rodd, via the radio, learned that it was the drifting airship which had broken loose at Trepassey.

He was also ordered by Read, who knew that Towers with the NC-3 and NC-1 was bound to be preparing for takeoff, to send a message, "Coming in for landing." This was not absolutely true—they were still fifty miles out—but Read hoped that it just might encourage Towers to wait for them.

But that was not to be. As the NC-4 circled the bay for a landing Read saw the two planes, obviously on takeoff runs with white water splashing in their wakes, heading into the wind. Almost despairing Read could not help but shout, "Wait!" though no one would hear him. Then, inexplicably, the two flying boats slowed down, turned around and headed for the supply ship *Aroostock*. All three planes nosed in near the ship simultaneously. Read was the last aboard, and after greetings, the first thing he did was thank Towers for waiting for them.

He had not been that considerate, Towers admitted. They had not been able to get the planes off the water in the crosswind that whipped Trepassey Bay. Well, the plane so many were calling "The Lame Duck" had finally rejoined them. As for the aborted takeoff (because of an overload of fuel, Towers was to learn later), Towers was philosophical: "I think everybody was glad we hadn't succeeded."

It is reported that even Albert Read smiled over the turn of events. He was not given over to the display of emotion, especially in the lighter vein. A Vermonter, he was taciturn, quiet, soft-spoken and extremely efficient at his job. Read was regarded as one of the finest navigators in

the Navy; he was also a certified pilot. A compact little man, just four inches over five feet tall and weighing barely 120 pounds, Read hardly fulfilled the popular conception of the intrepid airman.

From his days at Annapolis (Class of '07, in which he graduated fourth) he carried the nickname "Putty." This was bestowed upon him by a classmate who noted that, one summer, though Read had spent a good deal of time in the sun, he had returned untanned and with his complexion "looking like putty." From that day on Read was afflicted with the name, though few, particularly those of lesser rank, used it. That he responded to the name at all was the only soft spot in Read's New England starchiness. He was respected, admired, even regarded

OPPOSITE The NCs getting under way on their Atlantic adventure from Far Rockaway, New York, in the morning of May 8, 1919. (*National Air & Space Museum, Smithsonian Institution*)

LEFT The NC-3 churning up the water on a takeoff run. Leader of the flight, Commander John H. Towers, used this craft as the Flagship. (*National Air & Space Museum, Smithsonian Institution*)

with affection by his men, but few were encouraged to get cozy with Putty Read.

Towers, the flight's commander, was a more approachable, more relaxed man. He could understand Read's, and his crew's, delight in the delay in takeoff. He was unhappy, though, that the British had a bit more to laugh about, for few of the English pilots could bring themselves to take the NCs seriously. Hawker, visiting from St. John's to the north, jokingly suggested to Towers that they might best simply sail the NCs across—"Your planes look like they might be able to make it that way."

Towers laughed through tight teeth. He could imagine what the

OPPOSITE The NCs assembled, after tribulations, at Trepassey, Newfoundland. Their arrival was cause for mirth in the English camp; no one in it ever thought the planes would get into the air. (*National Air & Space Museum, Smithsonian Institution*)

RIGHT Flagship NC-3 proving the British correct. Overloaded, and with the winds wrong, the plane could not rise off the water. (*National Air & Space Museum, Smithsonian Institution*)

jolly Hawker would say after a fruitless day of waddling around the bay. He decided they would wait until morning; during the night the NC-4 had an engine changed and three split propellers replaced and was pronounced ready. They would take off for the Azores the next day, Friday, May 16, 1919.

Most of the day was spent in getting ready; engines were checked and rechecked. The planes taxied on the water during the morning and then Towers announced that they would start out around five in the afternoon. If all went well (for a change) they could expect to arrive at Ponta Delgada, the capital of the Azores, sometime in the early afternoon of the next day; this arrival was timed for a daylight landing.

In hopes of avoiding the fiasco of the previous day, the fuel supply of each plane was carefully measured before the planes moved seaward. The lightest of all was the NC-4 because of the presence of James Breese in the dual role of pilot-engineer; he had had plenty of experience with the NCs and understood the problem of weight, power and fuel better than anyone else. There was enough fuel to get them to the Azores, but no more than that.

The plan was for all three planes to take off simultaneously, if only to show those cheeky British, but as the big boats lumbered into a thirty-mile wind it became obvious that weight was still a problem. Breese, in the NC-4, was among the first to become aware of this and quickly tossed two cans of oil overboard (thus lightening the plane by seventy pounds); he had been saving them just in the event of an emergency. With the weight gone the NC-4 surged ahead of the NC-3, which supposedly was to lead the takeoff, and left the NC-1 behind also. Within seconds the NC-4 was airborne.

As he circled the bay Read saw the other two planes still struggling to get unstuck. Then he saw the "3" slow down and turn toward the *Aroostock*, followed soon after by the "1." As Read continued to circle (in touch with Towers by radio), a small drama was occurring down below.

Towers had begun ripping equipment out of the "3," first a long-range radio (they would still have the short-range), then a bag of mail being carried for the benefit of philatelists. Finally his eye lit on one of the two engineers they were carrying, the heavier one, Lt. Braxton Rhodes.

"What do you weigh, Rhodes?" he inquired.

"No, Commander, no!" Rhodes replied.

But it was, ultimately, yes, and Rhodes was bounced along with the radio, the stamp collector's bag and anything else Towers considered inessential. Having observed some of this from above, Read decided to land and find out what the plan really was. Towers was not in a very good temper, but he was determined that they would get off that day. Once again all three gunned engines and headed for the open sea. And once again the NC-4 was the first to get off, followed by Towers in the "3" and later by Bellinger in the "1." By the time they approached the open water Read had climbed to 600 feet, Towers was dragging at seventy-five and Bellinger had the "1" up to an altitude of ten feet, if that could technically be called altitude. They were so low that they had to traverse the regular shipping channel to avoid the hills around Trepassey Bay. His message radioed to the world as they got under way was, "With the help of God and in spite of the devil, we're going to do this little thing."

They were in the air at least, a little ragged as far as formation flying went, but they were pointed in the right direction and they were up and away from those gibing British.

The takeoff of the three NCs, naturally, had its effect in the British camp. Only sixty miles north of Trepassey they were still socked in by the weather. But a new urgency seized them as they realized that there was just the off chance that Towers and his men might make it. The instant the weather lifted they vowed they would set out themselves. If they could make the trip nonstop there was still the chance of beating the Americans across the Atlantic.

But for two days after the NCs had left the weather at St. John's continued to be recalcitrant. It was none too good over the Atlantic either.

For one thing salt spray had shorted out the running lights of the NC-3 and Towers had to fly without the protection of the red and green wingtip lights. This nearly resulted in a midair collision with the NC-1, but it was averted when one of the crew, noting the proximity of the "1," flickered a flashlight and the two planes flitted apart. From then on Towers ordered the planes to spread out. The smooth flying they had expected was a vain hope as the air grew rough; and so it went through the long night.

Morning brought no improvement, for then the fog began clotting up. The three planes were on their own and having problems. Sandwiched between fog and clouds, with the ocean somewhere around also —not to mention the peaks of the Azores, if they happened to be near them—it was an uneasy time. The turbulence made it difficult to take bearings, even if they could have seen the stars, and the fog obscured the Navy ships that were supposed to mark their progress with searchlights, star shells and other illumination.

All three crews began to wonder where they were. It would take very little variation from the course to cause them to miss the Azores completely. They could, perhaps, land and take some radio bearings if necessary, then take off again. All three began tentatively dipping through the fog searching for the ocean. In the fog, Stone, at the controls of the NC-4, became temporarily disoriented and the big boat slipped off into a spin. Read, trapped in his cockpit by centrifugal forces, was unable to attract Stone's attention. Not until they had fallen through the fog, and the sun broke through suddenly, did Stone realize that strange attitude

The NC-4, lighter than the other planes, is the first to lift off the surface of Trepassey Bay en route to the Azores. (*National Air & Space Museum, Smithsonian Institution*)

at which the plane was flying—and dangerously approaching a dive. He lifted the wing and pulled up above the fog.

Bellinger in the "1" and Towers in the "3" had decided to touch down momentarily—to determine their positions. Towers especially was way off course and Bellinger admitted to pilot Mitscher that they were lost. Master navigator Read seemed reasonably certain of his position and continued on toward the Azores. The "1" landed first and the crew found itself in very rough seas, indeed. The plane bounced and was swamped with water, drenching all hands, buckling struts here and there and filling the hull with two feet of water. They now knew where they were (about a hundred miles from Flores, their port-in-the-storm short of their destination Ponta Delgada), but they were not so certain that they were going anywhere. Bellinger ordered the pumps going to drain the hull, and the fabric of the lower wings was slashed to permit the waves to wash through; Mitscher remained at the controls to keep the plane under minimal control. Even so, the tail surfaces dangled uselessly and whipped around as the waves bounced the plane.

Shortly after the "1" had splashed down, the "3," some fifty miles away, did the same—even closer (though Towers was unaware of it) to Flores than the "1." The "3" came in hard: it brushed the crest of a wave, bounced to another crest and then, caught by the water, settled down in a deep trough. Water came crashing down and the hull cracked, engine struts buckled, wires snapped and went slack. Miraculously none of the crew was seriously injured. But like the NC-1, they were out of the running.

The "1," though damaged, was capable of moving through the water. This meant bailing out the water to keep afloat and hope to run across one of the destroyers. So they bounced, with some of the crew violently ill, for five hours before encountering a Greek ship, the *Ionia*, which lowered a lifeboat and took the six miserable men aboard. Despite a language difficulty, Bellinger made it clear that he would like the *Ionia* to take the NC-1 in tow. A rope was, under difficulty, fastened to the plane, but when the towing began the rope snapped, was refastened, and then a wing snapped. About at this moment the destroyer *Gridley* hove in sight, took the crew off and also attempted to pull the NC-1 after it. This only resulted in further damage to the plane in the still treacherous seas. Finally a hard decision had to be made. The plane could not be left, a drifting derelict and a menace to shipping; the *Gridley* turned away, built up steam, and rammed the plane. The NC-1 folded up and sank to the bottom.

It was then that the men heard that Read and the NC-4 had actually landed at Horta; there was some consolation in that. Putty in the Lame Duck, at least, had made it that far—if not to Ponta Delgada. But what about the "3"? There had been no word from Towers for several hours.

They had come down about forty-five miles out of Horta; besides the general damage to the plane it was soon discovered that a radio—the sending set, the receiver was all right—had broken down. They were able to hear the chatter of the nearby destroyers, no doubt searching for them, and the news of the other two planes, but what was happening aboard the NC-3 was a mystery to everyone but those who suffered the ordeal itself. It would last for sixty hours.

During this period of the blackout from the NC-3, when it was given up for lost, activity picked up back at St. John's, where the British pilots had been cursing their luck and the weather. On Sunday, May 18, the redoubtable Hawker, with Mackenzie-Grieve beside him in their single cockpit, took off in the *Atlantic* in the middle of the afternoon. The overloaded plane barely got into the air, narrowly missed a fence at the end of the field, then circled and dropped the landing gear, and headed out to sea. Hawker was the first of the British flyers to get off.

They were expected to be heard from some twenty hours later when they were due to arrive at Brooklands, England. But as with the NC-3, a sudden silence descended and days, not hours, passed by and it became obvious that something had gone wrong.

Two hours after the *Atlantic* had struggled off the field the *Raymor* was ready to go; there was still a good chance to beat the Americans. Raynham and Morgan climbed into the plane and began the takeoff; it was tricky because of a crosswind and the plane was heavy. Raynham managed to lift it off before they ran out of runway, but the wind caught the *Raymor* and lifted a wing, causing the plane to drift sideways. The landing gear touched the ground again, ripped away, and the *Raymor* plowed into the ground, its nose digging in and buckling the forward fuselage. Although, luckily, the plane did not burn, both men were injured, Morgan the most seriously, for slivers of glass from a broken compass had penetrated his skull. He returned to England for proper medical attention and as result of the accident lost an eye. Raynham, not as seriously hurt, was determined to try again. He had the *Raymor* rebuilt, renaming it the *Chimera*, and was ready, with another navigator, to try again a couple of months later. But during the takeoff the *Chimera* suffered a similar accident as it had in May and flattened out again—only this time without injury. Raynham decided that two strikes were sufficient and bowed out of the transatlantic race.

Kenneth Mackenzie-Grieve (left) and Harry Hawker, crew of the *Atlantic*, first of the English planes to get off after the NCs flew out of Newfoundland. (*Courtesy of National Museum of Science & Technology, Ottawa, Canada*)

Sunday May 18, 1919, had not been a red-letter day for the English. The *Atlantic* had flown out over its namesake and had vanished, the *Raymor* had cracked up; that still left the big Handley Page to carry on, but no attempt was made to get it off the ground—not that day, nor that month, for that matter. Meanwhile Alcock and Brown were still waiting for their plane to arrive by ship.

With Hawker and Mackenzie-Grieve missing and no word from the NC-3 a general gloom descended on the aviation world on that fateful Sunday.

Towers and his crew aboard the battered and broken NC-3 had not had a very good Sunday themselves. They had spent a miserable Saturday night being bounced and drenched; they had had to work for more than an hour in the rough waters cutting away one of the damaged elevators which had flapped so violently that there was a danger of capsizing. The water-logged wing fabric began sagging and water collected in little pools, adding to the strain on the already weakened wings and to the weight of the plane. The crew hacked holes into the fabric to let the water through. In the pounding waves the left wing float was washed away. This presented another danger, for the wing could dip into the water and, if broken away, would cause them to capsize. So they alternated, climbing uncertainly out onto the right wing to keep the plane in balance. It was not a pleasant perch and care was taken to attach themselves to a sound strut with a safety belt.

The Sopwith *Atlantic* used by Hawker and Mackenzie-Grieve in their unsuccessful attempt to fly the Atlantic. The plane was so designed that the landing gear was jettisoned after takeoff. (*Courtesy of National Museum of Science & Technology, Ottawa, Canada*)

Martinsyde *Raymor* being prepared for takeoff almost immediately after the *Atlantic* left St. John's. Crew was Frederick Raynham and William F. Morgan. (*Courtesy of National Museum of Science & Technology, Ottawa, Canada*)

With the coming of morning they were heartened to see the dim outline of land about forty miles distant. It was Pico of the Azores group, just slightly southeast of Horta and west of their original destination Ponta Delgada. Towers was forced to decide what they should do: they still had a little fuel and possibly could sail into Pico, provided the engines could start and provided the vibration did not disintegrate the NC-3. On the other hand they *were* drifting toward Ponta Delgada (about 200 miles to the east), even if they were ignominiously doing it stern first. There was still the chance of being found by one of the destroyers which, unfortunately, were searching for them 100 miles away from where they actually were, closer to Flores.

Towers elected to continue for Ponta Delgada; this meant another night at sea on short rations, drinking rust-flavored water from the radiators, and the misery of the tossing and dipping. During the night the wind came up and even though they faced in the wrong direction, they continued being pushed toward their destination. A wind shift, near morning, boded ill, for it threatened to blow them away from the Azores and out to sea. With daylight (Monday, the nineteenth) the wind shifted again and they were back on course. All eyes were anxiously turned to the northeast, except Richardson's, for he was seated at the controls, keeping the plane in trim, pointing into the wind and riding backwards.

Towers calculated their position and at nine in the morning announced, "We should be sighting land any minute now."

At 10:23 Boatswain Lloyd Moore, standing in the rear of the cockpit (now the front of their "boat"), jumped into the hull shouting, "Land —dead astern!" They were in sight of Ponta Delgada.

But they were not yet home safe. They could relax a little, perhaps

The *Raymor* after it failed in its takeoff. Both Morgan and Raynham were injured in the crash—although eventually Morgan tried again in a repaired *Raymor* (renamed *Chimera*), but it cracked up again and he withdrew from Atlantic flight attempts. (*Courtesy of National Museum of Science & Technology, Ottawa, Canada*)

eat a little better than they had for the past couple of days. Still they had the winds and waves to contend with and, as they approached the shore, there would be the reefs in their way and rollers close to the beach. Towers lessened their speed (by dropping a sea anchor to keep them from going too fast) and estimated at three o'clock, when they were still seven miles off Sao Miguel, the main island on which Ponta Delgada was situated, that they should be coming into the harbor within a couple of hours. They had ridden out of the fog, although the weather had not been kind to them. A sudden rain squall ripped away their sea anchor and the "3" yawed dangerously—a wingtip brushed close to the water and all hands snapped out of their premature sense of having arrived.

That they had not yet been spotted by one of the ships was rather unusual, although as one of the men suggested, "I don't think they are expecting us." All rescue ships, of course, were looking elsewhere, certainly not near Ponta Delgada. They continued drifting. It was about an hour and a quarter later that a lookout on the *Harding* saw them riding the waves into port. Suddenly the harbor blossomed with flags and lights, signals flashed, the *Harding* built up steam, whipped into action and began racing for them.

Towers ordered their ensign run up; if they were to be met by a ship of the U.S. Navy, then, tatters and all, they would be shipshape. Moore leaped onto the wing and reversed the flag (it had been up as a distress signal). Then a signal lamp was found and messages began flashing between the *Harding* and the NC-3.

"It's a miracle," the *Harding* lamp repeated over and over. Then came the offer of sending a boat out to pick them off the plane. Towers, with dignified pride, refused. "We came this far," he said, "we're going the rest of the way." So with the *Harding* standing by, just in case, the "3" continued drifting in. When they reached the breakwater a wave snapped their right wingtip float, which dangled by brace wires. Moore clambered out onto the wing and cut the wires; they now had no floats at all.

Towers ordered the aft engine started and its push helped to keep the wallowing plane on a near-even keel and gave them some control. He also suggested that the *Harding* stand by with a lifeboat and that the *Melville*, in the harbor itself, have a couple of punts ready to set under the wingtips, once they had arrived. Then he ordered two more engines started (a third was a lost cause) and these, on their buckled struts, caused the wings to vibrate severely. Moore, still out on the starboard wing, found himself lowered toward the water as the "3" began listing crazily. He moved to the port side—and that side teetered, sank under water. They were in danger of being swamped practically at their destination.

Lt. Comdr. Robert A. Lavender, realizing the situation, decided to counterweight Moore and dashed onto the opposite wing; in doing so he nearly ran into the propeller of the aft engine. But he weighed more than Moore and with the two men on either wingtip and three engines going, the NC-3 fluttered and seesawed toward the safety of the harbor. Holden Richardson then called Moore off his spot and changed places with him—he and Lavender were of about equal weight. Moore remained in the hull. Then the NC-3 moved into the port of Ponta Delgada, with copilot David McCulloch at the controls, Towers in the bow, two men dancing, gesticulating and shouting on the wings (they were not frolicking; Richardson and Lavender were trying to communicate with each other and moved constantly to maintain the delicate balance of the plane).

No one, of course, could hear anything as they came in; the harbor clamored with the sound of shouting, ship's horns and whistles, the roar of engines as motor launches darted around the harbor; there was a band blaring and even a 21-gun salute. Towers found it difficult to believe, all this festive din and the near-comedy as they wallowed in. Two punts had been positioned under each wingtip and groups of shouting sailors gingerly kept the plane's wings out of the water.

They had failed—the NC-3 would never fly again—but what a failure. They had flown over 1,200 miles and then had survived more than sixty hours in the open sea, through fog and gale, and had traveled 205 miles to be the first of the NCs to arrive at their first scheduled stop out of Trepassey. The saga of the crew of the NC-3 was unique in naval history. "The water cruise of the NC-3," Read said later, "was a trium-

The wave-and-wind-tattered NC-3 limping into Ponta Delgada, Azores, after a forced landing at sea and a 250 mile surface trip on the Atlantic. This mishap eliminated the NC-3, and flight commander Towers, from the flight. (*National Air & Space Museum, Smithsonian Institution*)

Closeup of the damage suffered by the NC-3 during its long Atlantic ordeal. (*National Air & Space Museum, Smithsonian Institution*)

phant demonstration of courage, expert seamanship and the seagoing qualities of the seaplane hulls. Sixty hours in a gale of wind and 30 to 40-foot waves, adrift in a machine designed for entirely different surroundings, the NC-3 overcame all difficulties and arrived in port safely."

As for Read and the NC-4, they had been grounded at Horta for days by fog. He and his crew were fêted by the town's dignitaries and populace, but that was not Read's way of life. He fretted to get away. When he heard that the NC-3 had finally come into Ponta Delgada, he was obviously relieved and happy with the news. When he heard of the plane's condition, his only comment was, "Well, I guess it's up to us."

But he knew better. According to Navy tradition, when the flagship is incapacitated, the commander merely moves his flag to another and retains command. That would mean that dour little Putty Read, who had brought the NC-4 to the Azores, would be bounced there by tradition. So be it, he felt, and made preparations to get away from Horta. This was finally accomplished on Tuesday, the twentieth, a day after Towers had brought the "3" into port. It was just a short hop—the flight was made in an hour and 45 minutes—but it had taken them from Saturday till Tuesday to do it.

The intact arrival of the NC-4 at Ponta Delgada, the reunion of all three crews, was reason enough for further celebrations and a new round of festivities began, somewhat to the dismay of Read, who hoped to be off again as soon as possible. Even so, he unbent enough that night to get mildly inebriated. The morning proved rather sobering. Before they could get under way, Read and Towers were called into the office of Admiral Jackson, the station commander. Word had come down from Washington, from the Secretary of the Navy himself, Josephus Daniels, that Read would continue in command of the NC-4.

Both men were stunned. Read was ready to step aside, in the traditional manner, to let Towers continue with the mission which he commanded. But no, Jackson said, that was not how the Secretary wanted it. Read then tried to get permission to carry Towers as a passenger. The answer was still no.

What had happened was that Read had become a national hero in the United States. The newspapers had been filled with the saga of the Lame Duck NC-4 for days; it had been the best press coverage the Navy had received since the war. To eliminate Read from the picture was courting a public relations disaster. Daniels could not be budged, not by his assistant Franklin D. Roosevelt, nor by Navy brass. Daniels was a former newspaperman, not a sailor, and cared little for briny customs.

Grimly the two men left Jackson's office, but first Towers ordered his ensign struck from the "4"'s lanyard. Although he saw that Read had spoken up in his behalf and had been willing to step down, the relationship between the two men—however innocent Read had been in the decision—would never be the same. So bitterly disappointed was Towers that he could never quite bring himself to be as friendly with Read again. It was not a deliberate turning away from their previous cordiality; it became a deeper, subconscious attitude on the part of Towers. Whenever he and Read met after that day in Admiral Jackson's office there was a slight cooling of the atmosphere and a stiffening, almost formal quality in their demeanor.

Putty Read was happy when a couple of days later Towers boarded ship for England; he had found it miserable reading the silent—if unfounded—accusation in Towers's eyes. But before he left, Towers found Read, put out his hand and said, "Good luck, Putty."

"Thanks, Jack," Read said. There wasn't more to say. Nor was there very much to do but wait. The weather had turned on them again and they sat out their time in port: Wednesday, Thursday and so on.

On Sunday, finally, there was good word. Almost out of nowhere news came that Hawker and Mackenzie-Grieve had been found! It was then learned that they had barely gotten 500 miles out of St. John's when engine trouble began to plague them. After some time Hawker realized that with an overheated engine they would neither be able to continue toward Ireland, nor could they return to Newfoundland. Seeking out the shipping lanes, he and Mackenzie-Grieve eventually found a ship (this was almost pure luck carried to an extreme). Hawker then splashed the plane down alongside the vessel and they were taken aboard. It turned out to be the Danish *Mary*, which to their disappointment had no radio; it would be days before anyone knew where they were. It was a week, in fact, when on Sunday, May 25, the *Mary* reached the Butt of Lewis, off the coast of Scotland, and flashed a message to a coast guard station there. The word soon spread through a suddenly joyous British Isles where everyone from King George V down to the cockney at the corner pub were certain "the worst" had happened. Everyone, that is, except Mrs. Hawker, who clung to the belief that her husband and Mackenzie-Grieve would appear again—and they did. Their progress from Scapa Flow (to which they had been taken by H. M. S. *Revenge* after being taken off the *Mary*) to Buckingham Palace was an outpouring of national emotion. Their train was stopped en route for speeches and noisy welcomes. On Tuesday, the twenty-seventh, they were received by the King and awarded the Air Force Cross; later they lunched with Lord Northcliffe, who presented them with £5,000 (half the original prize) for "a magnificent failure." (The drifting *Atlantic*, which could not be salvaged by the *Mary*, was found by an

Journey's End: The NC-4 sails into Lisbon Harbor to become the first aircraft to fly the Atlantic—May 8–May 27, 1919. (*National Air & Space Museum, Smithsonian Institution*)

American steamer, the *Lake Charlotteville*, hoisted aboard and brought to England, where it became a popular exhibit on the roof of Selfridge's department store.)

With all the excitement over Hawker and Mackenzie-Grieve it was barely noted in England, on the twenty-seventh, that Putty Read and the NC-4 had finally taken off from Ponta Delgada and 9 hours and 43 minutes later set down in the harbor at Lisbon. American headlines were ecstatic, however, led by *The New York Times*'s:

NC-4 WINS FIRST OCEAN FLIGHT FOR AMERICA;
9¾ HOURS FROM PONTA DELGADA TO LISBON;
HAWKER'S PLANE PICKED UP BY AMERICAN SHIP

Little, unsmiling Putty Read, his raffish crew and the once maligned NC-4 had succeeded in crossing the Atlantic Ocean by air for the first time in history. In nineteen days they had traversed 3,322 miles in 41 hours and 58 minutes in the air. The reception at Lisbon out-blasted those at Horta and Ponta Delgada, beginning with a 21-gun salute. There were wires from all over the world, including one from President Woodrow Wilson, at the Versailles Peace Conference, who said: "We are heartily proud of you. You have won the distinction of adding further laurels to our country."

Read was elated, but hoping, as the *Times* reported, to push off again the next day, destination: Plymouth, England. Before that, however, he unbent again and went nightclubbing with the crew. Jim Breese, particularly, enjoyed the good life that followed their historic stops and at one point during the convivial evening happily stated, "I may just take out citizenship papers."

Thanks to the weather, they remained at Lisbon for three days. On Friday, the thirtieth, they took off at dawn hoping to arrive at Plymouth before nightfall. They had been flying for nearly two hours when Breese noticed that one of the engines had begun to sputter and lose power. So they set down in what they learned was the Mondego River, near the town of Figuerra, still Portugal. They learned, too, that a radiator had sprung a leak, which was taken care of, but they also ran aground on a sand bar in the river. Though no damage was done, the wait for high tide made a takeoff inadvisable since it would have brought them into Plymouth too late for a daylight landing. Instead they took off as soon as possible and proceeded to Ferrol, Spain (a flight of a little over three hours), where the plane could be safely moored during the night—and, apparently, Jim Breese could enjoy the adulation of the populace.

The promised weather for the next day, Saturday, May 31, was, in a word, unpromising: fog and rain. Disappointed, Read made a comment to the effect that in the future "pilots ought to be trained in patience as well as flying." But, in a decision unusual with this self-contained, methodical man, Read got the NC-4 out of Ferrol early the next morning despite the weather.

They lifted off the water and quickly disappeared into the fog and rain. Over the Bay of Biscay the visibility was so poor that they never saw four of the six destroyers that had been deployed across their track. But they kept on, with Read plotting their course with characteristic precision. They circled Brest, the port at which thousands of American soldiers still awaited shipment home, but had to decline the port commander's invitation to drop in for a drink. Instead they continued toward England. Word came soon after that British planes were flying out to welcome and escort them in to Plymouth. Read radioed a warning: "Request British craft maintain safe distance until haze clears sufficiently for us to see them." Although the planes were aloft, Read never saw them.

Then Plymouth began forming out of the mist and, as they circled the harbor out of which the Pilgrims had sailed on the *Mayflower* nearly 300 years before, they saw the *Aroostock* moored awaiting their arrival. It had crossed over from Trepassey during their long flight.

The New York Times correspondent described their arrival:

> Flying straight for the *Aroostock,* the great plane turned west, flying along the whole length of the front, turning again around the western end of Drake's Island and again at the Citadel, and taxied into the sheltered Cattewater, where she anchored to a buoy in the very mouth of the River Plym and within a stone's throw of the Mayflower stone on the Barbican.
>
> As I swept up to her she looked like some huge, gray porpoise, covered with a staging of yellow, upon which small figures of human heads could be seen moving jerkily, while the British planes which had escorted her danced many lazy figures of sheer joy-riding and of the aviators' brotherly interest in the great victory achieved over the atmosphere and the mechanical difficulties.
>
> The streets were filled with cheering crowds all the way to the Grand Hotel on the Hoe, where, within sight of the greens on which modern Englishmen play Drake's great and historic game, the American aviators were welcomed to England.

The *Daily Mirror*'s headline ran: RAH! RAH! FOR READ, as the crew of the NC-4 was welcomed to London. Harry Hawker was on hand to greet them. He had conveniently forgotten his offer to eat the NC that succeeded in crossing the Atlantic. But he did say when he learned of

The first men to cross the Atlantic by air: E. Stone, E. Rhoads, W. Hinton, H. C. Rodd, J. Breese and A. C. Read, and an unidentified Naval officer. (*National Air & Space Museum, Smithsonian Institution*)

their success, "I am very glad they have got across. It was a jolly good effort."

Coming from the outspoken Hawker, this was no mean compliment. He meant it and they—Read, Stone, Breese, Hinton, Rodd and Rhoads—had earned it.

They had been The First.

2

". . . a terrible journey"

John Alcock and Arthur Whitten Brown shared a love for flying. Both had spent time in enemy prisoner-of-war camps during the Great War (after being forced down in planes), but otherwise they were opposites. The ruddy-faced, outgoing, laughing Alcock projected the image of the typical early airman (he was nineteen when he first flew in 1911); he came in third in the race Lord Northcliffe sponsored from London to Manchester and, when war came, he joined the Royal Naval Air Service. As a pilot he saw action on the Turkish Front. He became an expert in long-distance bombing (for which he was awarded the Distinguished Service Cross). It was, however, on one of these raids that Alcock's plane suffered engine trouble and he came down in enemy territory. Alcock spent most of 1918 in a Turkish prison camp. It was during this period that he began thinking about making a transatlantic flight.

Brown, six years older than Alcock, was a quiet, less demonstrative, more studious type of person. He was an American who had been born in Glasgow and who early showed a brilliant engineering gift. When war broke out in 1914 he gave up his American citizenship (no great sacrifice, for he had never lived for any length of time in the United States) and enlisted in the British army. Eventually he transferred to the Royal Flying Corps as an observer, serving as an artillery fire spotter and as reconnaissance officer. During one of these flights the plane in which Brown was flying was shot down by German fighters and he and his pilot were forced down behind enemy lines. The landing was a rough one and in it Brown received a severe leg injury which left him lame for life.

During his time in prison, like Alcock, Brown thought about flying the Atlantic and spent his time studying aerial navigation; the leg injury precluded any escape attempts. In fact, Brown's pilot was killed in trying—for the fourteenth time—to escape. Also because of his leg injury Brown was eventually repatriated, in the spring of 1918, and spent the rest of the war working with engines for the Ministry of Munitions.

When the war ended both Alcock and Brown left their respective military branches and sought work in the aviation industry. Each in his own time, and for his own reasons, gravitated to Vickers. Alcock had arrived first with his idea of flying the Atlantic, which he outlined to Maxwell Muller, manager of Vickers, who listened with a most sympathetic ear.

Soon after, Brown arrived with a letter of introduction (for he had had difficulty with his lame leg in finding work); he too spoke of the feasibility, with the proper plane and with skilled navigation, of crossing the Atlantic by air. Muller brought the two opposites together and the flight was on.

The plane selected was Vickers's Vimy, which had been designed late in 1918 as a night bomber. Powered with two Rolls-Royce Eagle engines, the plane was capable of lifting heavy payloads (originally bombs, but now fuel), and it was also able to remain aloft for long periods of time and maintain a speed of all of 100 miles an hour. It had come too late in the war to serve its original purpose, but with a few modifications it could be the plane for flying the Atlantic. All military hardware was removed to make room for fuel tanks (one of which, when empty, could serve as a raft); the two cockpits of the original plane were merged into one, making communication between pilot and navigator simpler. The original skid under the nose was replaced with a wheel, but that was removed eventually to lessen wind resistance and to save weight. The

OPPOSITE   John Alcock (left) and Arthur Whitten Brown, shortly after their arrival at St. John's, Newfoundland, in May of 1919. (*Vickers*)

gunner's cockpit in the nose was faired over to house one of the extra fuel tanks. One of the most "modern" innovations was the installation of a radio.

By mid-April, 1919, the Vimy was ready and Alcock took it up for a test hop and, according to his own account, "found it so satisfactory that it was packed for transshipment without delay. Strikes were the order of the day, however, and we were hung up for a considerable time at the London Docks. But at last we got off. . . ."

That was on May 4, 1919. The crated Vimy left a few days after. The crossing from Southampton was made on the *Mauretania* and, thanks to the captain, Brown was permitted freedom of the bridge where he picked up additional pointers on ocean navigation.

"We had arrived at St. John's early on the morning of May 13," Brown later wrote. "Thirteen, by the way, we regarded as our lucky number. The construction of our transatlantic machine was begun on February 13, it was number 13 of its class, and it reached Newfoundland on May 26 (twice thirteen). Our party, with mechanics, totalled 13 [ten workmen from Vickers, Ltd., an engine expert from Rolls-Royce plus Alcock and Brown]."

Three days after the Vimy crew arrived the NCs began their flight for the Azores which incited activity in the British camp at St. John's. This rush to be away made little concession to the weather and proper engine adjustments which may have been to some extent the cause of the crash of the *Raymor* and the coming down in the Atlantic of the plane of Hawker and Mackenzie-Grieve.

There was nothing for Alcock and Brown to do but wait for their Vimy and seek a decent airstrip, not a simple job because of the hilly and rocky terrain in the vicinity of St. John's. "Newfoundland is a hospitable place," Brown later observed, "but its best friends cannot claim that it is ideal for aviation."

With the Hotel Cochrane, in St. John's itself, as their headquarters, the two men spent many hours and drove "over hundreds of miles of very bad road" in quest of an "aerodrome." The town itself, Brown wrote, "showed us every kindness. We explored the town pretty thoroughly, and were soon able to recognize parts of it with eyes closed and nostrils open, for its chief occupation appeared to be the drying of very dead cod."

The enterprise engendered a festive air which was rather spoiled by the disappearance of Hawker's plane and the subsequent crash of the *Raymor*; but as Brown put it rather cryptically, "With one exception, there was the best possible feeling among the small colony of British aviators who had congregated at St. John's for the competition."

That exception was Adm. Mark Kerr, who commanded the party associated with the other bomber at St. John's, the big Handley Page V/1500. This group had rented the most suitable airfield in the vicinity of Quidi Vidi, especially for a large, heavily loaded plane. When word got out that Alcock and Brown were seeking such a field, Kerr offered the use of it to them and also to the advance party for another plane (one of those which never actually participated) for the consideration of each paying one-half the rent (thus making it rent-free to Kerr and company). But that wasn't all: they could use it only after the Handley Page had taken off over the Atlantic!

Alcock and Brown rejected this offer and did not find Kerr's offer at all "sporting." Meanwhile, with the arirval of the crated Vimy, there was some anxiety and both Hawker and Raynham offered their (inadequate) facilities to Alcock and Brown. It would do for the assembling of the plane—and actually could be used for taking off provided the Vimy was not heavily loaded, as it would have to be for the actual crossing attempt.

Erecting the big plane in an open field—sometimes from dawn to dusk—was hard work. It "went well till Friday, the thirtieth of May," Alcock recalled later, "when the weather broke. Rain poured down on us and eventually work on the machine had to be abandoned altogether. Till the following Monday evening it rained or snowed incessantly— four days of fierce gales."

A great camaraderie grew around this effort. The U.S. Navy offered to supply them the new Byrd sextant and one was ordered from Washington, although it did not arrive in time to be of any use on their flight. This was not the only hitch in the delivery service: an order had been placed for what Brown called "life saving suits" (probably life jackets) which, for some strange reason, were delivered to the Bank of Montreal where the carton was thought to contain typewriters and was stored in the bank's basement.

Newsmen, British and American, who had naturally flocked to St. John's, proved to be of great assistance "when extra manpower was required," helping with the lifting of various heavy parts, the wings and other such duties (including, when a field site was found, manhandling rocks and boulders). Brown was especially grateful to an American —"Mr. Klauber"—who supplied them at the last minute with a flashlight when their own failed.

One of the problems of working in the open was the gathering of crowds. "Many rubbernecks," Brown observed, "who seemed to have no other occupation, spent hours in leaning against the nearest fence and watching us. . . . The testing of the fabric's firmness with the point of an umbrella was a favourite pastime of the spectators. . . ." Despite these and other hazards the Vimy was finally assembled and ready for a test flight by the ninth of June.

In the meantime a larger field was found nearby at a place called Monday's Pool. It was not, in fact, much. But by "removing hillocks, blasting boulders, and levelling walls and fences," Alcock and Brown had an airstrip of about 300 yards in length (another 200 yards wouldn't have hurt at all). With luck, even with the loaded Vimy, they should be able to get out of that field.

Before a by now consistently large gathering of "rubbernecks" Alcock and Brown took off from the Quidi Vidi field on their first test flight. "The weather was on its best behaviour," Brown noted, "and our takeoff from the ground was perfect in every way. Under Alcock's skilful hands the Vickers Vimy became almost as nippy as a scout." The two Rolls-Royces hummed in gratifying unison as they flew out over the Atlantic where it "reflected the sky's vivid blue. Near the coast it was spotted and streaked by the glistening white of icebergs and whitecaps."

The craft and the engines performed beautifully; only the radio failed to operate. That could, of course, be checked later. Alcock swung the big plane easily inland and flew over Newfoundland again and, as Brown observed, "from above [it] looked even more bleak and rugged than it did from the ground." They spotted the location of their new airdrome with the aid of a smudge-fire which had been arranged as a signal. Alcock came in and brought the Vimy into the field; it touched heavily and rumbled over the still somewhat bumpy ground. Landing into the wind, they actually ran slightly uphill on the strip hacked out of the rocky earth. Even so, they practically traversed the entire strip and headed for a fence which ran alongside the road that skirted the field. Alcock gunned the starboard engine, which swung the plane around, and they were safely in their new air drome. They then alighted and pushed the Vimy down the hill to a more sheltered spot, "pegged it down, and roped off a space around it, to keep spectators at a safe distance."

They were thoroughly satisfied with their flight and, except for the radio, both men believed they were ready for the Atlantic flight.

The tempo of the activity increased, fuel problems required solving, the radio needed repairing and, just to be sure, another flight was accomplished on June 12—and again the only failure was with the radio. The plan, of course, was to get off on the following day, a lucky Friday the thirteenth. Meanwhile, they could see that things had picked up in the Handley Page camp also. The race was on. Various last-minute items were checked off: compasses swung, food and emergency supplies were put aboard, even affixing the Vimy with the official seal of the Royal Aero Club, thus, in the wry words of Brown, "insuring that we should not cheat by flying from Newfoundland in one aeroplane and landing in Ireland in another." Two final items were placed aboard in the special storage section in the tail, designed to remain above water for a good length of time should they be forced down: these were two stuffed animals, both black cats, named "Lucky Jim" and "Twinkletoe."

But to no avail. The overladen plane's landing-gear shock absorbers gave way and they had to be repaired, which required unloading, even to the point of siphoning off the fuel; the final coat of dope did not dry until Friday evening.

"A large black cat, its tail held high in a comical curve, sauntered by the transatlantic machine, early on the morning of June 14, and such a cheerful omen made me more than anxious to start." The words are Brown's; the black cat was the only cheerful omen. The weather was questionable: "Strong westerly wind. Conditions otherwise favourable."

Their strip ran east and west, so they would have to take off, if they did on Saturday, into the force of the strong west wind. They decided to wait until it died down (had the wind been less strong, they would have taken off, into the wind, and running downhill). By the afternoon, they had become restive and the wind continued rising. Since, obviously, it would not become any more favorable, they decided, about four in the afternoon, to get into their flying clothes and load all their equipment into the plane. An hour later Alcock gunned the engines. The heavy Vimy lurched and bumped over the rough ground.

A correspondent of the London *Times* described the takeoff: "Gradually increasing the pace, the Vimy slowly at first moved up the rather steep gradient of the aerodrome—100 yards—200 yards—300 yards—and the machine still moved forwards, but showed not the least desire to leave the ground. Pessimists who had foretold that, with its exceptional load, it could not leave an uphill ground in the face of a 40 mile an hour gale began to croak disaster, when suddenly and at just the right moment Captain Alcock operated his controls. The machine jumped off the ground, *zoomed* over the fence which was a few yards ahead, bounded over the eastern end of the aerodrome, and began steadily to climb."

Brown, in the cockpit beside Alcock, suffered some anxiety. The takeoff was bumpy as the engines strained for speed and Alcock held the nose down as long as he safely dared. The wind into which they flew was unpredictable, dropping from 40 mph gusts to nothing—and it would shift to the side, creating the possibility of the hazards of crosswinds, such as had wrecked the *Raymor*. Even after the Vimy had lifted uncer-

LEFT Assembling Alcock and Brown's Vickers Vimy, between rain squalls. The outer bay of the upper port wing is being fitted into place. *(Vickers)*

RIGHT As the Vimy nears completion great crowds of what Brown called "rubbernecks" converged on the plane. Their curiosity and probing were a menace to the aircraft. *(Vickers)*

tainly off the field—it had to, for there was little left of it—it settled downward when the wind died down. But Alcock managed to keep them airborne; they cleared the fence at the end of their run, nearly brushed some trees, skirted rooftops as they slowly climbed over St. John's. For a moment to the spectators it appeared that the plane was sinking into the trees and cries of "He's coming down!" were heard, but the Vimy continued to climb until, at around 800 feet, they pointed the nose toward the sea. They crossed the coast at 1,000 feet; now they were really certain they were on their way. This Brown attributed to "Alcock's clever piloting."

For the first hour the visibility was about as good as the weather report had promised; during this period Brown made all possible navigational observations while the getting was good. Then inexplicably the small propeller that drove the wind-driven generator, which supplied power to the radio, seized up and flew off into the sea. Alcock laconically observed, "This was indeed a cheerful beginning, and it accounted for our silence throughout the flight."

But that was, as a beginning, only the beginning.

They passed over a large fog bank as they flew deeper into the sky over the sea; soon there was no sea to be seen. Then the lowering clouds moved in. They were sandwiched between the two masses and now could no longer see sea or sky. Brown would have to navigate by dead reckoning.

LEFT Alcock (left) and Brown in flight gear waiting for the right weather for takeoff in the Vimy. (*Vickers*)

RIGHT Alcock stows a thermos bottle of hot chocolate aboard the Vimy just prior to takeoff. (*Vickers*)

BELOW ". . . zoomed over a fence which was a few yards ahead . . ." the Vickers Vimy taking off. (*Vickers*)

They droned through the approaching night, cut off from all possible human communication—even with themselves, for they had discarded their headphones because they were uncomfortable and inefficient. For the rest of the flight they would have to shout directly into one another's ear, gesture or write messages. A strange new sound caught their attention; from the starboard engine came "a loud, rhythmic chattering, rather like the noise of machine-gun fire at close quarters." The thought that came instantly to mind was engine trouble, the same thing that had stopped Hawker. Both men peered at the source of sound and saw a piece of the exhaust pipe break away into the wind; it was this piece of metal which was clattering. As they watched the piece became red hot, then white and liquid until it blew away into the slipstream. That left three cylinders emitting exhaust—and flame—directly into the air, increasing the engine noise and the chance of the fabric catching fire. There was nothing they could do, so they shrugged off the added roar and the threat of incineration (which, luckily, never actually became a serious one). Accompanied by the "insistent hum" of the engines, they proceeded eastward through the night. "The long flight would have been dreadful had we made it in silence," Brown wrote, "for, shut off as we were from sea and sky, it was a very lonely affair."

Soon the fog closed in so much that they could not see the engines from their cockpit, except for a slight, disconcerting red glow to starboard.

Once they left the fog behind, the clouds filled the space and continued to make navigation dependent upon dead reckoning. An occasional rent in the clouds above gave Brown a glimpse of the evening sun and if a patch opened below them he saw the Atlantic. The dead reckoning was off and they were further south and east than he had calculated. He passed a note to Alcock: "Can you get above these clouds at, say, 60 deg.? We must get stars as soon as pos."

They steadily climbed for more than an hour but the clouds above and below "grew denser and darker." It was after midnight—now Sunday, June 15, 1919—before Brown caught a quick shot at the Pole Star and Vega, which told them precisely where they were. They had drifted somewhat to the south of their intended flight plan and they were about halfway across the Atlantic. Things boded well, there was enough fuel, and they could look forward to the coming of daylight and a successful end to their flight unless something "entirely unforeseen" befell them.

It did. Quite suddenly they flew into a thick bank of fog "entirely unforeseen" by the weather predictions of the previous day. In an instant both men found themselves completely disoriented; they could not see the Vimy's wingtips, nor the nose for that matter, let alone the sky and the sea. There was, of course, no horizon. They had no idea which way was up, whether or not they were flying parallel to the sea or into it. Their instruments told them very little, since they had no really sophisticated instruments for blind flying. Only the fact that the air speed increased, the propellers raced and the engine roar crescendoed told them they were probably in a dive.

"Apart from the changing levels marked by the aneroid, only the fact that our bodies were pressed tightly against the seats indicated that we were falling." Alcock attempted to place the controls in neutral but actually had nothing to base this on. Brown strained his eyes hoping to find something that would tell them where they were in relation to the sea, but all he could see was the aneroid altimeter which rapidly indicated an alarming descent. They fell through nothingness until unexpectedly, about 100 feet above it, they saw the ocean. Everything was off kilter: the Atlantic was to one side, the sky on another and the horizon tilted at a right angle from the horizontal. They were flying at a crazy angle into the water.

Alcock grasped the situation immediately: he took one look at the ocean and the horizon and practically snapped the big Vimy (which for so large an aircraft was unusually sensitive to the controls) into a proper flight attitude. The low wing, which pointed directly at the water, came up; the nose twisted around and centered on the horizon and soon they were flying with all elements in correct propinquity. They were now so close to the surface that Brown could hear the ocean "as its waves swelled, broke and swelled again." Their compass, which had been spinning senselessly, stabilized and pointed in its proper direction; it told them that they were headed back for Newfoundland. Alcock turned the plane eastward and climbed away from the ocean.

But the unforeseens were not finished with them. Although it was technically sunrise, they could not see the sun as they continued to climb into the clouds. "And then came a spell of bad weather, beginning with rain, and continuing with snow . . . The snow gave place to hail, mingled with sleet."

This brought a new form of peril: icing. Some of the snow and sleet clung to the plane and clustered onto struts and covered the wing and fuselage with a glassy surface. The added weight of the ice was a problem, although that could be solved by descending into warmer air. But the greater danger lay in the accumulations of ice that covered the faces of certain instruments and gauges that Alcock had to see in order to keep complete control of the plane.

The instrument panel of the Vimy, though advanced for its time, was primitive by later standards. There was a reassuring clutter of dials and gadgets, but for some reason not all instruments were inside the cockpit. For example, the fuel supply gauge was affixed to one of the center section struts directly behind the cockpit. Alcock had to know what the flow of fuel was in order to avoid problems with the carburetor, among other variables. When he noticed that the face of the gauge had been covered with snow Brown simply crawled out onto the decking aft of the cockpit and, kneeling and holding onto a strut with one hand, cleared the instrument with the other. He later said that "the change from the sheltered warmth of the cockpit to the biting, icy cold outside was startlingly unpleasant." So was the "violent rush of air, which tended to push me backward . . ." but there was "scarcely any danger in kneeling on the fuselage, as long as Alcock kept the machine level."

Brown was forced to perform this feat several times as the snow and sleet blew into their faces. There were even more hazardous exploits, ignored by Brown when he later wrote of their flight and which might never have been known except that Alcock, immediately after they had landed, blurted it out to newsmen. There were other important instruments mounted on the inboard side of the engine nacelles; these carried the oil pressure and the revolutions per minute of the propeller of each engine. Flying practically blind as he was, Alcock could only judge whether or not they were diving (as their earlier scare had already demonstrated) unless he kept a wary eye on the rpm counter. If the count lessened it would mean they were climbing and in danger of a stall—which could mean spinning into the Atlantic.

There was only one way that these instruments—plus a couple of others, as well as the controllable engine shutter system—could be cleared and that was for one of them (Brown, since he was not the pilot) to leave the cockpit, clamber out onto the wing and chip away the ice with his pocket knife.

It was no great distance—barely five feet—but there were patches of ice on the upper surface of the wing and there were only bracewires to cling to until you reached the engine, which, of course, had a great four-bladed propeller swirling rapidly within inches of the gauges. Also there was the blast of the slipstream, plus whatever wind may have been blowing toward them (they were generally blessed with a tail wind, although in the storm the wind shifted crazily now and then). And there was Brown's lame leg.

No less than six times did Brown struggle out into the icy gale to chip away at the gauges and various tubes and air intakes that had been blocked by the ice; this as much as anything kept them airborne as they flew through the storm. At 5:00 A.M. at an altitude of about 11,000 feet, although still enshrouded in clouds and with their plane glittering with ice, Brown caught a quick glimpse of the sun through a sudden gap in the clouds. He made speedy calculations and determined that they must be approaching the coast of Ireland. About two and a half hours later he felt reasonably sure of their position and scratched out a message to Alcock: "We had better go lower down, where the air is warmer, and where we might pick up a steamer."

Icing on the wings had made aileron response sluggish and the warmer air would help to clear that up. There was still the thick cloud. If that extended all the way down to the ocean and if their altimeter was not precise, there was the danger of flying into the water. Against that contingency, Brown took the precaution of loosening his safety belt and "was ready to abandon ship if we hit the water."

Alcock put the Vimy in a flat gliding descent as slowly, with engines throttled back, they slipped downward through the murk. They exchanged anxious looks as the starboard engine popped and barked ominously. But throttling back cleared that up. They continued on downward, alert to every sound. The altimeter dropped from 11,000 feet to a thousand, where the warmer air freed the ailerons. But still they remained in thick vapor; the altimeter could be wrong, what with the atmospheric pressure as unsettled as it was. Suddenly they burst through the underlayer of the clouds—still 500 feet above the dark and restless ocean. Alcock throttled up again and was relieved to hear the starboard engine come to life with a healthy roar.

Brown went to work with his various instruments, checking against drift and what few sightings he had been able to take. He found that they were slightly north of their true course, gave Alcock the compass bearing and, it being then about eight in the morning, decided they would have breakfast. Neither man was hungry but they ate anyway, "partly to kill time and partly to take our minds from the rising excitement induced by the hope that we might sight land at any instant." Brown gave Alcock a sandwich, then some chocolate. Alcock flew with his right hand on the joystick and both feet on the rudder bar; he had been in this position for sixteen hours. And now that the flight appeared to be coming to a fruitful close he was forced to be even more heavy on the stick, for as the fuel in the aft tanks was used, the Vimy tended toward a nose-heavy flight attitude. He had to pull back on the stick to keep in trim.

Brown had turned to put the thermos and the uneaten food back into the little cupboard behind his seat when he felt Alcock's hand on his shoulder, forcing him to turn around. The pilot's face was cracked in a broad smile as he pointed in the distance. "I followed the direction indicated by his outstretched forefinger; and barely visible through the mist, it showed me two tiny specks of—land. This happened at 8:15 A.M. on June 15."

He put away his charts, his pages of computations, even "disregarded the compass needle. My work as navigator of the flight was at an end."

The specks grew larger as Alcock flew toward them—they were the small coastal islands of Eeshal and Turbot—and within ten minutes of their first sighting, they crossed over the Irish coast, flying at a height of 250 feet, just underneath the cloud mass. Brown was still uncertain as to their exact position until he spotted the radio antennae of the station at Clifden—they were only ten miles off their exact course. He indicated the direction to Galway, but it was obvious that in the mist there was the danger of flying into a hill. Alcock decided to land although they still had enough fuel for ten additional hours of flying.

They circled the Clifden radio station and Alcock selected a fine smooth piece of land close by. He turned into the wind and came in smoothly, engines off. "Already I was indulging in the comforting reflection that the anxious flight had ended in a perfect landing," Brown later confessed. Then came the moment for one more "entirely unforeseen" element. The landing spot Alcock had selected was not a field, but a peat bog; instead of a solid surface they were coming into a marsh. All was fine at first as the speed of the Vimy carried them along momentarily, but then suddenly the nose tipped and the tail rose and the plane dug into the soft earth.

Both men were tossed forward without warning. Brown laconically noted that he only avoided a "jarring collision with the help of my nose." Alcock hung onto the joystick and, in the impact, bent the metal post into the shape of a horseshoe. Luckily the crash had been absorbed by the nose of the plane, the covered-over forward cockpit, the extra fuel tanks and other structural additions, so that neither Alcock nor Brown had suffered any serious injury. However, a burst fuel line began filling the cockpit with gasoline, so the two men hurriedly climbed out of their plane. There was no fire however, just a sadly broken, almost dejected-looking, former transatlantic aircraft—the first ever to fly the ocean nonstop.

When a crowd gathered from nearby Clifden, Alcock and Brown had finished salvaging a few things from the flooded cockpit and had relaxed. There was time for a smile and Brown asked, "What do you think of that for fancy navigating?" They had covered 1,890 miles in 15 hours, 57 minutes.

"Very good," Alcock replied, grasping his partner's hand and shaking it. They had done it and it was beginning to dawn upon them. They had actually flown the Atlantic!

"Anybody hurt?" one of the newcomers asked and was assured that they were all right.

Then someone else asked, "Where you from?"

The reply, "America," was greeted with a nervous laugh. No one at Clifden, apparently, had heard of Alcock and Brown. Not until they had pulled a mail sack from the plane and showed that it had come from St. John's, Newfoundland, did it come to the crowd that Alcock and Brown had, indeed, flown the Atlantic. There were cheers and "painful hand-shakes" and the two men were taken to Clifden where they were able to inform Vickers, the *Daily Mail* and the Royal Aero Club of their success. Brown also sent a telegram to his anxious fiancee Kathleen Kennedy.

Then he was overheard saying, "We didn't do badly, did we?" and then, after Alcock said he was not a bit tired after the long flight, Brown said, "I am a bit fagged out."

Alcock gave two curiously disparate versions of some of the tribulations of the flight. In a version published three months later in *Badmington Magazine,* he reminisced rather rosily and wrote, "For ourselves, we experienced no discomfort, and with the exception of the failure of the wireless and that of the air-speed indicator with its resulting spin, we had no anxiety whatever."

However, in an article written the evening following their arrival, with the details of the adventure still vivid in his mind, Alcock had not been quite so sanguine. The article was practically a recitation of discomforts: no sun, fog, hail and snow, the plane sheeted in ice, the sleet that "chewed bits out of our faces" whenever they peered outside the cockpit; he even told of Brown's climb out onto the wing to chip away the ice (and later revealed to his brother that without that they would never have made it).

"We have had a terrible journey," he exclaimed. "The wonder is we are here at all."

After the misery had worn off, after they had rested, the wonder was practically all that remained. They were greeted by their countrymen as conquering heroes and were fêted, cheered and mobbed everywhere they went. The Secretary of State for War and Air, Winston Churchill, officially presented them with the *Daily Mail* check for £10,000 (which they shared with the Vickers mechanics who had made their flight possible). They were welcomed at Windsor Castle, where they were knighted, and visited London in great triumph.

It was a wonderfully heady time and they had earned it. But for Alcock it was an all too brief taste of glory. Both he and Brown were employed by Vickers, the latter in engineering and Alcock as a test pilot.

LEFT Alcock and Brown's Vimy straining for altitude over St. John's before heading out to sea. (*Vickers*)

BELOW The not very dignified ending of the first successful nonstop transatlantic flight by Alcock and Brown: June 15, 1919, Derrygimla, near Clifden, County Galway, Ireland. (*Vickers*)

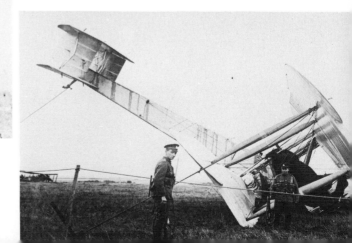

In December of that same year he was killed when a plane he was flying to a Paris air show crashed in the fog. Brown never flew again after the death of Alcock. He preferred a modest, glory-free life after their joint exploit. He settled down to a more sedate existence, married Kathleen Kennedy (their only son was killed during the Second World War; he had been a pilot). Brown died, aged sixty-two, in 1948.

By this time, though he and Alcock were all but forgotten, the air trail they had blazed in 1919 was filled with winged traffic.

3

Before the Storm

Because the *Daily Mail* prize had been captured, it did not mean that all the enticements were plucked. Even before Alcock and Brown had taken off, even as the fate of Hawker and Mackenzie-Grieve remained a mystery and the NC-4 lay weathered-in at Ponta Delgada, a new prize came out of the blue. Alan R. Hawley, president of the Aero Club of America, received a letter which read:

Gentlemen:
     As a stimulus to the courageous aviators, I desire to offer, through the auspices and regulations of the Aero Club of America, a prize of $25,000 to the first aviator of any Allied country crossing the Atlantic

in one flight, from Paris to New York or New York to Paris, all other details in your care.

Yours very sincerely,
Raymond Orteig

The letter had been typed on the stationery of the Lafayette Hotel and Orteig was the French émigré owner of that hotel as well as the Brevoort, where as a young man he had worked as a waiter. With all the transatlantic hoopla in the news Orteig later asked newsmen, "Where does France come in? I wanted to offer some inducement for a flight which would include France." One of his stipulations was that the flight must be made within a period of five years—that is, by the summer of 1924 (when no such flight materialized, Orteig extended the time an additional five years).

The success of Alcock and Brown did, however, finish all the ambitions for an Atlantic crossing of Admiral Kerr in his Handley Page bomber which had been left standing at the gate in Newfoundland. That watery avenue closed, Kerr elected to try for a different destination. New York was selected because no aircraft had flown between there and Newfoundland nonstop. While the further adventures of Kerr, Brackley, Gran and Wyatt lie outside the subject of this chronicle, suffice it to say that the plane took off on July 4 with two additional passengers (A. P. Arnold, an engineer, and C. C. Clements, a mechanic) and

Crew of the Handley Page in the plane's cockpit: pilot H. G. Brackley, navigator Trygve Gran and mission leader Adm. Mark Kerr. Note instruments (just above Gran's head) affixed to the engine; in time it would be learned that these belonged in the cockpit. (*Courtesy of National Museum of Science & Technology, Ottawa, Canada*)

headed southward. Engine trouble off the coast of Nova Scotia after dark brought them down in a field near Parrsboro for a landing which wiped out the landing gear, crumpled the wings and pushed in the nose—luckily without injury to crew.

With new parts shipped from England the Handley Page was repaired and ready to go again in October (still 1919) and actually made it to New York in an eleven-hour flight. Then, in November, looking for new worlds to conquer, Kerr decided to try for a nonstop flight between New York and Chicago which was sponsored by the Railway Express Agency. The idea was to make the first aerial express delivery between the two great cities. However, the weather, even as it did over the Atlantic, interjected complexities. The bomber was forced down twice en route—the first time all the express was transferred for delivery by train and the second was its own little saga.

The pilot, Maj. H. G. Brackley, took off from Mount Jewett, Pennsylvania, site of their first unscheduled stop, and headed for Cleveland. Their objective was Martin Field, but when they arrived over the city they found that directions had been misleading. In the deepening twilight, Brackley decided to set down in the North Randall Race Track. He did, but the fencing on either side of his improvised runway clipped away the wingtips and the plane came to fuller grief up against the grandstand. Again good fortune attended Kerr and crew and no one

The Handley Page taking off. (*Courtesy of National Museum of Science & Technology, Ottawa, Canada*)

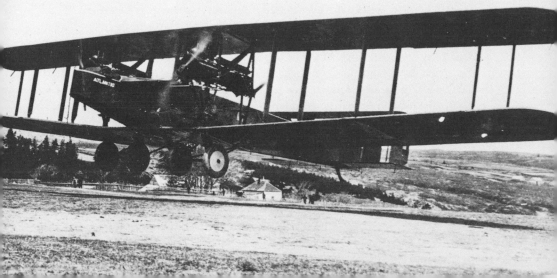

suffered serious injury—although all were ready to abandon any future record-breaking flights. Thus ended the last of the four British aircraft that had gathered near Lake Quidi Vidi, Harbour Grace, Newfoundland.

The entire front page, excepting for a small item and an insurance company advertisement, of the London *Sunday Evening Telegram* for June 15, 1919, was devoted to heralding the "Great British Air Triumph" of Alcock and Brown. There was even a touch of romance in such items as those headed "Flying To His Bride" and "Miss Kennedy Delighted" to add a further note of happiness.

The single item, not connected with Alcock and Brown, was still related, for it alluded to a transatlantic flight also. The body of the brief article read: "Last night, at about nine o'clock, the great airship R-34 left her shed at East Fortune aerodrome, Haddingtonshire, on a final trial flight in order to test the wireless apparatus and other mechanism prior to proceeding across the Atlantic. The maneuvers were carried out over the Haddingtonshire coast, followed by a flight over the Firth of Forth, and it is understood that the trial proved very satisfactory from every standpoint. The airship will probably attempt the Transatlantic flight in a few days."

The R-34, in fact, was not the only airship poised for an Atlantic flight. The German Zeppelin, L-72, under the command of *Hauptman* Ernst Lehmann, was ready to go also. The big airship (nearly 750 feet long) had been designed for just such a trip—originally to bomb New York City, in fact. It could certainly be expected to be in the running. Except that German government officials, hoping to put on a peaceful face under the scrutiny of the Inter-Allied Commission of Control, scrubbed the flight plans. It did not appear to be good politics, so soon after the war, to remind one of the victors of the Zeppelin terrors by having one of the monstrous airships pass over its original objective. Lehmann, however, insisted that his flight had been spoiled by the unsportsmanlike British, who wished to be the first to fly the Atlantic in an airship.

A wayward wind had eliminated the American competition, the C-5, and some form of political probity, the German; that left only the R-34. Actually, the design was based on a captured German airship, brought down by gunfire, the L-33. The R-34, though not as large as the scratched L-72, was 643 feet long and had a diameter of nearly 80 feet. Like the U.S. Navy flight of the NCs, the flight of the R-34 was carefully planned and thoughtfully manned. Commander of the airship was Maj. G. H. Scott, who hand-picked a crew of thirty; also aboard were such high officials as Brig. Gen. E. M. Maitland, an American observer interested in airships, Lt. Comdr. Zachary Lansdowne, British Maj. J. E. M.

Pritchard—and a weighty young man who would earn the distinction of being the first transatlantic aerial stowaway.

The R-34 cast off from its moorings at East Fortune, Scotland, at two in the morning of Wednesday, July 2, 1919. The long, slender airship lifted away from the earth and set course for Glasgow, its five engines sputtering away in general harmony. A heavy load of fuel (4,900 gallons weighing some sixteen tons) precluded any possibility of climbing to any great altitude, although the hills that lay in the path of the R-34 were cleared nicely. Weight and fuel were the critical items, and fuel was more precious than men. At the last minute Aircraftsman William Ballantyne, for example, was eliminated from the crew because he tipped the scales at fourteen stone (just under 200 pounds). The average speed at which the R-34 cruised was 45 miles an hour—top speed under optimum conditions (for example, no head winds blowing against its ample frontal area) was 65 miles an hour.

Chugging along at this good rate, the R-34, its upper surface skimming directly under thick cloud, crossed Scotland, then Ireland and finally went out to sea. The flight path was reasonably smooth, except for a bit of rising and falling of the nose because of the winds. The meteorologist, Lt. Guy Harris, climbed out of the control gondola and up through the body of the airship itself and poked his head out of the opening in the top for a peek at the weather. "The clouds fitted exactly over the top of the ship," he later reported to the navigator. "Any angel passing by must have been a bit astonished to see my disembodied head, like St. John the Baptist's on a plate."

The navigator, apparently in no mood for heavenly levity, retorted with "And if you step off the catwalk and fall through the bloody fabric they'll be a bit more astonished." It was the weather that interested him; and he got it. Harris predicted plenty of fog.

The erratic movement of the nose of the ship had its effect upon the unofficial passenger. Around eight o'clock in the morning, after the ship had been churning through the fog for six hours, all fourteen miserable stone of Aircraftsman Ballantyne were revealed when he gave himself up as a stowaway. He had hidden away among the fuel tanks on a narrow catwalk until he had become sick. No one, including Ballantyne himself, was much impressed with the fact that he was history's first transatlantic stowaway (a distinction for which he was later court-martialed).

Maintaining a speed of around 50 miles an hour, the R-34 continued on its course. It became almost routine as the day's schedule progressed. At meal times a small problem came up, since the dining quarters were located in the nose. If more than a dozen men ate at a time the weight caused the R-34 to become nose heavy; thus it was always necessary to be certain that the number of men in the mess was balanced by an equal

OVERLEAF The one-time Atlantic hopeful (with the name *Atlantic* since removed from the nose) in flight over the United States. (*Courtesy of National Museum of Science & Technology, Ottawa, Canada*)

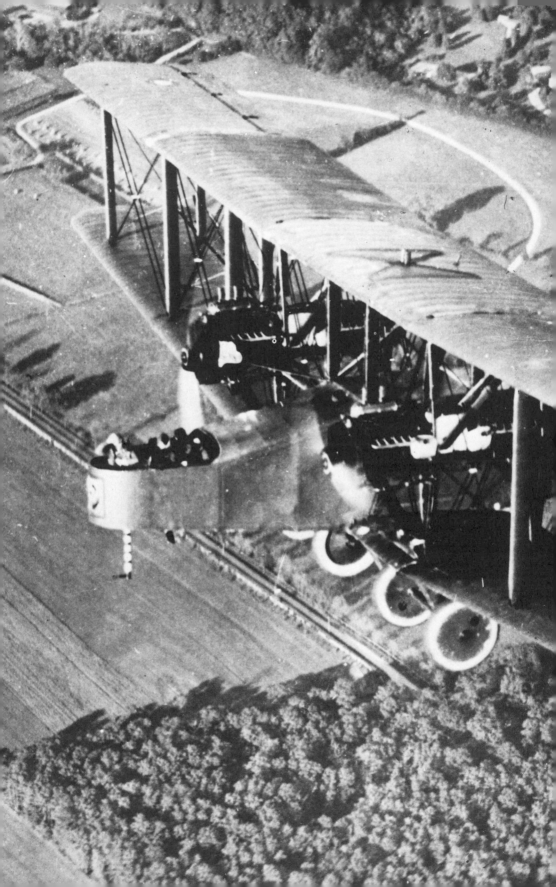

number in the aft section. Later in the day, however, the first serious
problem arose when an engine was found to have a cracked cylinder
jacket. There was no real solution to this while the airship was airborne,
although one ingenious mechanic solved the problem temporarily, in the
words of Alan Wykes, "by commandeering the steward's entire stock of
Wrigley's Spearmint, chewing it and using it to seal the crack in the iron."

Evening brought a worsening of weather and head winds, which
lessened the speed. The ship was shifted to a higher altitude where the

The end of the erstwhile *Atlantic*'s flying days after a landing at North Randall
Race Track, Cleveland, Ohio. (*Courtesy of National Museum of Science &
Technology, Ottawa, Canada*)

winds were less of a problem and visibility better. At daybreak of the
third day, Friday, July 4, they observed with wonder the great ice fields
that lay off Newfoundland; by Saturday they were passing over Nova
Scotia and on the way to New York. But then the storms and winds
intervened. Bucking the winds and dodging the most forbidding areas of
the storm, some of them violently electric, the airship with all engines
straining began consuming fuel alarmingly. It was buffeted about and at
one point men in the control gondola were not heartened upon looking
aft and seeing the tail curving, fishlike, in the strong winds. These winds
threatened, too, to blow the R-34 back out to sea, making the fuel
situation even more critical.

The imperturbable Scott waxed perturbed as was evidenced in a
radio message he sent that storm-tossed Saturday:

> Rush help. Making for Boston from Bay
> of Fundy at 23 knots. Come quickly. Gaso-
> line giving out. Send ship.

The U.S. Navy placed a destroyer in the waters of the Atlantic
between Nova Scotia and Massachusetts against the possibility that the

R-34 would be forced down at sea. The airship fought the winds and made for Chatham on Cape Cod, where preparations were under way for an emergency landing. At the same time, the landing crew that awaited the arrival of the R-34 at its original destination, Roosevelt Field, near Mineola, New York, piled into trucks and cars and raced for Montauk on the westernmost end of Long Island. They had been informed by Scott, very early in the morning of Sunday, July 6, that he had decided to pass Chatham by and would attempt to reach Montauk. "Will report time later," his message concluded.

After a frantic race, covering nearly ninety miles of what in 1919 could not have been very good Long Island roads, the crew, under the direction of Chief Frank Peckham, an American Navy man who had served aboard British airships during the war, arrived at Montauk Point. It was then about eight in the morning and they were cheered to have arrived safely, after several close calls which nearly ended them in roadside ditches, and to see looming out of the clouds the graceful form of the R-34. Peckham shouted orders as his crew took positions to grasp the lines that would be dropped from the airship and all eyes turned skyward. But the R-34 glided right over them, leaving them empty-handed and open-mouthed. Without a radio, they did not know that an unexpected shift in the wind had decided for Scott. They would continue on to Roosevelt Field after all.

When the R-34 arrived over Roosevelt Field there was no trained ground crew on hand, for Peckham and company were once again contending with the Long Island road system on the return dash. But the British were not without resources. As spectators watched the big airship hovering over the field, they gasped to see a man fall out of the gondola. In seconds a parachute blossomed over him and he floated to earth.

He was Major Pritchard, ordered by Maitland to drop down and organize a new landing party. Maitland would have done it himself (he was, in fact, famed in the service for making this rather unorthodox arrival at British installations), but he feared that this kind of performance before his American peers might cause them to think he was simply demonstrating a "cheeky stunt."

With Pritchard in charge, the R-34 was soon moored down and it was official. For the first time in history an airship had crossed the Atlantic—and by the more difficult east-to-west route. A distance of 3,260 miles had been covered in the not very startling time of 108 hours, 12 minutes. As for Pritchard, he accomplished two "firsts" that Sunday, July 6, 1919. He was the first man arriving by air from Europe to set foot in the United States, and the first to land safely in the United States by parachute from an airship.

The R-34 was, in fact, the first giant dirigible ever seen in the United

States and for three days after it was moored down, it was the center of attraction for crowds numbering in the thousands who came from long distances. But the job was only half done; on the Wednesday after the landing, July 9, the R-34 slipped its moorings in the early evening, and after taking a turn over New York, set course for home. With a good tail wind it made better time (despite the usual, and accustomed, engine troubles) on the return flight, to arrive at Pulham, Norfolk, in 75 hours, 3 minutes, on Sunday, July 13, 1919. The weather, for a change, had been kind to the airmen and, excepting the engine problems, the flight was relatively uneventful.

The historic fact was that the Atlantic had been crossed both ways by air, and advocates of the airship hailed the flight of the R-34 as a harbinger of the future when airships would regularly ply the cross-Atlantic air route in a great surge of commercial aviation.

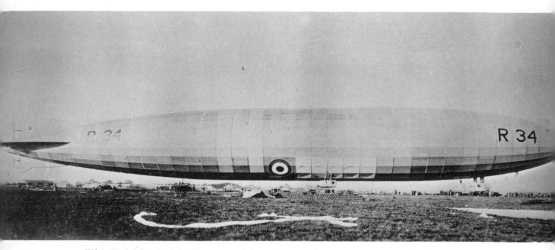

The British airship R-34 awaiting the word to go on its transatlantic attempt in July, 1919. (*U.S. Air Force*)

Major Scott was quoted in the newspapers as being "delighted" with the performance of the R-34 and pointedly said he believed it was "a good thing that Britain had collared first blood in aeroplane and airship single-hop flights." One of the immediate results of the flight was that the U.S. Navy placed an order with the British to construct a similar airship (this turned out to be the ZR-2, which broke up during a test

Closeup of the tail surfaces of the R-34. (*U.S. Air Force*)

ABOVE The R-34 passing over Long Island—also passing over American soldiers who were to have assisted in its mooring. (*University of Georgia*)

BELOW Mooring the R-34, Roosevelt Field, New York, July 1919; the finish of the first transatlantic crossing by a lighter-than-air craft. (*National Air & Space Museum, Smithsonian Institution*)

The history-making R-34, first aircraft to fly the Atlantic round trip. (*National Air & Space Museum, Smithsonian Institution*)

flight in 1921; the R-34 that same year suffered severe damage when it struck a Yorkshire hilltop and was eventually scrapped).

After the successful round-trip flight of the R-34 an inexplicable pause of five years followed; despite the Orteig prize, which expired and was renewed, no additional intrepid airmen appeared to accept the challenge until 1924. The achievements of the NC-4, the Vimy and the R-34 stood alone, almost as aerial flukes rather than the precursors of a new age in aviation.

To some degree this was true; luck played a role in all the flights. It supplied that element that aircraft design and engine reliability—what is frequently termed "the state of the art"—at the time lacked. No amount of intrepidity would compensate for the very real dangers that prevailed—including the wayward winds.

The hiatus applies actually to the North Atlantic, for the South Atlantic was traversed for the first time in 1922. While it did not lack intrepidity, it was not one of aviation's genuine early triumphs.

The South Atlantic did not attract airmen as the North did; there were no money prizes dangling at either end. Nor were there great cities in which the conqueror could be properly fêted should he be successful. This fact, also, made the South Atlantic route of no special economic value to the United States and Britain, these nations not having colonies of importance in South America. Compared with the shortest North Atlantic route, between Newfoundland and Ireland, a distance of 1,700 miles, the South Atlantic route, between the two bulges of North Africa and South America (Dakar and Natal, respectively), was about 200 miles shorter. This was not an unpleasant aspect, as it made the fuel situation less critical. Another pleasant prospect was the fact that the South Atlantic route intersected the Equator, which might have led one to believe that the weather over it might best be described as "balmy." Only experience would prove that this was a vain hope. The South Atlantic provided its full quota of stormy, treacherous weather.

However, the trade winds in the South Atlantic were favorable for an east-to-west flight (just the opposite of the North). There being little interest evidenced by American and British pilots in tackling the South Atlantic, it remained to other nations, particularly those with Latin American holdings, to show the way.

Two Portuguese airmen, Captains Gago Coutinho and Arturo de Cabral-Sacadura, were actually the first to fly across the South Atlantic, their selected flight plan running from Lisbon to Rio de Janeiro. The flight began on March 30, 1922, in a Fairey seaplane named *Lusitania*. They proceeded southward, reaching their first stop in the Canary Islands, then pressed onward to their second, the Cape Verde Islands, where they rested and waited for decent weather. This did not materialize until April 18. They headed out to sea and made it to St. Paul Rocks, a small group of islands about 500 miles off the coast of Brazil, where a Portuguese ship was stationed to assist them should they require it and to provide fuel. But St. Paul Rocks had no harbor and when the *Lusitania* landed it was engulfed by waves, bashed around, and immediately rendered un-airworthy.

There being no accommodations at St. Paul Rocks, Coutinho and Cabral-Sacadura boarded the warship and went to the island of Fernando de Noronha (which was about 200 miles off Brazil). There they awaited delivery of a replacement aircraft. When this arrived by ship, they boarded the plane and flew back to St. Paul Rocks to resume the flight where they had left off. Shortly after circling the little group, Cabral-Sacadura (who was piloting) suffered engine trouble and soon he and Coutinho were back in the water. An attempt to tow their plane by the cruiser *Republica* led to its ultimate destruction, so the two hapless airmen returned to Fernando de Noronha to put in more time waiting for a third plane. When that finally arrived they took off again and, wiser no doubt, decided not to backtrack and made straight for Brazil, where they landed on June 5, 1922. Although they were properly greeted by joyful Brazilians, the flight of Cabral-Sacadura and Coutinho, though a saga of a kind, was not an epochal flight—they had consumed at least two months and three aircraft to accomplish it.

Following this nontriumph, the Atlantic air remained relatively unruffled—at least by man-made machines—for another couple of years. The U.S. Army Air Service, not to be outdone by the Navy's initiative which resulted in the flight of the NC-4, dispatched four Douglas biplanes on no less than a round-the-world flight, a portion of which encompassed the North Atlantic. The four aircraft were named for cities: *Seattle* (where the flight began on April 6, 1924), *Boston, Chicago* and *New Orleans.* Flying westward the planes the two survivors at least—circled the globe in 15 days, 11 hours and 7 minutes. The *Seattle* came to grief early in the flight when it crashed into an Alaskan mountainside; the *Boston* came down in the Atlantic on the homeward-bound leg. In neither of these mishaps was any crew member lost or injured. The *Chicago* and *New Orleans* completed the circle upon arriving in Seattle on September 28. Considering the magnitude of the trip's mileage (27,553 miles), the small Atlantic stretch was merely an incident. Significantly the Douglas World Cruisers had flown the east-to-west route successfully, although fog was an ever present handicap. The *Boston* was forced down with engine trouble and was battered by waves before the crew, Lt. Leigh Wade and Sgt. Henry H. Ogden were rescued by a trawler, the *Ruby-Ramsey*, and ultimately the cruiser *Richmond*, which was stationed in the Atlantic for the purpose.

RIGHT Its wheels replaced by pontoons, the Douglas World Cruiser is lowered into the water for its transatlantic flight. (*National Air & Space Museum, Smithsonian Institution*)

BELOW A U.S. Army Air Service Douglas World Cruiser, two of which incidentally crossed the Atlantic during an epochal flight around the world in 1924. These craft could be equipped with either floats, as here, or wheels, depending upon the terrain over which they were to fly. (*U.S. Air Force*)

The *Richmond* was destined to play a larger role in the transatlantic. It so happened that at almost the same time that the Army planes made their Atlantic crossing, four Italian airmen had also embarked on a similar venture. They were Lt. Antonio Locatelli, in command and chief pilot, copilot Lt. Tullio Crossio, engineer C. Marescalchi and navigator R. Rissilo. For this attempt the Italian government, then much interested in the greater glory of an emerging Fascist Italy, provided the team with a German-designed and built Dornier Wal (Whale), a duo-engined single-winged seaplane. The flight began on July 25, 1924, when the Dornier lifted off the waters of the Arno near Pisa.

Well-planned, the trip went as projected, at no breakneck pace, and by August 17 the Italian crew caught up with the Americans fogged in at Reykjavik, Iceland. At the time, there were dark hints about how the Italians had hoped to steal some of the limelight away from the American crews and were, in fact, racing them across the Atlantic. This was not true, although it helped to sell newspapers. In fact the camaraderie of the air was amply demonstrated when Lt. Lowell Smith, in charge of the American flight and pilot of the *Chicago*, invited Locatelli to fly with them when the weather cleared enough to take off from Reykjavik. Thus would all three planes be able to fly in formation—the third being the other Army plane, the *New Orleans*—for mutual support. U.S. Navy ships were stationed in the waters over which they would pass, an added note of comfort—and for the Italian plane, as it turned out, the difference between life and death.

The three aircraft finally got under way on August 21. But the Dornier was capable of greater speed than the Army Douglases and, once airborne, left them behind. This did not sit at all well with some who saw this as an attempt to beat the Americans. It would actually have meant a waste of fuel for Locatelli to pace his swifter craft to the slower speed of the Cruisers. Whatever Locatelli's reasoning, the fact that he was lost to the sight of the Douglases caused him moments of soul-searching distress. When Smith and Lt. Erik Nelson and Sgt. John Harding, Jr. (the latter two in the *New Orleans*) arrived at Fredricksdal, Greenland, they were shocked to learn that the speedier Dornier had not yet arrived.

What had occurred was that about 200 miles off the coast of Greenland, the Italian plane developed engine trouble. Locatelli landed it in the icy waters to repair it and then learned that, ice-bound, they were unable to take off, there being no room in which to taxi. So the plane drifted for three days while the U.S. Navy searched for the missing crew. It was the *Richmond*, which had pulled the *Boston*'s crew out of the Atlantic, that found them. Since the plane could neither be lifted into the cruiser, nor towed, Locatelli elected to remove it as a possible hazard

Dr. Hugo Eckener, German pioneer in lighter-than-air craft, who successfully transported the ZR-3 (later *Los Angeles*) from Germany to New Jersey. Eckener was an important figure in the postwar resurgence of the dirigible although his career suffered because he fell out of favor with Hitler and the Nazis. (*National Air & Space Museum, Smithsonian Institution*)

to shipping by setting it aflame. It was a bitter ending to a flight that had almost made it.

The jubilation over the successful crossing by the *Chicago* and the *New Orleans* erased further attention to the hapless Italian crew, and the exploit faded into the dimmer pages of aviation history. The one flight proved that it could be done, but the other proved also that it did not happen every time. It was an ominous note for the future.

The year closed with yet another successful flight by an airship, the German-built ZR-3 (originally under construction for the Germans as the LZ-126). The ZR-3 was seized by the Americans (for use by the Navy) as part payment of the reparations according to the strictures of the Versailles Treaty. Germany was, of course, forbidden such activity for itself. The LZ-126 was a new Zeppelin—German Zeppelin crews destroyed seven airships after the war, many of which were to have been taken over by the United States. So it was agreed that the new ship would be produced by the Zeppelin-wise Germans and would be designated by the U.S. Navy, which intended using the 658-foot monster as a training ship, ZR-3. ZR stood for Zeppelin Rigid in Navy terminology. The ZR-1 would be American-built and would be known as the *Shenandoah*; the ZR-2 was the ill-fated British-built craft that had fallen into the Humber River with a loss of more than forty lives, among them Pritchard and Mailand of the R-34 flight.

The German-built ZR-3 (later the *Los Angeles*) would demonstrate plenty about German Zeppelin knowledge and technique. When it was ready it was placed under the command of one of Germany's outstanding airmen, Dr. Hugo Eckener, who was also managing director of Zeppelin. The great ship left its base at Friedrichshafen on the morning of October 12, 1924. Eckener chose to fly a less direct route than that which had been covered by the R-34, although one of the natural elements with which he would have to contend were the head winds of the east-to-west crossing. His flight went from Germany via the Azores, southward, then northeastward to Nova Scotia and finally south to New York. Despite the shape of the route, it was accomplished nonstop and covered more than 5,000 miles, about 1,000 miles less than the flight of the R-34. Eckener's route also took him through the milder head wind zones.

The trip could not have been more routine, and three days after leaving Friedrichshafen Eckener had the ZR-3 hovering over New York City; a bit later he eased the airship into its moorings at Lakehurst, New Jersey: it was October 15, 1924—the flight had taken 3 days, 2 hours and 56 minutes.

If there had been any misgivings about the welcome awaiting a postwar German crew arriving in one of their dreaded Zeppelins, they were dispelled by the frenzied reception at Lakehurst. Eckener and his crew were so joyously mobbed and cheered that they were genuinely surprised. The ticker-tape parade in New York City, as well as a number of spontaneous celebrations across the country, seemed to prove that the nation had, indeed, gone "Zeppelin mad." Even the President, reticent Calvin Coolidge, sent Eckener a long telegram in which he said, "It gives me and the people of the United States great pleasure that the friendly relations between Germany and America are reaffirmed, and that this great airship has so happily introduced the first direct air-connection between the two nations."

The flight served to rehabilitate the foe of the recent war in American eyes and succeeded to a great extent where diplomats had failed. A surge of pride was even noted in Germany, where warring political factions joined hands to praise Eckener, his crew and the ZR-3. The Allies thought twice about dismantling the Zeppelin works at Friedrichshafen (which Eckener managed to keep mildly busy producing kitchenware in the meantime). The flight of the ZR-3 would lead to a revival of the German airship industry. Of all the airships used briefly during the Twenties by the U.S. Navy, only the German-built *Los Angeles*, perhaps significantly, survived.

Thus did the period of near calm between the flight of the R-34 and the ZR-3 come to a happy end for the airship. No one had come forth to claim the Orteig prize, but in the interim preparations had been under way. It would usher in the initial phase of what newsmen eventually called "Atlantic Fever," a rash of Atlantic aerial derring-do. Like all temperature elevations, this one also harbored risk and imminent death, which had always been present in the earlier flights but for some enigmatic reason waited with uncommon patience.

4

"Great 1927
New York-to-Paris
Air Derby":
First Blood

Death had taken an Atlantic holiday since 1919, and generally rested during the period of slight activity into the middle Twenties. In June of 1925 Orteig renewed his offer of the $25,000 prize, with slight modifications. The award would be given to the "first aviator," with no specification as to wartime affiliation, who crossed the Atlantic "without stop" in "a land or water aircraft (heavier-than-air)" linking New York and Paris "or the shores of France." The renewal stimulated airmen on both sides of the Atlantic, shifting the scenes of activity to France and the United States. For some reason the British preferred sitting out this phase of the air race and were willing to rest on the early triumphs of Alcock and Brown and the R-34. Not that British airmen stopped flying in the middle Twenties; they had just chosen to fly other routes in the far-flung corners of the Empire. Besides, the sentiment was that so far as the Atlantic was concerned, it belonged to them anyhow.

When Orteig left for France in the summer of 1925 he announced that he hoped to arrive in time to observe the takeoffs of the various contenders from Le Bourget, the great airfield near Paris. There were several announced participants, but no takeoffs. High on the list of entrants were the names of such war aces as Paul Tarascon, François Coli (quite a pair, for Tarascon had lost a leg in the war and Coli an eye) and Maurice Drouhin, among others. On the other side of the Atlantic an organization calling itself the Argonauts, Incorporated, had been formed, the inspiration of Col. Harold E. Hartney, himself a war ace and postwar racing pilot, and especially of an Air Service Reserve pilot, Capt. Homer M. Berry. With Hartney assisting in lining up backers, Berry hoped to make an attempt for the Orteig prize. The syndicate was formed and the Argonauts approached a famed, though at that moment not very successful, aircraft manufacturer who had a small plant at Roosevelt Field, near Westbury, Long Island, New York, the Sikorsky Manufacturing Corporation.

Sikorsky's operation was a highly individual one. His entire staff was made up of Russian émigrés, many of them former noblemen before the Revolution. Sikorsky himself was an established designer of aircraft and, while the Sikorsky Manufacturing Corporation may have had all the earmarks of a Russian family affair, the planes so carefully turned out by these old-world craftsmen were outstanding. The major problem, often as not (and not necessarily unique, for all aircraft manufacturers in this period shared it), was finances. It is interesting to note that one of Sikorsky's most generous backers and a vice president in the company was the great pianist-composer, Sergei Rachmaninoff. It was the musician's money that made it possible to establish the company in "a leaky, old wooden hangar at a corner of Roosevelt Field," in the words of Sikorsky's biographer Frank J. Delear.

The Argonauts had contracted for a large twin-engined sesquiplane (that is, the lower wing was considerably smaller than the upper wing), one of Sikorsky's historic specialities. Sikorsky designated it the S-35, but decided that for a transatlantic flight a third engine should be added. By this time some rather drastic changes occurred in the Argonaut arrangements in addition to the plane, which had its fuselage extended for the mounting of the third engine in the nose and the wings modified.

Top-scoring French ace René Fonck decided he would get into the race; only unlike his French colleagues he felt it would be the wiser course to make the west-to-east crossing, with the wind. Upon arriving in the United States he managed to meet Hartney, who introduced Fonck

TOP   The great Sikorsky S-35 under construction for French World War I flying ace, René Fonck. (*Sikorsky Aircraft*)

ABOVE   Passengers and crew, following the first successful flight of the S-35: M. E. Gluhareff (one of Sikorsky's chief designers), Lt. Allan Snody (who was to have participated in the flight but withdrew), René Fonck, Igor Sikorsky, Robert Labensky (a Sikorsky engineer) and Al Krapish (also a Sikorsky worker). (*Sikorsky Aircraft*)

LEFT   The completed S-35 (*Sikorsky Aircraft*)

to the Argonauts and to the S-35 then being manufactured at Roosevelt
Field. Fonck was hired as the chief pilot of the venture, with the proviso
that the copilot (presumably Berry) would be an American. Fonck
agreed, at the same time making a statement on Franco-American
amity.

This worked well for a time and a full crew for the plane in progress
was selected by Fonck from hundreds of applicants. Berry was to be
copilot; his navigator, chosen by the U.S. Navy, was Lt. Allan P. Snody
(aide to the Navy's leading airman, Rear Adm. William A. Moffett); Lt.
George O. Noville would serve as flight engineer and Capt. John R.
Irwin as radio operator. The amity did not last. The problems began
when Fonck decided he would rather have Snody as copilot instead of
Berry, who immediately threatened a law suit (it was, after all, his idea
originally). Berry began making public comments decidedly inimical to
Franco-American amity, to wit: "No Frenchman, no matter how many
medals he has, can come over here and push me out of this flight."

For a time it began to look as if there would be no flight at all. Berry
then decided he would withdraw without a fight, giving as his reason
that the flight was the important thing, not personalities. The next to
leave was Irwin, for no known reason. Then Snody became ill—and he
withdrew. His replacement was another Navy man, Lt. Lawrence
Curtin. Noville, one day, stalked off the scene when he disapproved of
the type of lubricating oil which was to be used (there being a number
of advertising commitments made to help finance the flight). His place
was taken over by a Sikorsky engineer and friend of the designer, engi-
neer-mechanic Jacob Islamoff. Irwin's replacement at the radio was one
of Fonck's friends, Charles Clavier, who was anxious to return to his
wife and children in France.

During the squabbling and complete (except for Fonck) change of
crew, the "huge, elegant, efficient, and modern looking airplane gradually took shape in the old, leaky hangar," Sikorsky recalled. He was
uneasy over some points: the publicity, for one thing, which led to the
gathering of crowds at the Sikorsky "factory" at Roosevelt Field. He was
unhappy too because of the various publicity and advertising tie-ins he
was forced to make in order to finance his end of the project.

The publicity led to the announcement of other embryo Atlantic
flights hoping to beat Fonck to the Orteig prize. The pressure to be off
and to hurry with the completion of the plane introduced an ominous
note, which also disturbed Sikorsky. There would have to be too many
compromises.

The S-35 was ready for preliminary testing in August of 1926, nearly
a year after Fonck had arrived in the United States. After a series of
ground tests, including taxiing, the plane was taken up by Sikorsky and

Fonck for a flight. Only two engines were used (the plane not being heavily loaded) and Sikorsky found that "in spite of that the plane took off very easily and performed well in every respect. During the second flight, we climbed several thousand feet high and made a flight over New York. There were practically no corrections or adjustments needed after these test flights.

"Much work, however, was still left to be done; the installation of additional gasoline tanks, of various equipment, and of the auxiliary wheels which appeared to be needed for the takeoff of the overloaded plane. The wheels were to be released and dropped after takeoff."

The modifications required to certify the Atlantic airworthiness of the S-35 would, of course, add weight. The new fuel tanks would not only contribute to the load, but so would their contents. It was Sikorsky's plan to proceed with the tests, step by step, increasing the load gradually to ascertain the takeoff capability of the plane. The weight of the fully outfitted transatlantic aircraft would also put a great strain on the landing gear; Sikorsky hoped to program a series of tests on that aspect of the flight also. It was then September, not too happy a weather time over the Atlantic, and Sikorsky looked forward to a winter of testing so that Fonck could get off in the spring.

But too many factors had begun to intrude. The most serious—and the least to do with aeronautics—was the wide publicity given to the preparations, the announcement of rival airmen considering the same effort and the general excitement. It was as if some great amorphous giant insistently pushed all before him. Despite their better judgment the men involved with the planning and preparation of the flight were caught up in the urgency and glare of the publicity. All proceeded as if, indeed, there were an actual schedule to meet.

Certain weight tests were simply not carried out (this meant filling fuel tanks with water—which then had to be drained out and the tanks and fuel system cleaned) because, should Fonck decide to leave, the plane might not be ready to fly. Finally that day did arrive—September 15, 1926—and the S-35 was gassed up fully to take advantage of a momentary good weather spell. Then a fuel tank was found to be leaking and the takeoff was canceled—followed by more dreary weather.

On September 20 another good weather period was promised and, after a late evening discussion, it was decided that Fonck and crew would try to get off early the next morning. They tried to get some rest as Sikorsky and his men prepared the plane. "Around midnight," Sikorsky later wrote in his biography, "I climbed into the pilot's cabin and carefully and slowly taxied the huge, beautiful ship to the end of the runway, where it was turned and the pumping of the fuel began."

OVERLEAF One of the hazards of well-publicized transatlantic flights: crowds, a constant source of worry to pilots. Some members of crowds had little inkling of what a whirling propeller could do should one walk into it. Moving aircraft without brakes, too, could be a hazard to a heedless crowd. The group in the photo has gathered for a ceremony, blessing of the S-35. (*Sikorsky Aircraft*)

This photograph dramatizes the fuel requirements of a transatlantic flight. The plane became one massive flying fuel tank. (*Sikorsky Aircraft*)

Through the night the laborious fueling-up continued in a glare of floodlights; barrels and barrels of aviation fuel were poured into the several tanks—2,500 gallons of it. As this proceeded Sikorsky would walk out to "the top of a small hill at the edge of the field, hoping to find some wind. Even a little breeze in the right direction along the runway would have greatly assisted the takeoff. But there was none at all."

Before daybreak, after hundreds of automobiles had been driven to Roosevelt Field, Fonck, Curtin, Clavier and Islamoff appeared in their flying gear. A path had to be cleared for them to the plane. The weather report was only fair, but unless Fonck was willing to spend more days waiting he would have to settle for it. He chose to begin, so all boarded the plane. The three engines were warming and within moments Fonck began moving the plane along the runway. Sikorsky had by then become just another member of the mob that had gathered at the field and sought refuge on the small hill. There was now a slight breeze, but it was a tail wind—which would be no help in the takeoff.

The heavily laden S-35 moved along the runway, and just about at the halfway mark spectators saw dust erupting in its wake. One of the auxiliary landing gears had come loose and was dragging. This slowed the plane down so that it reached the end of the runway before it had attained flying speed. Fonck could not turn (and, of course, had no brakes—they did not exist then), nor could he throttle down. There was a mob of people to consider: if he turned, the plane would plow through them; if he cut the engines he would lose control and accomplish the same thing. There was nothing else to do—keep going. For a moment a cheer went up as it appeared that the plane would lift off—then it

Fueling up the S-35, a time-consuming job, considering the quantity of fuel that would have to pass through the tiny hose. (*Sikorsky Aircraft*)

Charred wreckage of Fonck's S-35 after it crashed and burned while attempting to take off, taking the lives of Clavier and Islamoff. (*Sikorsky Aircraft*)

settled down, out of sight of the spectators on the field, into a gully beyond the far end of the field. And then, as the spectators watched, for just a moment nothing happened. The plane did not appear again. But suddenly a great blast of red flame shot into the air; a cloud of black smoke mushroomed upward.

When the first spectators arrived at the scene of what was by then an inferno, they found only two men, Fonck and Curtin, who had been able to scramble out of the cockpit. But neither Clavier nor Islamoff, who had been stationed inside the fuselage, had been able to get out. The heat generated by 2,500 gallons of burning aviation fuel made it impossible to get into the plane and the two men were almost instantly incinerated. The Atlantic Fever had claimed its first two fatalities.

The investigation which followed the crash absolved Fonck of any blame (there were some hints of "irresponsibility" and "incompetence"; the desire to take off before all testing was completed, on the one hand, and lack of experience in the handling of so large an aircraft, on the other). Curtin was one of those who testified in favor of Fonck and the decision was that it had been "an unfortunate accident." If there was any single factor responsible (other than the rush to be first) it was the crucial one of overloading. While the plane was perfectly airworthy, the question of weight was never fully explored before the flight. Two less men in the crew would have made a great deal of difference, perhaps; especially to the two men who might have been left behind, Clavier and Islamoff.

Fonck was still determined to make the flight—and Curtin was willing to assist again as copilot—and to try again in a Sikorsky. A new plane was begun, the S-37, with this plan in mind, although with the proviso by Sikorsky that a thorough testing program be completed before the flight was attempted. Before the plane and the testing were finished, however, the need for the first plane to join New York and Paris by air had been taken care of by a young pilot no one had ever heard of before. Fonck then quietly withdrew from any further such ventures, content to enjoy his role as France's greatest living ace.

The crash of Fonck's plane, and the usual fall and winter weather, curtailed further considerations of a transatlantic flight for 1926. But the winter months were not totally wasted, for schemes were hatched, plans made and dreams dreamed. By January of 1927 the filing of entries for the Orteig prize began, the first being made by Lt. Comdr. Noel Davis of the Massachusetts Naval Reserve Station at Boston. He had been one of the first in the previous year also, but his initial project had never materialized. Now he had some backing from the American Legion (which just happened to be holding a convention in Paris the summer of 1927). As his navigator Davis had selected Lt. Stanton H. Wooster.

The second entry was simply signed C. A. Lindbergh, of St. Louis. Little more was known about him than that.

Not in the Orteig running, but talking about flying the Atlantic as a purely scientific venture, were Navy explorer and pioneer Comdr. Richard E. Byrd and his chief pilot Floyd Bennett (both of whom had made history in 1926 by flying over the North Pole).

Preparations proceeded also on the other side of the Atlantic, although the team of Tarascon and Coli, handicapped by financial difficulties, broke up. Coli, not easily discouraged, found another partner in the colorful Charles Nungesser (second only to Fonck in France's listing of aces). One of France's most dashing airmen, Nungesser had talked aircraft manufacturer Pierre Levasseur into modifying one of the planes he produced for the French Navy into a transatlantic aircraft. Initially, and characteristically, Nungesser planned to make the flight solo, but was convinced that merely flying a plane was not the whole answer; someone had to make certain that it traveled in the right direction. It was then that Coli, without money and without a pilot (Tarascon having been injured in a crackup), joined Nungesser.

There were other names of airmen being mentioned as transatlantic contenders during the early spring, among them Clarence Chamberlin, Bert Acosta, Maurice Drouhin, Dieudonné Costes (in France) and more daily. Again the air filled with the sound of engines and a deadly urgency.

Byrd, unconcerned with the race and the prize money, exhibited a prudence and an attention to detail worthy of a scientist. He was not, of course, a pilot, but rather the organizer of projects of something more than stunt status. He had missed out on the NC flight, he had almost been a passenger on the C-5—and, parenthetically, luckily missed being aboard the ZR-2 when it fell into the Humber. Fortune sometimes grimaced upon Byrd, and then it smiled. His polar flight in May of 1926 placed his name among those of the immortal explorers.

As a kind of celebrity Byrd had little trouble getting a backer for his flight—Rodman Wanamaker, the same air enthusiast who had stood behind the Curtiss *America* project of 1914. For Byrd he purchased a trimotor monoplane from the Atlantic Aircraft Corporation, the American branch of the Dutch Fokker Company. This plane also would be named *America*. Fokker himself had come to the United States to oversee some of the final arrangements.

Byrd had used Fokker's first trimotor (which Fokker had produced simply by hanging two engines on the wing to augment the single engine in the nose: thus the first Fokker trimotor) for his epochal polar flight. Certain actions in connection with that flight had not pleased Fokker, who had, he later stated, sold the plane, which "had proved such an excellent ship that I wanted to fly it myself," to Edsel Ford, who financed the Byrd polar expedition. Fokker forced himself to part with the plane for $40,000 on the condition that the Fokker trademark be left on the nose. To his dismay (and to the consternation of his publicity-loving heart) the aircraft was named the *Josephine Ford*, for Ford's three-year-old daughter. "Little Miss Ford rode to fame and the North Pole on the wings of Mr. Fokker," was the designer's acerb comment later. This is curious in light of the fact that photographs taken during the period

Floyd Bennett (left) and Richard E. Byrd, being welcomed after their flight over the North Pole in May of 1926. Soon after, they began discussing the possibilities of an Atlantic crossing by air. (*National Air & Space Museum, Smithsonian Institution*)

of the flight and after reveal the name of Fokker prominently displayed on the leading edge of the wing, on the fuselage and, in giant letters, on the underside of the wing, for the benefit of any passing Eskimo.

Obviously the relationship between Byrd and Fokker was not particularly cordial. The new plane differed from the previous one mainly in that the wingspan had been stretched from the original 63 feet to 71, to achieve more lift in order to carry the great load necessary to a transatlantic flight.

The wing was constructed at Fokker's plant in Holland while the fuselage was built at Atlantic Aircraft's facilities at Teterboro, New Jersey. It was there that the entire plane was assembled. When it was completed Fokker was on hand to oversee the test flights. While he had little regard for Byrd as an airman, Fokker did recognize Floyd Bennett as the outstanding flier he was. He would fly the *America*; George Noville would serve as flight engineer and Byrd as navigator. The newspaper-generated Atlantic Fever of the period played its part: newsmen seemed to swarm over airports demanding choice items—which then appeared in strangely garbled versions in print. They referred to the by then several flight preparations as the "Great 1927 New York-to-Paris Air Derby" and proceeded to whip up enthusiasm, public curiosity and myth.

"I was shadowed," Byrd wrote of this time later. "Questions were put my family and friends about me to find out what I had 'up my sleeve.' Exaggerations and rumors flew about thick and fast. Caustic criticism of other entrants was attributed to me. Presently I found that instead of being a technical explorer I was some sort of frenzied political candidate. At least that was the impression I got."

Finally, out of desperation, Byrd asked Wanamaker to hire a press agent to try to get matters straight. "I must add that I think representatives of the press, later on when I had a chance to explain things, sympathized with my position. But at that time their owners and editors had to get news. The public demanded it, due to its great interest in the forthcoming flight."

Word had come from the factory that the *America* was ready for its first flight; Byrd and his two colleagues hurried over to New Jersey to be on hand. None other than Anthony Fokker himself was to serve as test pilot. The events that followed have suffered in the telling because of two different versions, one Byrd's, the other Fokker's. According to Byrd's version, all three men took it for granted that they would be taken on the first hop (a rather unusual procedure, true, but it was not as if the Fokker was not an already proved design). According to Fokker's version, first Bennett, then Noville, and then *finally* Byrd (the implication is obvious) invited themselves aboard. "I should have refused," Fokker rationalized after the event, "because without any load in the rear, and with an empty main tank, the ship became nose heavy with the two pilots' seats full. But as I had flown somewhat similar ships under the same conditions without difficulty, I agreed." It was at this "last minute" that Byrd, according to Fokker, "rushed over in a comradely spirit, wanting to come along. It was so proper for a commander to take his chances along with his men that I couldn't say no."

With Fokker at the controls and Bennett in the copilot's seat to his right, with Byrd standing directly behind Fokker and Noville behind Bennett (the latter two clinging to the seat backs), the plane got off the ground nicely. Byrd takes up the story of the test flight: "So long as the engines were running everything went all right. But the moment they were cut off the plane felt nose heavy. Noville and I saw Bennett licking his lips. This is the only sign Bennett gives when he is nervous—which, I may say, is very rare. . . ."

Fokker, too, was having his moments: "What I had not sufficiently figured on was the larger wing of this particular ship. The combination of large wing, empty tank, and small supply of gas in the wing tanks made the speed of landing so slow that the efficiency of the elevator was lower than normal. But, coming in for a landing, I had an instinctive feeling of danger, and told Bennett to go to the back. He refused, however, paying no attention to my suggestion."

It was impossible for Byrd and Noville to move further aft because of a large fuel tank that had been installed behind the cockpit; it was this tank which was empty. When the nose-heaviness of the plane was noticed, Fokker gunned the engines and came in for another approach. The plane touched down about fifty feet short of the spot selected by Fokker and raced along the runway. To his "surprise the tail was not settling as we lost speed, but very slowly rising. Instantly, I realized the possibility of nosing over. I had something less than a second to decide what to do."

According to Fokker, he did what would have to be done: he cut the engine switches to minimize the possibility of fire should they turn over as he feared and at the same time pulled back on the controls to bring the tail down. There being a dual system in the Fokker, the other "stick" in the adjoining seat, of course, held Bennett fast to his seat.

Byrd's account was somewhat different: "I caught hold of a steel upright just back of Fokker's seat—kept my gaze concentrated on the air speed meter. We were going a mile a minute. The wheels touched the ground. Instantly I saw Fokker rise and make frantic efforts to jump out. Bennett was trapped as Fokker occupied the only exit. There was no way Noville and I could even try to get out."

"Maybe Byrd was excited and imagined this," Fokker countered, "a description more worthy of a layman than a supposed technician." The point would be difficult to determine; it would seem unlikely that Fokker would have tried to leap from a moving aircraft—but, on the other hand, Byrd, a man of noted integrity, would hardly have tried to besmirch Fokker's reputation without some foundation. Fokker would not want his name clouded with the shame of a captain who had deserted his ship and would, on the other hand, not be above a little exaggeration or two. It was, however, a more serious issue of whether or not the name of Fokker had been prominently displayed on the *Josephine Ford*. Byrd may have, indeed, been confused in the last minutes of their landing but Fokker, in his account, made a point of blaming practically everyone aboard the plane except himself for what came next—and referring to Byrd as a "layman" was an exaggeration in itself.

The plane skimmed along the ground at around 100 miles an hour, and instead of its tail bouncing to the ground, it persisted in rising as they moved (Fokker blamed this on Bennett, also, saying that Bennett had not trimmed the elevator properly). The farther they ran, the higher the tail rose until it flipped over completely. There was a blinding crash as the nose struck the ground and the engine crushed in the nose—only the fact that the propeller deflected it to the right, away from the cockpit, saved Fokker and Bennett. "Something struck me a stunning blow on my head and in the small of my back," Byrd later wrote. "It was Noville thrown forward from the sudden stop. The impact snapped my arm like a match stick. Then dead silence."

This was broken when Bennett gasped, "Look out for fire." He was still trapped in the copilot's seat, where the fuselage had crumpled under the weight of the engine. Only Fokker managed to get out unhurt. Byrd and Noville tore their way out of their compartment and, according to Fokker, "Noville ran away from the wreckage screaming, holding his body in agony. He had been internally injured when thrown against the wall." Byrd, meanwhile, rushed back to the plane to find Bennett in his seat hanging head downwards. His face was badly bloodied and he was covered with oil.

"Guess I'm done for," he told Byrd. "I'm all broken up. I can't see and I have no feeling in my left arm."

Byrd disagreed with his friend, but subconsciously believed that Bennett was right. However, after carefully wiping Bennett's face of the oil and blood, the injured pilot was able to see. But his leg was in bad shape, with compound fractures which would take weeks to mend. Noville's injuries seemed such that for a time he was not expected to live and then it was thought he would require surgery. However, it turned out that he had suffered torn stomach muscles and, in time, he was ready for another try. Byrd set his own arm on the way to the hospital.

When the smoke cleared away Byrd and Fokker were no longer friends. Even their accounts of the damage to the plane differed. As for that, Fokker found, "It wasn't so extensive as I had feared. A few panels in the wing were punched in; two propellers were bent, the rudder askew, and the nose crushed in. We were able to complete repairs in two weeks."

Byrd said, "The damage to our plane was serious. It took a month of day and night toil to get her back in shape again."

While this went on, for however long (the crash having occurred on April 16, 1927), other contenders in the "Air Derby" began moving ahead, in the United States as well as France. Nungesser and Coli were nearly ready to go, Fonck's new Sikorsky was being built and almost daily the press reported the activities of a Charles A. Levine who was seeking a pilot to fly a Bellanca-designed plane which his firm, Columbia Aircraft Corporation, had produced. Although Levine had selected the navigator, Lloyd Bertaud, he managed to keep his, and his company's, name before the public by making the selection of the pilot—either Clarence Chamberlin or Bert Acosta—a cliff-hanger.

"The choice will not be made until the last minute before the flight," Levine explained, "and it will then be determined by lot. Both pilots will appear upon the field in flying togs. Their names will be written separately on slips of paper. One slip will be drawn. The name on it will decide the flyer." In a later outburst of candor Levine said, "I want both boys to have their heart in their work up to the last moment and if one of them is chosen now, the other would probably be sore."

Two days later, on April 24, the issue was temporarily settled for one and all. After the Bellanca had been christened *Columbia* with a bottle of ginger ale (prohibition was then in full force), two girls, aged nine and fifteen, were taken aloft by Chamberlin—chosen by lot?—for a little flight. During the takeoff part of the landing gear tore away, leaving the plane with only one wheel. Chamberlin, an adept pilot, managed to bring the plane down, first on the single wheel and then, when speed was lost, scraping on the wingtip. This was managed without injury to his two young passengers or himself and with only slight damage to the plane. But for the time being it ended Levine's lottery.

Two days after Chamberlin's mishap, the *American Legion*, the Key-stone Pathfinder which was to carry Noel Davis and Stanton Wooster, was ready for its final testing before the actual takeoff. Davis was determined to test the aircraft completely (the vision of Fonck's crash haunted all of the entrants) and said, after a most successful first flight early in April, that "the plane handles beautifully, but we want to test it thoroughly; we are not going to leave anything to chance."

For the test Davis and Wooster, with the *American Legion* fully loaded, selected Langley Field, Virginia, on April 26. As the big tri-motor lumbered down the runway it was obvious that it was having trouble getting airborne. Once off the ground it was still in trouble, for it appeared that it would not clear a line of trees that stood just beyond the end of the runway. There had never been any problem before in lifting over the trees, but the *American Legion* had never been as heavily loaded before. All of Davis's efforts to climb had no effect and he kicked the rudder bar to avoid striking the tree tops. The turn caused

Keystone *American Legion* in which Noel Davis and Stanton Wooster crashed to their deaths during a test flight at Langley Field, Virginia. (*National Air & Space Museum, Smithsonian Institution*)

the plane to lose what little air speed it had and it stalled. Nose down it fell into a marsh with a great splash. There was no fire—obviously Davis had cut the engines and they had fallen into about four feet of water. The wing was crumpled and the nose was bashed in. By the time help came both Davis and Wooster were dead; trapped in the crushed cockpit, they had drowned in the marshy waters of a Virginia swamp.

So, one by one, were the large trimotored aircraft eliminated from the "Air Derby," Fonck's Sikorsky, Byrd's Fokker and Davis's Keystone (Chamberlin's Bellanca had a single engine). These multi-engined planes were considered the best type for a long flight, for it was believed that if a single engine conked, that was the end of everything, while if one engine stopped in flight a trimotor could make it on the other two engines. But even with three engines the big planes were found to have a problem lifting heavy loads. It was a crucial factor.

As far as was known, the elimination of the *American Legion* left only Nungesser and Coli to make the Paris to New York flight. Their

preparations were closely followed by American newspapers and fervently reported in the French press. Nungesser and Coli would carry the banner of France across the sea, it was believed, and their every word and deed became familiar to every patriotic Frenchman.

Their Levasseur, with its all-white finish, was named *L'Oiseau blanc* (the *White Bird*). It was powered by a single 450 horsepower Lorraine-Dietrich twelve-cylinder engine; the upper wing spanned forty-eight feet. The fuselage design was interesting, for the forward section under the nose was formed as a planing bottom and watertight compartments in the fuselage made the plane a kind of primitive flying boat. The landing gear could be jettisoned after takeoff, to reduce air resistance and weight slightly and to make ditching in water simpler. It was possible also to lock the propeller in a horizontal position for the water landing—for it was the plan to end the flight in New York harbor.

Nungesser was banking heavily on the reliability of the single engine, believing that success depended more on one engine in which he had complete faith and a relatively light aircraft than on a three-engined monster with all its load—including fuel.

OPPOSITE François Coli (left) and Charles Nungesser in the cockpit of their *White Bird* before setting out on their attempt to fly the Atlantic. Their insignia was obviously a twitting of the Grim Reaper—who won after all. (*Musée de l'Air, Paris*)

BELOW Levasseur PL-8, named *The White Bird* by its crew, Nungesser and Coli. The landing gear was dropped after takeoff. (*Musée de l'Air, Paris*)

By the end of April, following a series of load tests, Nungesser announced that he and Coli would get off "by the end of the month." There were, of course, some questions. To begin with they were going to attempt the tough east-to-west route; another was the great strain of the long flight on the engine—would it hold up? No one had ever flown 3,600 miles on a single engine. The maximum range of the *White Bird* was 4,000 miles, which left little margin for error in navigation or for the weather. Their plane would not carry a radio or much survival equipment. "I am thinking of flying to New York," Nungesser was supposed to have said, "not of saving my skin. You fly with fuel, not with wireless sets." And the plane was built for floating, just in case.

The two airmen were popular heroes and even if Nungesser did not make the statement about flying to New York and not saving his skin, it was the kind of thing expected of him and Coli. They were seen in the right places—and Coli was especially noticeable with his eye patch; they joked and laughed a lot in public and appeared to disdain the obvious dangers that the flight posed. Behind the scenes, however, they carefully measured out their fuel supply, closely watched the weather and the antics, some of them fatally tragic, of their rivals across the sea. The news was either inciting, as each new entrant appeared to be the first to be ready, or grim and melancholy as each was eliminated.

When the time arrived for the *White Bird* to take off from Le Bourget, word got out and by midnight the area swarmed with vehicles and people. The crowd was filled with Parisian celebrities, ranging from nightclub entertainers Maurice Chevalier and Mistinguett to boxer Georges Carpentier. At three in the morning, May 8, 1927—Joan of Arc Day—the *White Bird*, fueled to capacity with 880 gallons of highly volatile liquid, was pushed out of its hangar. The ground crew placed it at the far end of the runway facing in the direction from which, it was hoped, the wind would blow at takeoff time. The crowd cheered mightily at this first sign of action in several hours. There was, too, an ominous note which indicated that finally, after all the announcements of impending departure, the moment was near. Several fire engines were positioned along the runway and an ambulance was parked at one end.

It was nearly another two hours before the airmen themselves arrived, in full flying gear, seated in an open touring car. The crowd roared again; Nungesser even caught a single rose tossed by a girl and threw her a kiss.

There were last-minute embraces and handshaking and the last word on the weather. This was not quite so promising as it had been the night before. An area of depression had formed in their original path and they would have to alter course a bit to the north to avoid it.

Otherwise, things were more or less equal—mostly less, for as morning approached the sky was broken with the flashes of lightning from the distant storm. Despite this, the two men took their places in the cockpit, standing momentarily for a final photograph before takeoff—the very prototypes of the dashing airmen of the period.

It was 5:18 A.M. Nungesser started the engine and let it warm up for some time. The sound was good and he signaled for the wheel chocks to be pulled. The *White Bird* trundled, then gradually picked up speed, lifted off the ground, then settled down again. The runway was beginning to be used up and there were five tons of man, machine and fuel to get off the ground. The plane rose again sluggishly and bounced down for the second time; there were only a couple of hundred yards remaining of the half-mile runway. Near the end of the runway the *White Bird* lifted for a third time and stayed airborne; the wheeled gadget that had been placed under the tail to assist in the takeoff careened away. But the plane still struggled with what appeared to be near-human reluctance, then cleared the inevitable trees at the end of the runway and, although not climbing, remained well above any ground obstacles. Military planes, acting as honorary escort, flew in formation alongside the *White Bird* until it reached Etretat. Dipping their wings and waving, the French Army pilots turned away as Nungesser and Coli headed across the English Channel. It was on the French coast that the *White Bird*'s landing gear was dropped as Nungesser brought the plane down low before heading out across the first stretch of water.

Five hours later word came from Ireland that the plane had been seen off that coast heading into a strong Atlantic wind.

Then nothing.

There was wild jubilation in all of France when *La Presse* came out in the evening of May 9 with a special edition in which the headlines heralded the arrival of Nungesser and Coli in New York harbor. The description was excitingly detailed: flag bedecked ships in the harbor, a squadron of fighter planes as escort, then the splashing landing in the water within a hundred yards of the Statue of Liberty. A perfect landing; then, as if they could not for the moment fathom their success, the two men stood as if dazed in the cockpit. Then they embraced with the realization of their accomplishment. A motor launch, *La Presse* continued, arrived at the *White Bird* to take them ashore where they were wildly greeted by waiting mobs waving American and French flags. The two men were mobbed by newsmen and photographed by newsreel and still-cameramen. These photographs would grace the front pages of *La Presse* as soon as they could arrive, by fast ship, from America.

The announcement in *La Presse* led to one of the most frenzied celebrations ever to occur in France. Paris especially simply stopped functioning as a major center of the economy in an eruption of champagne corks, celebrations, parties and parades. It was a proud moment for the Republic; their own airmen had been the first, fittingly, to link Paris and New York by air.

But the promised photographs of the arrival of Nungesser and Coli did not come by the next fast boat; they never arrived. Nor, tragically and poignantly in the aftermath of the jubilation that *La Presse* had ignited, had Nungesser and Coli arrived.

The *White Bird* had simply vanished into the Atlantic mist and was never seen again.

5

Lone
Eagle

In less than a year the Atlantic aerial sweepstakes had claimed six lives. The inadvertent, though cruel, hoax played upon the people of France by *La Presse* injected bitterness into what had once been light-hearted international rivalry. Both nations scoured the Atlantic waters for Nungesser and Coli for days following their disappearance—and from time to time hopes rose when now and again the sighting of a white aircraft was announced. Word came from ships at sea that the plane had been seen flying long after its fuel should have given out.

Emotions ran high and low, from fiery anger to deep gloom. The copies of *La Presse* still unsold were seized in the streets and burned. They were dire hints intimating that one of the causes of the loss of the two French airmen was that the U.S. weather bureau had deliberately withheld its reports—which rumor was immediately scotched by the French weather bureau. From Paris a worried Ambassador Myron T. Herrick informed the State Department that he feared any more attempts to make the New York to Paris flight at that moment might very well be "misunderstood and misinterpreted" in France; he suggested a suspension for a time in the "race."

On the west coast, at San Diego, a young airman watched the headlines covering the preparations for all the transatlantic flights and the rapid succession of those that told of the fate of Nungesser and Coli. He was twenty-five-year-old Charles A. Lindbergh, the youngest of all Atlantic contenders. An aviation enthusiast since boyhood, he made his first flight at the age of twenty. Within days, Lindbergh began flying lessons and before the year was over embarked on a barnstorming tour of southern Nebraska—and later other western states. During this tour Lindbergh did some wing-walking, parachute jumping and other such diversions which it was hoped would attract the yokels to the field from which he and a friend operated, to be taken up at a price of $5 a ride.

The next year, 1923, Lindbergh bought his first plane, a government surplus wartime JN-4, Jenny. In this plane he barnstormed through the south and west and even assisted his father, Congressman Charles A. Lindbergh of Minnesota, in his political campaigning by air. It was the senior Lindbergh's first experience with flying, after which he no longer voiced objections to his son's aerial activities. Shortly after, Lindbergh also treated his mother to her first flight.

It was while barnstorming through southern Minnesota that Lindbergh met some men who had been trained to fly as members of the U.S. Army Air Corps. Impressed with the "hangar flying" tales of piloting the powerful de Havillands, and observing them in flight, Lindbergh "longed to fly one of them." He enlisted as a cadet and, by the following year, had won his Air Corps wings and was commissioned a second lieutenant in the Air Corps Reserve.

Lindbergh's next step, between barnstorming sessions, was to join the newly formed Robertson Aircraft Corporation as its chief pilot (there being two others to round out the total flying staff). Robertson began operations officially in April of 1926, linking St. Louis and Chicago, and quickly built up a good record of on-time mail deliveries. The planes were modified wartime DH-4s, rather unhealthily referred to as "Flaming Coffins." But it was the weather, particularly during the winter months, that most plagued the young airline—air routes then were quite primitive and made little provision for night operations. Consequently on those few occasions when the mail did not get through all the way by air it was because of fog and icing. More than once Lindbergh was forced to circle a fogged-in area, hopefully seeking an airfield, and then, with the fuel low, would head for what he guessed was an unpopulated section and simply take to his chute.

Neither he, nor anyone else, was injured in these emergency jumps—although Lindbergh himself had close calls while the abandoned plane circled around him as he descended. The planes piled up but Lindbergh made certain that the mail was salvaged and placed on the first train.

It was on one of his less thrill-packed mail flights that Lindbergh got an idea. "I first considered the possibility of the New York–Paris flight while flying the mail one night in the fall of 1926. Several facts soon became outstanding. The foremost was that with the modern radial air-cooled motor, high lift airfoils and lightened construction, it would not only be possible to reach Paris but, under normal conditions, to land with a large reserve of fuel and have a high factor of safety throughout the entire trip as well."

The plane he had in mind was a Bellanca powered by the new Wright Whirlwind engine; it would probably have the range and the engine was the epitome of reliability, certainly the finest radial (as opposed to the clumsier in-line) air-cooled (in-lines were water-cooled) engine available.

As he winged through the night, Lindbergh rationalized the idea. He felt perfectly qualified to make such a flight himself; he had been flying for nearly five years, he had logged nearly 2,000 air hours, he had flown under all conceivable conditions and had faced nearly every possible situation in the air, from storm to night flight. He had even picked up a knowledge of navigation as an air cadet. All of these points could be placed in the plus column.

On the negative side there was the very impressive economic point that he did not own a plane capable of a transatlantic flight and did not have the money with which to buy one; he was not a "name," like Fonck or Byrd or Chamberlin or Nungesser. And, despite his nearly twenty-five years, the tall, slender Lindbergh looked more like a boyish air enthusiast than an experienced Air Corp lieutenant, barnstormer and mail pilot.

He found his staunchest supporters, practically upon landing, among the air-minded in St. Louis, including Frank and William Robertson, who, like Lindbergh himself, were willing to put up hard-earned money. But so were certain members of the business community: banker Harry Bixby, broker Harry Hall Knight and insurance executive Earl Thompson, all of whom flew or owned planes of their own. They, in turn, were able to bring others into what became the Spirit of St. Louis Organization: Harry F. Knight, Albert Bond Lambert (for whom Lambert Field was named), J. D. Wooster Lambert and E. Lansing Ray. These men contributed much to the project, more even than money, for they also believed that Lindbergh could carry it off. He had, of course, convinced them on the simple argument that a flight to Paris, sponsored locally, would place St. Louis prominently on the growing aviation map. And, he added, if he just happened to be the first to make it, the prize money would bring a return on their investments.

And so it grew, first with a $1,000 contribution from Lambert, added to $2,000 Lindbergh himself had taken out of his savings. When the real money men came in with both their knowledge and interest in aviation, Lindbergh's major concern became the flight itself, the plane and such technical subjects, not finances.

The first step, of course, was to find a plane that could do the job. Lindbergh had his heart set on a Wright-Bellanca—a plane designed by Giuseppe Bellanca and powered by the Wright engine. Another possibility was the Fokker trimotor—although Lindbergh's plan was to make the trip alone and in a single-engined plane. Still any plane that could do it, provided the price was reasonable, would be worth looking into. One day Lindbergh learned that Roy Russell, Fokker's salesman, was visiting Lambert Field. Seeking him out, Lindbergh broached the subject of a New York to Paris flight.

Russell was happy to inform him that, indeed, Fokker had given thought to such a project and could produce a trimotor, to be delivered the following spring, for $90,000. Russell even added the contingency that Fokker would have to pass on the competence of the crew of such a plane.

Lindbergh pretended not to have heard that remark. He tried to make it plain that he did not want a custom job; wouldn't a standard Fokker be capable of the flight? Russell argued that a proper transatlantic craft would require a larger wing, extra fuel tanks and a stronger landing gear—the standard Fokker was simply not built for such work.

How about a single-engined plane? Lindbergh countered.

"Fokker would not be interested in selling a single-engined plane for a flight across the ocean," Russell answered with an undisguised finality, and that ended Lindbergh's interest in the Fokker as a possible plane for his flight. (When Fokker learned of this conversation later he commented wryly, "It was a joke on us. . . .")

Lindbergh hadn't found the discussion very amusing; Russell was no amateur and his professional attitude did count for something. There was still the Bellanca at Wright and only one way to look into that. Lindbergh boarded a train and went to New York—where he did see Bellanca himself (who assured him he was certain his plane could make the 3,600 miles between New York and Paris); Bellanca was sympathetic to Lindbergh and assured him of all cooperation. Then there was the Wright Corporation, which was not at the time really interested in manufacturing aircraft—the Bellanca had been built merely to demonstrate the Whirlwind engine. They had no idea how much the Wright-Bellanca would cost; Lindbergh returned to St. Louis slightly frustrated and continued communicating with both Bellanca and Wright by telegram. It was by then already December of 1926. The status of the plane itself was rather fuzzy, for Lindbergh had heard that the Huff-Daland Company was interested in buying it. Then Bellanca offered to build a trimotor for $29,000. And finally word from Wright: "Regret that we do not desire at this time to have Wright Bellanca used for transatlantic flight . . ."

That was, at least, definite. Lindbergh's hope was that Bellanca had found himself a factory and if he could build a trimotor, why not a single-engined plane powered by a Wright Whirlwind? He was certain that multi-engined planes were too complex and subject to more problems than a single-engined plane. The major problems, he explained to Knight and Bixby, were the weather and taking off with a full load. The Whirlwind had averaged 9,000 hours of operation before breaking down; it would not be an engine failure that would spoil his flight.

For the moment, in fact, it appeared that it might be the inability to acquire a plane. The manufacturers were especially wary because of the publicity which would come to any plane used in such a flight. If there was a failure, having their names splashed across the front pages of every newspaper in the country would not be good public relations. Besides, who was this kid Lindbergh?

Disappointed, Lindbergh began sounding out other manufacturers who produced the kind of plane he hoped to use in his flight. He had heard pilots talking the praises of a new Travel Air that had some of the same qualities of the Bellanca. A telegram only prompted another definite No. Then there was another company which made a high wing monoplane on the West Coast, a small firm named Ryan Airlines. On February 3, 1927, Lindbergh dispatched his first inquiry to Ryan, signing it (with permission) Robertson Aircraft Corp. That, at least, would carry a bit more weight than an individual. The replies from Ryan were remarkably encouraging and it appeared that the company took Robertson Aircraft Corp. seriously: there was a promise of a transoceanic aircraft at a cost of $6,000 for the airframe alone to be completed within three months, perhaps less. The engine would bring the cost up to about $10,000, which was within Lindbergh's budget. However, there was some question of Ryan's ability to fulfill the promises and the usual response, "I never heard of the Ryan company."

About at this same time word came again from Bellanca, who had left Wright and formed a new company, Columbia Aircraft Corporation. His financial backing came from a youngish (twenty-eight) millionaire Charles Levine, who had made his money dealing sharply in war surplus materials. He had taken up flying some years before as a student of Bert Acosta and had accumulated some time in a Jenny, although even his colleagues never knew if he had actually soloed or not. It was not as an airman, however, that Levine had joined up with Bellanca; he was a money man and a promoter.

Lindbergh immediately set out for New York to meet with the officials of Columbia Aircraft Corporation. There in an office in the Woolworth Building he was introduced by Bellanca to Levine and to Clarence Chamberlin, Bellanca's good friend and a pilot himself. The subject of the sale of the Bellanca plane for a New York to Paris flight was broached immediately. Levine believed the plane was worth $25,000 but was willing to sell it, with certain provisos, for $15,000, thus contributing the remainder to the flight. Although Lindbergh did not have the money with him, and was not successful in talking the price down, he was almost certain his backers would be willing to put up the additional money.

He boarded the next train for St. Louis and found himself right in believing his partners would back him up. Armed with a cashier's check for $15,000 he again boarded the very next train and sped back to New York.

The part played by railroads in this flight has hardly been emphasized, but Lindbergh did spend a great deal of time traveling by rail—certainly not his favorite mode of travel. Nor was New York his favorite city. His next meeting with Levine was one of the most frustrating in a long series of frustrations. Lindbergh had barely placed the check before Levine when he was informed that while Columbia was willing to sell the plane, Columbia was also to decide who would fly it.

Lindbergh stood there "dumbfounded." This was as preposterous a proposition as he had ever heard. Levine continued, "We can't just let anybody pilot our plane across the ocean."

Lindbergh, all but boiling, explained that he could see no point in buying a plane merely for the "privilege of painting the name of St. Louis on the side."

Levine countered with an idea dear at least to him, that the St. Louis organization would "have all the credit for the flight, all the publicity." Publicity was one of his fixations.

Lindbergh was firm; either the plane was for sale or not.

Levine assured him it was for sale—but with his own crew, and advised Lindbergh to think it over.

There was no thinking over to do, Lindbergh replied, picked up the check and left. As he did Levine suggested that he phone at eleven the next morning, after thinking things over. After a miserable night Lindbergh did call. Levine's first words were, "Well, have you changed your mind?" Lindbergh hung up on him.

Discouraged by Levine's bombshell, disheartened by the bitter mid-February weather of New York, depressed by the hurrying crowds, Lindbergh left town again to make the 1,000-mile train trip to St. Louis. As far as he could see the situation was nearly hopeless. He was almost

Giuseppe Bellanca's handsomely designed WB-2, the second of the Wright-Bellanca aircraft. It was this plane, after Bellanca and Wright parted, upon which the Columbia Aircraft Corporation was founded with money furnished by Charles Levine; it was also this plane that Lindbergh hoped to purchase for his New York to Paris flight. Lindbergh found dealing with Levine exasperating and turned to other firms for his plane. (*National Air & Space Museum, Smithsonian Institution*)

convinced that Levine had a plan in mind to let Chamberlin fly the plane to Paris. Lindbergh had no plane at all; he was far behind everyone else now. He began considering a Pacific flight, for by the time he did get a plane the Atlantic would have been flown, the Orteig prize won and all point to the dreary weeks of planning, train trips and frustration would amount to nothing.

When he suggested a switch to the Pacific, Lindbergh was overruled by Bixby and Knight. No one had yet actually made the Atlantic flight and it would be spring before anyone could begin trying. Maybe, after all, Ryan could come up with a plane—and in a short time—capable of such a flight. Having been rejected by such an imposing array of name manufacturers—Fokker, Wright, Columbia—Lindbergh had to gird himself before he could take on Ryan, the company of which one of his partners had "never heard."

Lindbergh arrived in San Diego on February 23, 1927, to see if (a) Ryan could build the plane he had in mind and (b), if so, would they permit him to buy it? His first sight of the factory was not especially impressive, for Ryan Airlines was located on San Diego's waterfront in a jumble of warehouses, factories and fish canneries. The first man he met as he entered the office was a slender youthful designer named Donald Hall, the firm's chief engineer. There was something quietly impressive about Hall, however. It was the same with other members of the firm, B. F. Mahoney, president, Hawley Bowlus, who managed the factory and supervised the construction of Ryan aircraft. There were others, too: A. J. Edwards, the dynamic head of the sales department, and Walter O. Locke and John van der Linde, who were young supervisors.

Hall and Bowlus were probably the two most essential to the project. The former worked out the design of Lindbergh's plane and the latter was in charge of its construction. At the time Lindbergh arrived work had been developing on a new Ryan design, an advanced cabin monoplane in a series that would be called the Brougham (the derivation is not very clear; a brougham was initially a closed carriage with an open driver's seat. The original design may have been the same, though unlikely, with an enclosed cabin and the pilot seated out front in the wind and rain, a common practice in those days).

Out of the basic design of the Brougham Hall evolved the aircraft that was to become the *Spirit of St. Louis.* Modifications altered the fuselage, added several feet to the wingspan and a new (for Ryan) type of landing gear capable of standing up under the weight of extra fuel. Between them Lindbergh and Hall agreed that it was possible for Ryan to build the plane required within a period of about two months and, with Mahoney's help, arrived at a cost figure of $10,580, including the price of the latest Wright J-5 Whirlwind.

The enthusiasm, spirit and cooperativeness at Ryan impressed Lindbergh. "I believe in Hall's ability; I like Mahoney's enthusiasm. I have confidence in the character of the workmen I've met," he wrote in his *Spirit of St. Louis.* There was absolutely no haggling over price; there was no questioning of Lindbergh's ability as a pilot. There was no suspicion on either side. On February 25, 1927, Harry H. Knight replied to a wire from Lindbergh, informing him that the partners agreed that they should purchase the new Ryan monoplane.

Hall was "rather startled" to learn that Lindbergh planned to make the flight alone—without the essential navigator. But then, Hall quickly saw, the lack provided more space for fuel tanks and for the extra weight of fuel. All nonessentials were stripped away; there wasn't even a front windscreen. Lindbergh wished to have the main fuel tank installed directly under the wing inside the fuselage directly behind the instrument panel. This would place the concentration of weight nearly at the center of gravity of the plane itself for better longitudinal stability. Two more tanks were installed in the wings, near the roots, and a third in the center section.

Before him Lindbergh would have a fairly sophisticated (for the time) instrument panel. There were windows on either side of the cockpit and for an additional view of where he was going a small periscope was built into the instrument panel and could be projected sideways from the fuselage to give him a better view of the area directly in front of the plane. In landing he could operate as did most pilots in cockpit planes, craning his neck out of a window to keep his eye on the ground.

While Hall worked on the design and, shortly after, Bowlus supervised its construction in the Ryan factory, Lindbergh plotted a Great Circle course across the Atlantic on a drafting table. There amid the sounds of labor in the shop, the aroma of aircraft dope and decaying fish, Lindbergh connected lines and dots between New York and Paris.

As work progressed on the plane—with plenty of dedication from Ryan employees, who willingly put in long hours of overtime to speed the work—Lindbergh kept informed on the "Air Derby" via the newspapers. He read about Byrd, Davis and Nungesser, wondering if he himself would ever get to fly the Atlantic. He read of a great endurance flight in Levine's Bellanca, piloted by Chamberlin and Acosta; so clearly Levine and company too were considering the flight. Then came the more dismal reports of Byrd's crash, the wiping out of the Bellanca's landing gear, the deaths of Davis and Wooster.

On the day Lindbergh read of this tragic event (April 26, 1927), his plane was being taken out of the Ryan factory to be assembled for test flights. There were some hitches; in order to get the fuselage through the factory door one of the landing gears had to be removed. The wing was an even greater problem, for in adding ten feet to the standard Ryan wing (it measured 46 feet), it was difficult to get it out of the loft of the old cannery. Instead of tearing out part of a wall a simpler solution presented itself: a railroad track ran alongside the building, so a number of Ryan workmen—and Lindbergh—manhandled a boxcar until it stood just outside the loft's double doors. Then the wing was carefully lifted out onto the boxcar; a derrick was used to place it in a truck. Finally both fuselage and wing were hauled out to nearby Dutch Flats where Ryan tested its planes and where the *Spirit of St. Louis* was finally assembled.

Charles Lindbergh planning his flight to Paris; at the same time Donald Hall, who snapped this photo, designed the plane in which Lindbergh hoped to do it. (*Ryan Aeronautical Library*)

It was a compact, handsome little plane—all silver, with trim lines and a pleasing configuration. The long nose, which housed the engine and its internal gadgetry plus a fuel tank, was covered by a soft aluminum cowling, as was the propeller spinner. Incidentally, one of the reasons for the fuel tank's placement in front of the pilot was to minimize the possibility of injury to the pilot in the case of a crash. If a plane nosed in which had the tanks in the fuselage behind the pilot, there was all too often the chance of his being crushed by the weight of the tanks and fuel. All the struts on the plane were carefully streamlined with light aluminum; even the wheels were covered over with fabric, laced and doped taut. It was believed that such careful attention to streamlining had added ten miles an hour to the speed of the plane.

Two days later, on April 28, 1927, exactly sixty days after work had begun on it, the *Spirit of St. Louis* was given its first test flight at Dutch Flats. Lindbergh climbed into the little cockpit feeling that both he and the plane were on trial that day. Would the plane perform as it had on paper and, if not, would he be pilot enough to counteract any problem?

Chief mechanic van der Linde cranked the prop and Lindbergh revved up the engine. The compact cockpit, so unlike any he had occupied before, seemed strange to him with its total lack of any front view and the complexity of instruments. But the engine sounded fine. When the revolutions per minute rose on the tachometer, he tested the magnetos by cutting them one at a time; and the engine roared back to full life as soon as he cut them in again. The *Spirit of St. Louis* was ready to go; he signaled for the wheel chocks to be pulled away, and the eager young mechanic, Doug Corrigan, nimbly avoiding the whirling propeller disc, yanked them away. Hand delicately on the throttle,

Uncovered fuselage of the plane Hall designed for Lindbergh; structure was of welded steel tubing. (*Ryan Aeronautical Library*)

The new aircraft, with new Wright Whirlwind J-5C engine installed, emerges from the Ryan factory— once one of the landing gear legs has been removed to make that possible. Young aviation enthusiast Douglas Corrigan stands second from left; factory manager Hawley Bowlus, in charge of the aircraft construction, is fourth from left. (*Ryan Aeronautical Library*)

The wing of the new Lindbergh plane has just been hoisted out of the former fish cannery in which it had been built. Because of the span it could not be taken down to the first floor and was taken out of a second story window onto a boxcar, and then placed on the truck for delivery to Dutch Flats for assembly. (*Ryan Aeronautical Library*)

The fuselage of the new Ryan monoplane the NYP (New York to Paris) is towed out to Dutch Flats. (*Ryan Aeronautical Library*)

Assembling the *Spirit of St. Louis*, Dutch Flats. Lindbergh is fifth from left; manhandling the tail is a young Ryan employee named Corrigan. (*Ryan Aeronautical Library*)

All responsible for the *Spirit of St. Louis*—officials and employees of Ryan and Lindbergh (with hat)—pose before the finished plane. (*Ryan Aeronautical Library*)

OPPOSITE Lindbergh expresses his pleasure in his new plane. (*National Air & Space Museum, Smithsonian Institution*)

Lindbergh moved the plane down the runway; more power, and the little plane quickened to powerful life. In less than 200 feet it darted off the runway and climbed swiftly. Lindbergh noted with satisfaction that there was a clear power reserve and then began running the plane through a careful series of tests, making notations so that future small adjustments could be made.

During the tests a Navy Curtiss Hawk flitted over to study the strange new gyrating craft. Through his upper window Lindbergh watched the Hawk diving down on him. He flipped the *Spirit of St. Louis* into position to meet his attacker. For several minutes the two planes skylarked as the two men, unknown to each other, engaged in mock combat over San Diego. They broke off and Lindbergh brought the plane down again at Dutch Flats (the next day newspapers reported that he had just barely escaped having a midair collision with a Navy plane). The single big problem was instability (the tail surfaces were comparatively small), but this did not bother Lindbergh. He would have to fly the plane every minute and this would certainly help keep him awake on any long flight.

The next test phase was devoted to weight lifting: could a fully loaded *Spirit of St. Louis* get off the ground? For the load tests Lindbergh flew over to the Army's Camp Kearney about eleven miles from San Diego. The runway was smoother than Dutch Flats or Rockwell Field on North Island and therefore more suitable for a fully loaded takeoff. The possibility of disaster lurked in the blowing of a tire and the smoother the surface the better.

A small mishap delayed the tests. Before landing at Kearney, Lindbergh made some speed tests over San Diego Bay, noting everything carefully on his clipboard. But just as he began heading for the Army field a gust of wind carried the board—and all its valuable data—out the window. Lindbergh followed it down until it fell into the brush near a small hill. Circling the spot, he noted a few check points and then landed at Kearney and phoned for another plane to be sent over. It would be impossible to land the *Spirit of St. Louis* in the spot where the clipboard had fallen. A slower plane would do, however. Lindbergh found the clipboard from the air, but on landing could not find it, although he knew it was nearby. Leaving his coat as a marker he took off again in the other plane, a Standard, and circled again, spotting both the coat and the board. When he landed, Lindbergh found he had been within twenty feet of the wayward board. He quickly took off and flew back to Camp Kearney where Hall carefully studied the retrieved data sheets.

It was worth the effort, for redoing the original tests would have consumed a good deal of time; there was very little time left for the load tests. The day had begun to wane and there was little wind to assist in the takeoffs. The men hurried, filling the tanks—adding fifty gallons for each new takeoff—until a nearly full load of 300 gallons weighed down the *Spirit of St. Louis*. As the weight increased Lindbergh noticed a greater roughness in the takeoff as the shock absorbers and wheels sustained more punishment; the greater weight required a longer run also. But within twenty seconds, which consumed 1,023 feet of runway, the plane left the ground, "but the tires took a terrible beating and the landing was even rougher than the takeoff."

Lindbergh rejected another fifty-gallon load; he was confident that the plane could take off fully fueled (even though when he planned to leave New York the load would amount to 425 gallons of fuel). Judging from the various curves and calculations on their data sheets the *Spirit of St. Louis* was ready for its flight to Paris.

Lindbergh, too, was ready to leave for the East but poor weather over the Rocky Mountains kept him grounded. The speed and load tests— and the clipboard search—had occurred on May 4; as he impatiently awaited a good turn in the weather Lindbergh read about the departure from Paris of Nungesser and Coli on May 8. Certain that these two fine airmen were bound to arrive in New York the following day Lindbergh again turned to studying the charts and plans for a cross-Pacific flight. He even considered fitting the *Spirit of St. Louis* with pontoons.

The weather held no promise for the ninth—nor was there much

RIGHT Ready for fuel load testing at Camp Kearney. (*Ryan Aeronautical Library*)

BELOW A slight touch of commerce, characteristic of most record-making flights of the Twenties which depended on sponsorship. Pouring fuel into the tank is H. J. van der Linde (later factory manager for Ryan); standing below are O. R. McNeel (who had been in charge of welding on the plane), George Hammond, a student pilot, Lindbergh, Donald Hall, Ryan's chief engineer and designer of the plane, and A. J. Edwards, at the time sales manager for Ryan. (*Ryan Aeronautical Library*)

hope for Nungesser and Coli by this time—but on May 10 Lindbergh was able to set out for St. Louis. He believed he owed it to his sponsors to make a long flight if only to show he was capable of it—and thus put an end to several demands that the flight be canceled because of Lindbergh's inexperience.

Except for a few unexplained but anxious moments when his engine ran roughly, the cross-country flight was without incident. After 14 hours and 25 minutes in the air Lindbergh set the *Spirit of St. Louis* down at Lambert Field; it was the fastest cross-country flight to that time. He stayed in St. Louis only overnight and the next day, May 12, he hopped to New York, landing at Curtiss Field, Long Island, after a seven-hour flight. It was official now; Charles A. Lindbergh was in the race to Paris.

After his record-smashing transcontinental flight Lindbergh became even more of an object of curiosity and newspaper scrutiny than before. Though Byrd, in his repaired Fokker, and Chamberlin, in his repaired Bellanca, were also in the running, it was the youthful, genuinely shy and modest Lindbergh (with his diffident air of mystery) who fascinated. His name, in various spellings—Lindenburgh, Linberg—appeared on the front pages across the land. This did not bother the young pilot as much as some of the other press-coined *sobriquets* such as the "Flying Kid," or worse, the "Flyin' Fool." Familiarity bred further familiarity and he became known to everyone as "Lindy" or "Lucky Lindy" or "Slim" (the one nickname used by many of his intimates). The slightly manic journalism of the period began its work. There was plenty of time for this, for after Lindbergh's arrival a week of poor flying weather settled down over the East Coast.

Between bouts with reporters Lindbergh attended to the necessary preparations for the flight—and it seemed that every time he took off in his plane the press announced that the Flyin' Fool was off for Paris with a "toothbrush and a comb" in his pocket. There was still much to do; there had been a little trouble with the earth inductor compass, so the Pioneer Instrument Company sent a representative to the field to be on hand when Lindbergh arrived. He was Brice Goldsborough, an expert in the field, who one day in the near future would attempt his own transatlantic flight. Besides Goldsborough there were other specialists on hand, sent by their companies, to look after every possible contingency associated with fuel, oil or engine. There was even an agent who represented a young dancer and who wanted her to be photographed doing a split on the propeller of the *Spirit of St. Louis* to "symbolize the flight between New York and Paris." Lindbergh did not concur.

His one major concern was the weather, special reports of which were supplied by the New York weather bureau's Dr. James H. Kimball, who himself became a kind of minor celebrity during the upsurge in the transatlantic flurry. Soon pilots and newspapers referred to him simply as "Doc." Lindbergh was sure his plane was as ready as possible—although it would never be able to get off from tiny Curtiss Field with a full load of fuel. This problem was graciously solved by Byrd, in adjoining Roosevelt Field, who offered Lindbergh the use of his own runway. Of course Byrd and Chamberlin in their respective craft were poised, too, and depending upon the weather, it all became a question of who would get off first.

But Byrd was ever cautious and unhurried and Chamberlin's flight was disrupted by internal squabbles which led to law suits, injunctions and general delays.

By May 19 Lindbergh grew rather restive; he was ready and had been waiting for good weather. But the day opened drizzling, the sky was overcast and the weather over the Atlantic was reported to be foggy and stormy. With little to do but dodge reporters, Lindbergh slipped away to Paterson, New Jersey, to visit the Wright plant; he had plans to see a popular musical comedy, *Rio Rita*, in the evening. It had even been arranged to visit the show girls backstage ("It ought to be great fun").

Around six in the evening, however, Lindbergh checked in with Doc Kimball and learned that the low pressure area over Nova Scotia and Newfoundland was receding and that the chances were good that the fog would clear up. Instead of going to the Ziegfeld Theater Lindbergh hurried back to Curtiss Field, where he arranged to have the *Spirit of St. Louis* partially fueled up, checked and towed over to Roosevelt Field. He was surprised to see no activity in the camps of Byrd and Chamberlin. Certainly they must have had access to the same weather report as he. Of course, the report was not exactly promising, but it was the best so far—and might not last. Lindbergh planned to take off in the morning and went to his hotel to rest. Word had already spread and the lobby was jammed with reporters, autograph collectors and a man who wanted Lindbergh to sign a movie contract promising thousands of dollars.

It was midnight before Lindbergh reached his room. There was too much on his mind for sleep; a friend had cautioned him about the reception to expect at Le Bourget. A successful flight by an American so soon after the loss of Nungesser and Coli would not bring out the best in the French. Another friend arrived shortly after Lindbergh had stretched out and was barely dozing to ask the question, "Slim, what am I going to do when you're gone?" There was no sleep for Lindbergh that night.

Just before three in the morning, May 20, 1927, Lindbergh arrived at

Curtiss Field. Men had worked through the night to get the plane ready. Lights glowed in the hangar housing Chamberlin's Bellanca; Byrd's hangar was dark, although he had scheduled further tests later in the day. Lindbergh studied the dark sky, still not promising. He prodded the ground: muddy. It had been decided to lash the tail of the *Spirit of St. Louis* to the back of a truck, cover the engine with a tarpaulin and haul it to Roosevelt. Carefully the plane was moved to its starting position followed by policemen, reporters and a few curious onlookers. They formed a dreary *cortège*, sloshing through the mud, their raincoats dripping, moving slowly through the darkness. "It's more like a funeral procession than the beginning of a flight to Paris," Lindbergh would later recall.

He hoped to get off at dawn, to take advantage of whatever weather breaks Doc Kimball had promised. But the weather had taken its toll—the engine was thirty revolutions short of full power because of the dampness. There was a slight tail wind, nothing serious but not good. The plane was placed at the extreme west end of the runway, facing east. The only obstacles to clear were a tractor at the far end and, just beyond that, a telephone line. To take off westward would mean having to clear the hangars of the field and a settlement of houses. Should the *Spirit of St. Louis* not get off properly going west the results could be disastrous. Unless the tail wind increased dangerously Lindbergh decided to chance it eastward.

The field was a bit sticky and the plane was heavily loaded; the wheels were greased to keep the mud from adhering. The wheels bulged slightly under the heaviest load they had ever sustained. Lindbergh sensed the difference in the "feel" of the plane, the fragility of its structure and its wings which had to lift 5,000 pounds (a thousand more

LEFT Lindbergh about to leave California on his way to St. Louis and New York. Seeing him off are (left to right): Donald Hall and A. J. Edwards, of Ryan, and Lt. Col. Harry S. Graham, commanding officer of Rockwell Field, North Island, California. (*Ryan Aeronautical Library*)

RIGHT The *Spirit of St. Louis* takes off from California. (*Historical Collection, Title Insurance and Trust Co., San Diego, California*)

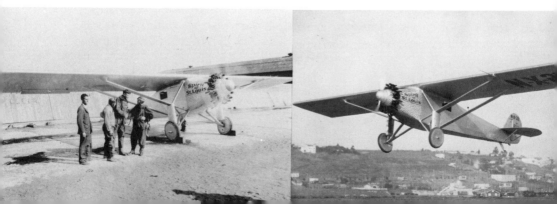

than at Camp Kearney). He found very little comfort in knowing that if he decided to call it quits no one would question his decision, no one would censor him.

At the same time he realized that it would be nearly another month before there would be a period of full moon, so essential to his navigation—for he had decided not to add to the load of the plane various navigation instruments he could not use. He would have enough to do just flying the plane.

Seated in his plane, vibrating with the power, but just a little too little power, Lindbergh had a decision to make. The gray sky was uninviting, the narrow runway looked tiny and short. But there were Byrd and Chamberlin to consider. Questions and answers churned up in Lindbergh's mind as he methodically weighed one problem against the other; there were doubts. And then some inner voice said *Go*, something told him that the wheels *would* lift out of the mud, that he *would* get to Paris, that "it *is* time to start the flight."

On either side of the plane anxious men, ropes in hand, kept their eyes on Lindbergh. First on the left, then on the right, a hand signaled to pull the chocks. He had fastened the seat belt, pulled the goggles over his eyes and sighted down the runway from the left window. The *Spirit of St. Louis* began moving slowly, almost reluctantly, as if the throttle had little effect. Mechanics tried to assist by pushing on the wing struts on either side and Lindbergh worried that their help could very well buckle the struts. "The *Spirit of St. Louis*," he thought, "feels more like an overloaded truck than an airplane."

A hundred yards of runway were consumed and though the speed had increased, it was still far short of flying speed. The straining engine lacked that extra power which had been so evident during the early

LEFT   Still smiling, Lindbergh flies the *Spirit of St. Louis* over San Diego. (*Ryan Aeronautical Library*)

RIGHT   An air view, which Lindbergh himself may have seen as he approached Curtiss Field, of the impressive Byrd establishment at nearby Roosevelt Field. When Curtiss proved to be the wrong field for a takeoff, Byrd generously gave permission to Lindbergh for use of his facilities at Roosevelt. (*National Air & Space Museum, Smithsonian Institution*)

flight tests. He speculated on the possibility of the landing gear collapsing under the heavy load and the bouncing of the run before the wings could take up some of that burden. There *was* better response to the controls as speed picked up little by little. At the halfway mark the plane tentatively lifted off, but then settled down again, splashing water and mud onto the fuselage. He had almost made it—and nearly 2,000 feet of runway still stretched comfortingly ahead of him. Once again the *Spirit of St. Louis* strained into the air, remained haltingly airborne for a longer period than before and then, impetus gone, fluttered down for a briefer return to earth. Then easing back on the stick, he pulled the *Spirit of St. Louis* gently off the runway—a thousand feet away were the telephone wires beyond the end of the field—and closer, the tractor near the runway's end. The engine ran smoothly and the propeller sliced the air with greater efficiency, the controls were alive to his touch. He did not try to climb too steeply, even nosed down slightly to pick up speed without strain. The tractor flashed by, fifteen feet below; then in seconds he passed over the wires with twenty feet to spare. But there was a small tree-covered hill ahead—gingerly he pushed the stick and rudder to bank to the right to avoid that obstacle. He had to be careful; the slightest loss in flying speed or lift and the flight could end in a sudden swift drop and a burst of flame.

He exulted in the plane's airworthiness, despite the small margin of risk on which everything balanced. The longer he remained airborne the better the engine responded; he could even throttle back slightly without serious loss of air speed—a hundred miles an hour. The controls felt good to his touch and the instruments read right; he moved the rudder to place the plane on the correct course on the Great Circle Route to Paris. It was 7:54 A.M., May 20, 1927; Lindbergh and the *Spirit of St. Louis*—"we" as he came to call this perfect combination of man and machine—had been airborne for all of two minutes. Before them lay 33 hours and 28 minutes of lonely flight.

Because he had not slept the previous night, it would be the almost overwhelming craving for sleep that would be Lindbergh's greatest enemy during the flight. The *Spirit of St. Louis* and its Wright Whirlwind performed to perfection. So, indeed, did Lindbergh, but he was no machine. The tensions, excitements and lack of sleep over several days might easily have vanquished a lesser man. Nor was the success of the flight dependent upon simple physical stamina—although that became a critical factor which could have decided the outcome—but rather upon a complexity of elements: skill, courage, intelligence under stress, self-confidence. Perhaps the one simple factor was the will to survive. And even that was nearly canceled now and again when the desire for sleep seemed even more inviting than life itself.

The weather, as could always be counted on over the Atlantic during the period of the pioneer flights, contributed its own peculiar hazards. Initially there were no problems; over Long Island the morning mist began to clear and as he flew from Cape Cod toward Nova Scotia Lindbergh enjoyed perfectly clear weather. With the Whirlwind turning smoothly and the propeller turning 1,750 times a minute he could set his course (which to remain on the Great Circle required a change every hundred miles, or about every hour), study the landscape of New England, sometimes—particularly once when he was over the Atlantic—from as low as ten feet above the water. There were fishing boats in the water as he skimmed the surface and he pulled the plane up, adjusted his periscope out the left side of the fuselage to keep an eye on the path before him. Prudently he lifted the *Spirit of St. Louis* above mast height, and then higher. Flying close to the water was tiring, for he had to be constantly alert with his hands and feet firmly on the controls. A wheel or wingtip touching a wave could be disastrous.

Over Nova Scotia he encountered the first stormy areas; but, despite some bumpiness and the necessity of flying through storms, Lindbergh was easy in mind, knowing that he was pretty much on course. Nova Scotia also marked his second phase of decision; the first had been back at Roosevelt Field, where he could have aborted the flight, the second was Nova Scotia, which he had selected as a haven should the engine sound rough, or if fuel problems arose. But all was mechanically fine and he pushed on for Newfoundland.

Flying over the open ocean, after leaving Nova Scotia behind, Lindbergh began to feel the first craving for sleep; nothing really serious though. By the time he reached Newfoundland it was eleven hours since the takeoff and he had covered 1,100 miles. He flew slightly off course in order to pass over St. John's so that the fact that he had come that far would be known should he, for any reason, have trouble over the Atlantic. While flying over St. John's Lindbergh's thoughts dwelled on the historic setting for the flights of Read and the NC-4, Alcock and Brown —Hawker and Mackenzie-Grieve: that last was not a comforting thought, however. It was at this point, also, that Lindbergh's navigational skills would be put to the test. Over the United States he could refer to ordinary road maps, but over the Atlantic he would have to depend upon his instruments, his mental dexterity—and intuition. Besides keeping his eye on fuel consumption, he would have to watch the compass to which he would apply such variables as the magnetic variation and the drift off course contributed by the wind.

St. John's was ninety miles south of the Great Circle, and Lindbergh felt that the deviation might have been a fuel-consuming lark. But still it had not been a bad idea. Should he be forced down in the Atlantic his rescuers would know at least where to begin searching. He had decided to trade a radio for fuel so there would be no means by which he could communicate with anyone in the event of trouble; but still the thought that he had expended a little fuel to fly over St. John's nagged him. But it was a bit late to worry about that; the *Spirit of St. Louis*—"on schedule, plenty of fuel, and a tail wind"—flew out to sea.

In twelve hours he had covered one-third of the distance to Paris; his real Atlantic adventure was about to begin. There were no other reference points except those afforded by the sky and sea—and his instruments. The only reality lay within the small cockpit of the *Spirit of St. Louis*; everything outside it was real, too, but it shifted and changed and did not conform at all to his skill. The gods of sea and air could not care less. "We" were strictly on their own; Lindberg was alone in a small, not really proved, airplane over the vasty expanse of the Atlantic Ocean. The questions that would have to be answered in the next twenty-four hours or so were: Could the plane and the engine endure for that period? What were the true weather conditions over the remaining 2,400 miles? Could he keep the plane on course? Would the instruments function properly, for his navigation would necessarily depend upon them? Could he remain awake?

All of these questions were, of course, answered and have become a part of the history, even legend, of aviation. But when Lindbergh nosed the *Spirit of St. Louis* out over the Atlantic on the evening of May 20 he had no certainty, despite his own self-confidence and his confidence in the aircraft and its engine, that the answers would come out in his favor. Neither he, nor any other man before him, nor any plane, had been put to such a test. Leaving Newfoundland with its iceberg-cragged coastal waters behind, he had made another decision. Over the Atlantic he would have only one other to make: either to press onward for Europe, or to turn back while still within flying distance of American soil.

The coming of darkness, with no moon at first, and the building up of fog prompted him to ease back on the stick to climb above the clouds. Despite the blackness Lindbergh saw storm clouds in the near distance and continued to climb until he reached 10,000 feet—even that was not high enough and he was forced to fly directly through the swelling thunderheads. As he did he believed he could depend on his senses for direction, but realized also that his instruments must make all his ultimate decisions. When he flew over the last landmark, he had been perfectly on course; with that as a reference, and taking certain buffeting from the wind into consideration—plus an appreciated tail wind—he could remain at least nearly on course even in utter blackness.

The dials of the instruments glowed in the dark and the cockpit grew colder. The altimeter read 10,500 feet and it was very cold; a sudden thought came to Lindbergh: if it was cold inside the cockpit, what was happening out in the night air? He removed a glove and put his hand through the side window and felt sharp needlelike stings. It was as he feared and shining the beam of a flashlight out the window confirmed it: ice was forming on the plane, making it heavier and altering the configuration of the wing. Ice could disfigure all of the aerodynamic qualities of the plane, could falsify the instrument readings, could be fatal. Lindbergh turned the plane around in a half-circle to retrace his path through the thunderhead and to seek a lower altitude at which the ice did not form. He considered changing course but saw that to the south and north loomed similar cloud formations, some rising even higher than the one he had so blithely flown into ten minutes before. Once again he weighed the wisdom of turning back, but only momentarily. Eye on compass, which swung crazily, he managed to make sense of it and, once again on course, weaved around the ice-filled clouds. He steered by the stars since both compasses behaved erratically because of the electrical disturbances surrounding him.

After fifteen hours of flight, and at the midpoint between land ahead and behind, Lindbergh finally saw the moon. The haze drifted away, the clouds were left behind, he could set the plane, despite the still jiggling compasses, on course. The ice had all but melted from the plane in the warmer air, the compasses began to settle and a pleasant warmth enveloped the cockpit. And with it entered Lindbergh's dearest enemy: sleep.

The steady drone of the engine, the monotony of staring fixedly at the instrument panel and simple aching fatigue made sleep a nearly consuming passion. An alert part of him—which he called "spirit" as opposed to body and mind—would catch him drifting off and forced him into watchfulness. He would try to exercise in the cramped cockpit: remove his helmet, rub his head, put a hand out the window to direct a cool draft of air to his face, stamp his feet. This was temporarily effective, but his eyes would droop, close and he would slip again into momentary somnolence. That the *Spirit of St. Louis* had deliberately been left unstable proved wise: whenever Lindbergh slipped into a doze, or relaxed his grip on the stick, the plane snapped into a dive or a climb, jerking him back to wakefulness. Even so, the mere routine of flying became boring and sleep-inducing as he checked the fuel consumption, switched from one tank to the other to make for good weight distribution, or checked compass headings and make the hourly change to keep to the Great Circle.

After the eighteenth hour he had reached the halfway mark of the flight itself: 1,800 miles flown and the same number yet to go. As he flew toward the dawn Lindbergh sensed something illusory, something not

quite real, about his experience. Time, which had always been so important to him (not in the convention "time is money" sense, but in terms
of fuel consumed and miles flown), time seemed nonexistent, as if he
were "flying through all space, through all eternity" with no destination
and no starting point. He flew out of a short night into a dawning
day.

Suddenly he was jolted out of this reverie when some vigilant part of
his being warned him that he was about to smash into a great white
wall. But he had only drowsily flown into a cloud. His mind, though,
had been jarred back to the business at hand and he rapidly scanned the
instruments to be assured that he had not strayed off course as he flew
blindly through the ghostly mist. Fifteen minutes later (time had taken
on value again) he emerged from the cloud into a magnificent cloud-
studded and dazzlingly blue sky.

Daylight to some extent lessened the craving for sleep. The necessity
of watching the instruments while flying through cloud mountains
sharpened his consciousness. Through a hole in the clouds he caught a
glimpse of the ocean, flecked with white, then dipped the wing and
dropped down to estimate wind velocity and drift. Fifty feet from the
water he could see heavy water as a wind of perhaps sixty miles an hour
lashed the surface with gale force. It was a much too unfriendly setting
for so frail a craft as the *Spirit of St. Louis,* so after making calculations,
he pulled the nose back upward and climbed. As he studied the chart,
estimating his position, the waves below vanished completely as he was
enveloped in a thick fog.

The plane shuddered and capered in the turbulence. Lindbergh was
still too close to the water in such air, so he pulled back on the stick and
climbed to 1,000 feet. Still fog-bound, he saw nothing. As he flew blind
he sensed that one wing was too low, but the instruments told him the
plane was, in fact, in level flight; he chose to believe the instruments and
not his fog-disoriented instincts. Cut off again from all normal references
to the world beyond his cockpit, Lindbergh again was forced to struggle
with his body's importunities for rest.

For several hours he droned through an ethereal nothingness: a flight,
it seemed, into eternity. But as he experienced it then, for some fleeting
moments it seemed to be a flight into welcome oblivion.

> Sometimes, shut in by fog, the impression of movement ceases, and I seem
> to be just hanging in space—unrelated to any outside point of reference,
> hypnotized by the instruments, deluded by the noise and vibration of the
> engine into the belief that I'm flying rapidly across an ocean between two
> great continents of the world. How fantastic it is to think that if I sit
> here long enough, juggling these needles, France will lie below—like a

child's imaginary travels in a parlor chair. Over and over again, I fall
asleep with my eyes open, knowing I'm falling asleep, unable to prevent it . . .

His sleep-haunted mind conjures up "ghostly presences" which speak
to him "with human voices."

All sense of substance leaves. There's no longer weight to my body, no
longer hardness to the stick. The feeling of flesh is gone. I become inde-
pendent of physical laws—of food, of shelter, of life. I'm almost one with
those vaporlike forms behind me, less tangible than air, universal as
aether. I'm still attached to life; they, not at all; but at any moment some
thin band may snap and there'll be no difference between us . . .

He lost interest in keeping the log of the flight as he hovered in the
mist; there were occasional, brief glimpses of water. He even imagined
that he sighted land, islands complete with trees, but he logically dismissed these mirages for what they were, as he forced himself to attend
to the navigation and fought off sleep.

As the fog dispersed somewhat he descended nearer the water, at
times as close as ten feet above the waves. This helped to keep him alert
and to check the drift. Once he was almost certain he saw some creature
bobbing on the surface, a porpoise perhaps; later he was absolutely sure
he saw gulls flying. He envied their ability to sleep on the water. Such
signs of life indicated that he must be approaching land. In the twenty-
seventh hour since takeoff he spotted another object on the water which
materialized into a boat, then many boats of a small fishing fleet. That
definitely meant the proximity of land.

He nosed the plane down and circled the first boat, saw no one and
flew on to the next, circled that one also with the same result. There was
not a sign of life. Then a head poked out of a porthole, wide eyes staring
skyward. Lindbergh throttled back to cut the engine noise and glided
closer to the inhabited boat, realizing in the same instant that perhaps
the man in the porthole might not understand English.

Even so, he swooped in close and shouted, "Which way is Ireland?"
There was no response and he made several equally fruitless passes over
the boat. It was difficult to understand why the decks of the little boats
were not aswarm with curious seaman—unless the holds were packed
with superstitious sailors hiding below decks.

Puzzled by the mystery fleet, but not wishing to waste the time and
fuel, Lindbergh placed the *Spirit of St. Louis* back on the proper course.
Doing this he flew into a series of rain squalls while peering into the
distance for a glimpse of the land he knew must be near. The rain was
refreshing on his face, the cool air helped to curb the need for sleep.
And then—after nearly twenty-eight hours of constant flying, and less

The *Spirit of St. Louis* over the Atlantic, as it may have appeared on the morning of May 20, 1927. (*National Air & Space Museum, Smithsonian Institution*)

Instrument panel of the *Spirit of St. Louis*; not a part of the panel itself is the magnetic compass which dangled practically in Lindbergh's eyes. What appears to be a small television screen is the horizontal periscope through which, when it was extended, Lindbergh could achieve a limited frontal vision. Otherwise, since there was no windshield, his vision was confined to the views from the two side windows. (*Ryan Aeronautical Library*)

than an hour since the strange encounter with the fishing boats—he discerned on the distant northeastern horizon a shadowy broken form. Could it be another mirage? But no, it remained in place, steady and immobile, as he flew closer. He banked the plane and flew toward what he was certain was land.

Could this be Ireland? he wondered. If so, he was more than two hours ahead of schedule. He swept in low over an eroded coastline, then climbed to clear the hills and compared his map with the outlines below. It was indeed the southwestern coast of Ireland in the vicinity of Dingle Bay—he had crossed the coast a mere three miles off course. He circled over the first evidence of humanity he had encountered in over a day; his once sleep-accursed eyes drank in the vistas of neatly fenced fields, of sheep grazing, of friendly arms waving, of simple cottages and gardens.

Completely wide awake, Lindbergh rejoiced in the fact that he had a mere 600 miles to go. From that moment on he would never be cut off from humanity, from help if he required it.

From Ireland he flew southeastward, crossed over southern England (marveling over the compact tidiness of the farms compared to the sprawling ranches of the American West), then, as darkness approached, traversed the narrow waters of the English Channel. As the sun began to drop below the horizon, he flew over Cherbourg at an altitude of 2,000 feet. Finding Paris presented no navigational problem, and soon it appeared in a glow of light; it was then thirty-three hours since he had taken off from Roosevelt Field, an ocean—a lifetime—away. It was almost ten in the evening in Paris (nearly five in the afternoon in New York). Lindbergh did not resist the impulse to circle the Eiffel Tower before heading for what he hoped (according to all the instructions he had received at home) would prove to be Le Bourget Airport. He located a dark patch, remarkably close to Paris, he thought, which could have been an airfield. He was puzzled, however, for there were no flash-

Lindbergh, showing the strain of his flight—and reception—at Le Bourget Field, Paris. (*Musée de l'Air, Paris*)

ing beacons as was the custom in America. And, strangely too, there appeared to be congeries of lights converging upon it from all directions, thousands of them, unevenly spaced and which he assumed were factory windows. He questioned the wisdom of building such a congestion of factories so close to a large, busy airport.

Still he thought perhaps he might have been mistaken and continued circling a little longer. But he found no other spot near Paris which so resembled the goal he sought as that first dark patch. He approached it again, gingerly manipulating the throttle, cutting power on the approach. It was, indeed, an airport. And as he came in closer Lindbergh could recognize details which assured him he was right. To his surprise he found that the great myriad of lights he had thought belonged to factories actually were the headlights of automobiles, literally thousands of them, which jammed the roads to and around Le Bourget. He could not understand that at all.

He had located a small floodlighted area on the field and headed the *Spirit of St. Louis* for that. Approaching a strange airport, his every nerve was alert for all possible contingencies—farm implements and cows, for example—as he made out the forms of hangars, parked aircraft and other vehicles common to an airport—and a fine smooth runway before him under the lights. Inexplicably, he felt almost like a raw pilot coming in for his first solo landing—as indeed it was: the first night landing in the *Spirit of St. Louis*.

They were below the hangar tops, wheels probing for the earth, one hand on the stick and the other on the throttle, ready to pour on the fuel should something untoward occur. Man and plane descended into the near darkness; the wheels touched gently, bounced slightly, touched again, and then the comforting feel of the tail skid scraping the earth ("Not a bad landing . . ."). But it was eerie moving at high speed in a strange airport in almost complete darkness. When the speed diminished, Lindbergh whipped the plane around to taxi back to the lighted area. The plane stopped rolling for a moment then, with engine up, moved toward the light.

He had actually made it: in 33 hours and 30 minutes he had become the first man in history to fly nonstop and alone from New York to Paris.

And then bedlam. As he ground-looped the plane to head for a hangar he was appalled to see the entire field ahead of him swarming with excited unheeding humanity. If for the past thirty hours he had longed for human companionship, Lindbergh was being compensated with a vengeance. The significance of the mistaken "factory lights" around Le Bourget dawned with shocking suddenness as tens of thousands of cheering Frenchmen, who had broken through steel fences, bore down on him.

Fearful of what the turning propeller would do to such a mob, he quickly switched off the engine before the crowd engulfed him. Trapped inside the plane, he peered out at the faces that filled the side windows, listening to a chorus of voices calling his name. Even more ominously, he heard the sound of snapping wood and ripping fabric as the *Spirit of St. Louis* trembled and shuddered under the press of the mob and suffered at the hands of souvenir hunters.

Unable to make himself understood, Lindbergh tried to get out of the cockpit to organize a crew of men to get the plane to safety. His feet never touched the ground as he was seized and lifted overhead and carried triumphantly in jubilation. This mad tumbling went on for nearly a half hour before he was put down. The welcome was as warm as it was frenzied—there was absolutely no evidence of any bitterness over his success where Nungesser and Coli had failed. It was as if Lindbergh's safe arrival, in a sense, helped to compensate for their loss.

Thus, frenetically, Lindbergh remained airborne for a half hour after he had landed and then—"on European ground at last"—he stood on terra firma, intact though flabbergasted by the riotous reception. Then someone snatched the helmet off his head and an American reporter donned it. He, mistaken for Lindbergh, soon became the crowd's center of attention. Someone pointed and shouted, *"Voilà Lindbergh!"*, drew off the adulators and, in the confusion, Lindbergh was slipped to safety by two French airmen. Meanwhile the fake Lindbergh was carried on the collective shoulders of the mob to the official reception committee, where he was to be introduced to Ambassador Herrick.

Lindbergh, though safe himself, was concerned with the fate of the *Spirit of St. Louis*; it would have been an irony to have come all that way only to have his plane destroyed by human hands. In fact, it was even then being pushed into a hangar, not quite intact but in good shape for all that. Great patches of fabric had been torn from the fuselage and a piece of the engine was gone, but no serious damage had been done.

Lindbergh remained under wraps, hidden away in a darkened hangar, and, though there was a language barrier, one of his first inquiries was of Nungesser and Coli. There had been no word of the French airmen, but the very fact that the question had been asked deeply moved the French. It was but the first gesture of the countless number that were to follow that endeared Lindbergh to the French and that would later

OVERLEAF   "We," as Lindbergh chose to call the combination of man and machine which made the first solo nonstop flight from New York to Paris. Following his historic flight Lindbergh returned to the United States, then embarked on good-will flights across the country as well as to Central and South America. These flights contributed greatly to a resurgence of aviation in the late Twenties. (*Ryan Aeronautical Library*)

captivate the English, the people back home—and the world. If mankind needed (certainly America did at that moment, what with the tales of bootlegging, graft and gangsterdom monopolizing the headlines), if there was a need for an unassuming, poised, youthful hero, he had arrived at Paris the evening of May 21, 1927, in the unique person of Charles A. Lindbergh.

Gem of the
Ocean

The great public outpouring of adulation that engulfed Lindbergh swept all before it. There was little room in the public heart for anyone else but the slender youth who somehow managed to retain his dignity and self-respect despite the wide acclaim to which he was subjected. Although he appeared to be naïve in the ways of the world, he certainly side-stepped temptations (in the form of large sums of money) to sell his soul. He did not even enjoy the role of supercelebrity; he endured it but it did not impress him.

The celebrations, fêtes, receptions and honors accorded him upon his return to the United States were overwhelming. His presence, for a brief moment in time, relegated unwholesome news—political scandal, gang

RIGHT   Italian airman Francesco Marquis de Pinedo, who successfully crossed the South Atlantic and who might have been a contender in the North Atlantic Orteig sweepstakes had not bad luck overtaken him in Arizona. (*National Air & Space Museum, Smithsonian Institution*)

OPPOSITE   Francesco de Pinedo's *Santa Maria*, a Savoia-Marchetti S-55 twin-hulled flying boat, on a good-will tour of the United States after its transatlantic flight. The plane was accidentally destroyed by fire while moored in Roosevelt Dam, Arizona. (*U.S. Air Force*)

wars, murder and other folk mores of the American Twenties—to the back pages of the newspapers. He was showered with praise, medals, honors and offers; those he found acceptable, he took with good grace—the unacceptable he refused with equal courtesy. Publicity, a life in the limelight, the stage and screen (with all their monetary potential) repelled him. His one abiding dedication was to aviation and, having provided the greatest impetus to its development since the flight of the Wright brothers, he rejected all offers except those connected with the further evolution of aviation.

Unwittingly, however, he spurred others on in a real rash of Atlantic Fever, others who were not as skilled, nor as wise in preliminaries. His very reticence and composure, not to mention his youthful good looks and the ability to speak simply, with obvious integrity and brevity, endeared him to a massive public which in its characteristic inconstancy barely noticed that other airmen were risking all and contributing also to aviation's expansion.

A hapless victim of the Lindbergh idolization was a great Italian airman named Comdr. Francesco Marquis de Pinedo who, with two other of his countrymen, Capt. Carlo del Prete and Lt. Vitale Vacchetti, successfully crossed the South Atlantic in February, 1927, just about at the same moment that Lindbergh was undergoing his ordeal with Charles Levine over the purchase of the Bellanca. While the three men had not accomplished an aviation "first," and took ten days to reach

Brazil after leaving Italy, they *had* made the flight and were well received in South America—which they toured before finally arriving at New Orleans on March 29, 1927. (At about this time Lindbergh was studying the Wright Whirlwind that had just arrived in San Diego from Paterson, New Jersey; the *Spirit of St. Louis* was in its final month of construction).

Commander de Pinedo (who had earned glory as early as 1925 when he made a record flight from Rome to Melbourne and Tokyo) cagily made no reference to the Orteig prize. Ostensibly the flight was a goodwill tour, joining Fascist Italy with South America and the United States. De Pinedo and his crew were well received all along their route. Their plane was an impressive sight in itself—a Savoia-Marchetti 55, a twin-hulled flying boat of some 78 feet 9 inches of wingspan and which measured 52 feet 6 inches from tip of hull to tip of tail. Originally designed as a torpedo-bomber, the Savoia-Marchetti proved itself, properly modified, a good record-breaking aircraft. Italy was at the time anxious to build up propaganda for its new government and airmen. De Pinedo was among the most celebrated and his good-will tour—and the possibility of capturing the Orteig prize—would serve well, indeed, in the cause of Italian glorification.

The plan was to make their way to New York by a roundabout route, a stop which took the *Santa Maria*, as the plane was named, to Roosevelt Dam (near Phoenix), Arizona. It was here that disaster struck, which pretty much spoiled all the good will, at least that accumulated in the United States, of the tour. In filling the tanks for a flight to Phoenix, de Pinedo discovered that they had ordered too much fuel; he spilled the surplus into the water. Minutes later, one of the teen-age boys who had offered to help tow the *Santa Maria* to its mooring spot lit a cigarette, tossed the match into the water—a normal gesture—and the *Santa Maria* was soon ablaze and sank beneath the surface of the lake. John Thomason, the match-tosser, stoutly denied igniting the fuel-skimmed water and soon accusations of an anti-Fascist plot began emanating from Rome.

Diplomatically matters were pretty touch-and-go for a while until a newsman, Fred Gray of the *Arizona Republican*, suspecting the truth, talked with young Thomason and finally got him to admit that he had inadvertently burned up the *Santa Maria*. All was quickly forgiven (the plane had been insured by Lloyds of London) and, rejecting an offer of replacement by the United States, de Pinedo ordered another Savoia-Marchetti—the *Santa Maria II*—which was shipped from Italy by boat. Ominously, it arrived under heavy armed Fascist guard, in the eventuality that young John Thomason might be hanging around the New York docks, carelessly smoking.

By this time it was early May, the *Spirit of St. Louis* had been completed, tested and Lindbergh was awaiting a break in the weather before flying to St. Louis. De Pinedo, too, was testing the new flying boat and then, finding all well, took up his barnstorming of American cities. He returned to New Orleans and then began proceeding northward for New York. By this time the press was caught up in an outbreak of Atlantic Fever and, for some reason, de Pinedo made no effort to enter the Orteig sweepstakes. After New York, the *Santa Maria II* flew on to Trespassey Bay—the date was May 20, 1927. As he waited for decent weather conditions, de Pinedo may very well have heard the *Spirit of St. Louis* (though this was never reported and Lindbergh did not mention seeing a flying boat in the bay; his route took him north of Trespassey Bay, closer to St. John's).

When the *Santa Maria II* did finally get off, it was May 23 and the world was caught up in a Lindbergh delirium and gave scant attention to de Pinedo and his doughty crew. Worse, bucking head winds, the plane ran out of fuel and came down 300 miles short of Horta, their destination in the Azores. Luckily a ship chanced to be passing by and took them in tow for three days (it was reported that the Italian dictator Benito Mussolini spent sleepless nights during this period), bringing them into Horta, battered but safe.

After a few days spent on repairs, de Pinedo took off for Rome, arriving there on June 16, 1927. Celebrations of the flight were pretty much confined to Italy, for Lindbergh was still news and other, more spectacular, flights had been made by that time also. That the flight had fallen short of glory-mongering was all too obvious and may have contributed to de Pinedo's eventual fall from grace. Mussolini found a new favorite in Italo Balbo, who received government backing for his later mass flights. De Pinedo did not quit aviation, however, and on September 2, 1933, in taking off on what he hoped would be a world's long-distance flight, his plane careened into a fence and burst into flame, and he died. Embittered by his treatment in Italy, and in practical exile as the Italian ambassador in Argentina, he had been too anxious to prove himself. Early in the takeoff run it was obvious that his plane was not under complete control and swerved erratically from side to side until it left the runway to smash into the fence. There had been time for de Pinedo to cut the throttle and abort the flight, but he had tried too hard and lost.

De Pinedo and his *Santa Marias* had not been taken seriously as contenders in the Atlantic race, although he had, with qualified success, crossed it twice. The only serious Lindbergh rivals were Byrd and his *America* and the Bellanca owned by Levine, who liked to keep his pilots dancing, named *Columbia*. But then a boy flew in from the West and left them at the gate.

Byrd was not terribly perturbed; he had refused to enter the Orteig competition—nor was he in any hurry to get off while Lindbergh was suffering the attentions of the world. Not so Charles Levine, for he had ambitions as well as problems.

When he initially backed Bellanca in December, 1926, Levine had visions of providing the general public with Bellanca-designed aircraft and hoped, for a time, of landing the contract for the mail route between Chicago and New York. He purchased the Wright-Bellanca, the plane that gave Lindbergh many an anxious moment, from Wright, established the Columbia Aircraft Corporation and took Giuseppe Bellanca with him. Bellanca, on his part, took with him a friend of several years standing, Clarence Chamberlin, an ex-Iowan barnstormer, who had flown for Wright and had accumulated a good number of hours in Bellanca aircraft.

Levine, the germ possibly implanted by Lindbergh, at some point early in 1927 began thinking about the New York to Paris prize. He had plans, but they did not include Chamberlin, feeling that the pilot was not photogenic enough and, as put by Chamberlin, "would not film well after the big adventure." Obviously Levine believed in planning ahead with a vengeance, with a sharp eye on the publicity potential, which, in turn, could be traded in for show business dollars. The period was one in which vaudeville flourished throughout the land and it was Levine's destiny to contribute a touch of farce to the history of aviation.

If public relations was a Levine preoccupation, his personal relations with pilots was quixotic and the game he played was a kind of aerial musical chairs. His design for a transatlantic flight was shaped to begin with an initial record-breaking duration flight with the Bellanca, thus breaking ground in the area of publicity. His choice for the pilot of this flight was Leigh Wade, who had gained fame as pilot of the *Boston* of the U.S. Army's 1924 round-the-world cruise. That he was not as familiar with the plane as the relatively unknown and unphotogenic Chamberlin, despite Bellanca's objections, made little impression on Levine. But eventually Bellanca prevailed and Chamberlin was considered as a second pilot. Then Wade, infected by Levine's penchant for "headliners," began searching around for a bigger name pilot from his Army days to supplant Chamberlin; this wasn't so bad, so far as Levine was concerned, but then Wade began making peculiar noises about bringing in another friend to serve as general manager and his own public relations man.

Exit Leigh Wade, enter Bert Acosta, Levine's flying instructor and, like Chamberlin, a fine flier. During the brief tenure of Wade, Chamberlin had continued carrying out various preliminary tests and the plane was ready by the second week in April. Certain "experts," however, disagreed. "They predicted," Chamberlin later wrote, "that we wouldn't be able to get off the ground, and I think that most of them expected us to crash as Fonck's big plane had crashed at the end of the mile-long runway which ends at the bluff where Curtiss Field begins. One of the Curtiss engineers estimated before the take-off that the Bellanca 'ceiling' with the load she carried for the duration flight was 600 feet *below sea level!*"

But on April 12, 1927, the overloaded Bellanca took off before much over a quarter of the runway had been traversed and climbed easily out of Curtiss Field and remained well *above* sea level (with 375 gallons of fuel) for 51 hours, 11 minutes and 25 seconds to establish a new world record for endurance (held till then by France's Maurice Drouhin and M. Landry).

Levine now had two pilots, each of whom had acquired a degree of headline value. But he continued to have other ideas, announcing soon after the two had landed that *one* would be chosen as the pilot of the plane for the transatlantic flight, but that the other would be replaced by an experienced navigator-pilot, Lloyd W. Bertaud, a famed airmail pilot. At the same time Levine made it known that the choice between Acosta and Chamberlin would be made by tossing their names in a hat and deciding on the day of takeoff which would be the pilot. Chamberlin, however, had his doubts, for he knew that privately Levine "declared that Acosta and Bertaud, who were both tall and powerfully built in contrast to my own slender physique, would make a much better screen impression than I to make the flight together because of the motion picture offers that would pour in as soon as they landed in Paris." Chamberlin had passed the Air Service requirements, he had gone through the traditional barnstorming phase and had helped to set a new world's endurance record—but he had failed his screen test.

Witnessing such shenanigans from the sidelines, Bellanca was aghast (even hardened newsmen thought the name-in-the-hat trick was rather low) and informed Levine that should Chamberlin be left out of any transatlantic flight Bellanca would resign from the Columbia Aircraft Corporation. Bertaud introduced his own little variation on the theme when he attempted to bring in a friend, Harry L. Chandler. This would have eliminated *both* Acosta and Chamberlin.

At the same time, Bertaud and Chamberlin disagreed over a couple of fundamental points: the former hoped to carry a radio in the plane (which Chamberlin regarded as excess baggage and a source of danger should anything electrical go wrong) and, rather than fly the shorter Great Circle route, Bertaud thought it best to fly directly from New York to Paris over nearly 1,500 additional miles of ocean. Levine sided with Bertaud on the radio primarily because he had already sold certain rights to a newspaper syndicate which would have liked radio flashes from the plane en route during the crossing. As the radio barely had the range to reach even ships at sea (if the Great Circle route was used), it seemed to have little value except to displace its weight in fuel. On his part, Chamberlin vowed that if he were to go and the radio was installed in the Bellanca, he would "rip the thing out myself and throw it away" once they actually got under way.

By this time April had all but dwindled away (and, unknown to the bickering Bellanca crew and Levine, the *Spirit of St. Louis* was nearing completion in San Diego). Sunday, April 24, was selected for the christening of the plane, which would be done by Levine's nine-year-old daughter Eloyse with a bottle of ginger ale. The Brooklyn Chamber of Commerce, of which Levine was a member, had posted a prize of $15,000 which could be added to the Orteig prize, should anyone succeed in flying to Paris. After drenching herself with the ginger ale and dubbing the Bellanca *Columbia*, Eloyse Levine asked if she and a friend, fifteen-year-old Grace Jonas, daughter of the president of the Brooklyn Chamber of Commerce, could be taken up for a ride.

This seemed a reasonable request, so with the two girls plus mechanic John Carisi aboard, Chamberlin took off in the *Columbia*. During the takeoff a pin sheared off a shock absorber, the left landing gear strut dropped down and the wheel sagged uselessly under the plane. Chamberlin was unaware of this and had he landed the plane in that state the result would have been a crackup. Another pilot, Dean C. Smith, raced to his plane with a mechanic carrying a wheel in pursuit and both took off.

For a time Chamberlin and Carisi mistook Smith's intentions: at first they thought Smith only wanted to race them (not very logical, for the Bellanca was much swifter than Smith's Curtiss Oriole) and the girls greatly enjoyed the manner in which Smith and the mechanic, when they flew alongside the *Columbia*, "acted funny." Both men in the Oriole were frantically waving their arms and the mechanic held a wheel in his hands. Chamberlin very quickly caught the import of their odd behavior and found himself in an unenviable spot: two very young passengers in danger, with their families anxiously watching from below, not to mention Giuseppe Bellanca himself and practically all of the Brooklyn Chamber of Commerce.

No little trouble was contributed by a well-meaning motorcycle policeman also. Because they carried 350 pounds of bagged sand in the rear of the plane to balance it (since they were flying without a normal load), Chamberlin asked Carisi to pass them to him so he could toss them out and lighten the plane for the landing.

> An energetic motorcycle cop, who seemed very anxious to help, caused me more worry than any other part of my predicament. He saw the sand bags falling and got the idea I was dropping messages to the people on the ground. He steamed over to pick up the notes and would dash from one sand bag to another like a dog chasing sticks. I was afraid one would land on him and break his neck, but somehow I managed to keep him from guessing just where the next one would drop. They told me later he came back with a manufacturer's "O.K." tag, which a factory inspector had fastened on one of the bags, and assured the anxious crowd that everything was all right.

Below them thorough emergency arrangements were under way as an ambulance and "trouble wagon" (equipped with fire-fighting equipment, axes and other tools) hurried across the field. By this time Mrs. Levine and Levine's parents, plus Jonas, realized that something was very wrong; the junior Mrs. Levine, particularly, became overwrought. A second plane took off with the message "Land at Mitchel" scrawled on its side. It was thought it would be wiser to land at Mitchel Field nearby rather than at crowded Curtiss. Chamberlin circled to expend as much fuel as possible—at the same time Carisi and Grace Jonas were rendered miserably air-sick—and then brought the plane in with hardly a bump on the single wheel.

The two girls, slightly disappointed that they had not been treated to the crash Chamberlin had promised them, were lifted out of the cabin. Before they drove off both girls came back to Chamberlin, bemusedly inspecting the damage to the plane, to say, "Thanks for the ride, Mr. Chamberlin."

The incident was thrillingly covered in the press and more and more pressure was put on Levine to assign Chamberlin the post of pilot on the transatlantic flight. Levine was "considerably nettled" by this; he was not overjoyed either when a day or so after the emergency landing Bert Acosta turned in his resignation, giving as his excuse (among others) the fact that he weighed more than Chamberlin (he also weighed *less* than Bertaud, but Acosta was undoubtedly rather tired of the bickering). The field was narrowed down to Chamberlin and Bertaud.

In fact, this really settled nothing, for Levine and Bertaud continued to have their disagreements. Bertaud had made an arrangement with a writer to help him with his story to be sold to the same news service with which Levine had made his agreement and which included all details of both pilots on the flight, whoever they were. Levine's ultimatum was simple: either get out of the private agreement or out of the flight. Bertaud decided to remain with the *Columbia*.

Then on what seemed to be the night before they were to take off, Levine arrived with a contract drawn up by his attorney for both to sign. According to this unique document, Chamberlin and Bertaud were each to receive $150 a week for a year after the flight "during which time Levine was to act as our 'manager' and we were to be under his direction in whatever vaudeville, motion picture and other contracts he could arrange for us as a result of the flight. If our earnings exceeded by a large margin our weekly salaries, he would give us such 'bonuses' as he saw fit. In addition, Levine was to get half of the so-called 'prize money' which was up at the time of the flight—the awards offered by gasoline, oil and accessory companies for using their products; the North American Newspaper Alliance news rights contract; and the prize posted by the Brooklyn Chamber of Commerce [they were not entered in the Orteig prize competition because of the ruling that a sixty-day advance notice was supposed to be filed and there had not been time for that in the Bellanca camp; interestingly, Lindbergh had taken off before the sixty days had expired and was thus, technically, not eligible for the prize. The restriction was waived, of course]. There was no life insurance provision to protect our wives in case we proved to be another Nungesser and Coli."

Whatever they thought of the terms, the two men signed the contract, so eager were they to make the flight. But all was not to be well for Levine, despite his legalistic victory; the weather turned sour and the flight was grounded. It gave Bertaud time to ponder the contract he had signed; as an air-mail pilot he could easily have earned the salary offered by Levine—without the additional risk of flying over an ocean. Then one fine day Levine announced to the press that "every nickel of the prize money goes to the *Columbia*'s pilots." Bertaud then decided to get his own lawyer. Word of the Levine-Bertaud feud began trickling to newsmen, who rather delighted in roasting Levine.

A meeting was called and a better contract was devised (under the vigorous urging of the Brooklyn Chamber of Commerce) which would assure the pilots all of the prize money (close to $100,000 by then) and provision for their wives "in case of disaster." This seemed fine indeed and boded well. But, in the meantime, Byrd had returned with the repaired *America* and Lindbergh had arrived in the *Spirit of St. Louis*. This was grist for the news mill: "What promises to be the most spectacular race ever held—3,600 miles over the open sea to Paris—may start tomorrow morning. Three transatlantic planes are on Curtiss and Roosevelt Fields, within a short distance of each other, ready to take to the air . . ." and so on.

But the newly agreed upon contract for Bertaud and Chamberlin was not forthcoming from Levine. Whereupon Bertaud's lawyer drew up a temporary injunction in the Brooklyn Supreme Court which restrained Charles A. Levine and the Columbia Aircraft Corporation from making any flight to Paris in the Bellanca without Bertaud, with proper contract, aboard. The injunction was returnable on Friday, May 20. Here was a double irony: the *Columbia* might have gotten off the week before, except that Levine did not wish the flight to begin on a Friday the thirteenth; the second irony was even more devastating. It was on the morning of Friday, May 20, that Lindbergh took off for Paris.

As a further irony, Bertaud's injunction was dismissed summarily and the *Columbia* was free to fly, but Lindbergh was by that time over Nova Scotia. Also, as far as Levine was concerned Bertaud (the more photogenic pilot he himself had brought into the picture) was through. That left only Chamberlin—and who?

Not that Levine's afflictions were finished. Bellanca, distressed over the legal wranglings and over the fact that another plane had preceded his to Paris, washed his hands of the whole thing and resigned. Lindbergh had already safely arrived at Le Bourget when the Bellanca was being readied for flight in a mess of confusion. Byrd had offered use of his runway at Roosevelt Field for the takeoff, but his watchman had not been advised of the approach of the *Columbia*, towed, as had been Lindbergh's plane, from Curtiss Field by truck. The uninformed watchman refused to permit the plane on the runway. To add to the bedlam, the Nassau County police, also not informed of the intent of

Levine and company, were disturbed because they were unable to control the crowds that swarmed around the plane. To make things worse, Police Chief William Beckert and John Carisi, who was trying to get the plane under way, had words and even began trading punches to respective noses before being pulled apart.

Levine, meanwhile, upon being informed of Bellanca's withdrawal, went into a blue funk and simply never showed up during the commotion. Chamberlin was determined to go—had always wanted to go; he would have preferred being first, but that Lindbergh had already accomplished this did not lessen Chamberlin's determination. Besides, it was still possible "to beat Lindbergh's record" by flying farther.

Even so, with near chaos unloosed around him, Chamberlin called off the flight. To relieve the strain on the *Columbia*'s landing gear Carisi jettisoned about 150 gallons of fuel onto the field, pushed the plane out of harm's way, checked on the crowd and, to assure no future calamity from a careless smoker, set the pool aflame. A great burst of fire and smoke shot up and distant spectators were certain the *Columbia* had come to grief, among them Chamberlin's wife Willda. There were even rumors that Levine, disgusted with the turn of events, had put a match to the plane.

But Levine, Chamberlin and the *Columbia* persevered—and so, disobligingly, did the poor weather. For nearly two weeks after calling off the flight, Chamberlin had to wait around for a decent turn of weather. The time was spent with Levine in the plane flying over Long Island. An air of mystery enveloped the plans of Levine and, as plans for a transatlantic flight proceeded, there were no further announcements made about it, nor was the name of Chamberlin's copilot mentioned; Levine, for a change, admitted he was tired of making announcements.

Not until June 3 did the weather map over the Atlantic, thanks to the indefatigable Doc Kimball, look promising. Chamberlin had the *Columbia* fueled up, supplies loaded aboard, *two* sets of flying gear placed in the cabin, food (including the cure-all chicken soup) and various equipment, including a rubber boat, although without paddles. Chamberlin's maps had been carefully prepared by Bernt Balchen (one of the other "name" pilots Levine had approached earlier, though without success). Like Lindbergh, Chamberlin went to his hotel to rest, but found it impossible. By five in the morning, June 4, 1927, he arrived at Roosevelt Field.

Charles and Grace Levine appeared around the same time; Levine wore his usual business suit and Mrs. Levine was decorously attired as befitted a former beauty queen of Brooklyn. Chamberlin was dressed for business, too, in a leather jacket, knickers and colorful golf stockings. When reporters demanded to know the name of Chamberlin's partner,

Levine answered that the navigator would "climb in just before she goes."

As the plane warmed up Levine joined Chamberlin in the cockpit to discuss the final arrangements. The pilot throttled the Whirlwind and the plane moved tentatively ahead as he tested the "feel" of the engine, the balance of the aircraft, controls and other such checks. The Bellanca had a tendency to swing from side to side as it moved along the runway. That was bad enough, but the police were having trouble keeping the crowds away. He turned the *Columbia* around and came back to the starting point. An apprehensive Grace Levine sighed in relief. For a moment it had appeared that her headstrong and foolishly fearless husband would turn out to be the mysterious "navigator" of the flight.

The police managed to clear the runway as the ground crew turned the heavy plane around; all helped except Carisi, who stood on a wheel arguing about something with Levine. The argument became quite heated although its burden was lost to the crowd in the roar of the Whirlwind. Chamberlin "shoved the throttle open again. John and his arguments both were blown out of the way as the *Columbia* started down the field once more."

Keeping the bucking plane under control was difficult, and the proximity of clots of people bothered Chamberlin. But he managed to pull the plane up before striking the markers along the runway. These were stakes a mere three feet high, topped by a star. The *Columbia* had lifted so slightly that its propeller could not have cleared the marker it passed over; by a miracle the plane passed over just at the fraction of a moment the propeller was not in a position to strike the marker. Once in the air the plane became the perfect flying machine it was designed to be.

When this occurred it suddenly dawned on Grace Levine that the unnamed co-airman of the *Columbia* was none other than her husband. Frantically she sought the crowd for someone to assure her that it was not true. "He's not going?" she asked, and then fainted into the arms of a Nassau County policeman.

But he was going, and it had been arranged long in advance. When it appeared that the entire project would collapse with pilot trouble, particularly with the defection of Bertaud, Levine broached Chamberlin with yet another offer. Why not take Levine along on the flight, if not as a navigator, then at least as the first transatlantic passenger? For this privilege he would pay Chamberlin $25,000 and would insure him for $50,000. Chamberlin found little wrong with that; at least he would be in command of the flight, without any disagreement over whether or not to carry a radio or over which route. Besides, while neither he nor Levine were very strong on navigation, it would have been difficult to miss the entire continent of Europe if their compasses were reasonably accurate. Levine was not exactly dead weight either; he could take his turn at the stick to relieve Chamberlin. That was why, during the two weeks after Lindbergh's flight, Chamberlin spent so much time aloft with Levine, teaching him some of the niceties of flying the Bellanca and the use of the various instruments. Levine had one other quality: he did not know the meaning of fear.

This was demonstrated soon enough as they flew over what they hoped was Cape Cod (although its configuration did not jibe with their map) and the earth-inductor compass went out. The instrument was their one most important navigational device (it had cost Levine $1,125 and lasted a mere 200 miles), which left them with the conventional, not too precise magnetic compass. Chamberlin gave serious thought to turning around and heading back. His job, he felt, was "to fly Mr. Levine to Europe and not just *try to fly him there.*" On the other hand, returning to Long Island could end forever his chances of a transatlantic flight. Then, too, there was Grace Levine to consider; certainly she "would never let her 'hookey-playing hubby' start another transatlantic flight, and I recalled vividly her threat to burn up the plane." Once Levine had jokingly mentioned to his wife that he might make the flight and she informed him she would burn the *Columbia* if she thought he really meant it.

Somehow returning to New York represented a fate worse than death to both men; but Chamberlin, though willing to chance the Atlantic with one not very dependable compass, thought it best to explain to Levine the gravity of their predicament. "If we flew out to sea and found no land, I didn't want to be blamed for getting him wet."

"Go ahead," Levine told Chamberlin. "I'd rather be in Davy Jones' locker than go back and face those newspapermen. They didn't think I wanted to fly to Europe anyway." The only unreasonable manifestation Levine exhibited was to curse the earth-inductor compass, its makers, and any and all connected with it every time his eyes rested on the bouncing, useless needle. He was also a bit put out when he learned that Chamberlin carried a rubber boat but no oars for it. The pilot rationalized this by explaining that they added weight and besides, should the boat be required, "it would be too far to row back" anyhow.

Checking their position by the sun, they flew on and when they reached Nova Scotia " 'on the nose' . . . our morale shot up like a free balloon." Before long they were flying out over the Atlantic in a route roughly parallel to Lindbergh's. The major difference was that there were two of them and could spell one another at the controls. They had slipped into flying coveralls and helmets (which had been hidden in the plane before takeoff). Behind the cockpit was the "shelf," actually the top of the main fuel tank, which served as a cot during the relief periods. Behind that, near the center of the plane, was a seat and a table on which Chamberlin worked out their position—such as it was—on their chart. This aspect of the flight was quite informal. Luckily, the Bellanca was a remarkably stable plane in the air and required little effort to control; there were stretches as long as a hundred to two hundred miles when neither man so much as touched the rudder or the control stick, according to Chamberlin.

Fog was, as always, a problem, and it took an experienced pilot to keep an eye on all the instruments simultaneously, thus in turn keeping the *Columbia* in level flight at a safe altitude. Chamberlin of course handled this part of the flying; but Levine contributed his full share. It would be wrong to label him simply the first transatlantic "passenger," although in fact that is what he was.

With the coming of day the weather cleared and they had a magnificent view of the ocean and began sighting ships. The third was the great liner *Mauretania* which they buzzed and circled to enable the passengers and crew to identify them and send word back to New York that they had been seen safely flying over the Atlantic. Chamberlin then did some novel navigating; he turned to the shipping page of the previous day's *New York Times*, checked the *Mauretania*'s sailing information (it had left Cherbourg the day before), and estimated that they were now about 350 miles from France. All this time they were flying alongside the ship, pacing it and in fact flying back in the direction of the United States. Then Chamberlin "turned presently and pointed the Bellanca straight over the center of the big liner and on back through the middle of her wake. This path, I knew, led straight past the Scilly Islands and Land's End into the English Channel and so on to Germany."

They had agreed on Berlin as their destination—a city beyond Paris, which would win them a distance record. Besides, when Lindbergh made his flight he visited only France, England and Belgium—all wartime allies of the United States. Chamberlin and Levine selected Berlin because Lindbergh's orders to return (from President Coolidge) canceled any visits to Germany that he had originally intended. This had led to a little bitterness on the part of the Germans; Levine and Chamberlin hoped, with their flight, to compensate for the diplomatic oversight.

A half hour after setting course on the *Mauretania* they spotted another ship some ten miles distant. "We couldn't read her name, of course, but we knew she was the *Memphis*, carrying Lindbergh back to a triumphant home-coming in America. Levine wanted me to fly over and 'jazz her up,' but it meant wasting fuel for twenty-five miles and I shook my head. I had been fooling around over the Atlantic long enough and was all for getting along with the flight."

By sunset, the end of their second day in the air, they had passed over Land's End, crossed the Channel and flew into thick weather over the Continent. It was here that their luck, wildly good so far, took a bad turn. Steering a compass course for Berlin and climbing as high as possible and "leaning" the fuel to assure them enough to get to their destination, the two men prepared themselves for the final lap of the flight. But Chamberlin, to his discomfort, found that even at 21,000 feet the clouds towered above them. Rather than risk flying blind through the clouds, he chose to fly "back and forth, killing time, until day should break." Near exhaustion after flying at a high altitude which not only caused the controls to react flabbily but also induced a mild anoxia, Chamberlin decided to take a nap around dawn. Turning over the controls to Levine he said, "See what you can do with her for a while; I've got to get some rest." Chamberlin slipped back onto the shelf for a breather. Levine had only to continue killing time till full daylight when Chamberlin hoped they could see well enough to set out for Berlin.

Chamberlin had barely settled on the shelf when he sensed danger and awakened to find the plane gyrating through the mist. Levine had flown into a cloud, lost his sense of orientation and stalled the Bellanca which, although it could not spin (thanks to its designer's ingenuity), was in a steep spiral heading earthward. Chamberlin scrambled back into the cockpit.

"Even in the time it took me to slide down off the tank into my seat, the Bellanca's wings had started shuddering and shimmying as if they would be ripped away from the fuselage of the sturdy little ship at any instant. Her balanced rudder, oscillating in the terrific dive, was whipping the rudder bar back and forth with leg-breaking force and shaking the rear end of the plane with such violence that I expected the whole tail to be torn off.

"Never in my life have I felt that death was so close or been so badly scared. Levine, on the contrary (with that odd failure to realize that flying has its hazards, which is so characteristic of him), was enjoying the experience hugely." Realizing that the plane had gotten completely out of control, Levine simply turned off the engine and released the controls, hoping no doubt that nature would take its course and right the plane. To Chamberlin's astonishment Levine sat there, hands and feet off the controls, laughing—he thought it funny that the plane should be acting "like a bucking bronco." Chamberlin could not bring himself to join in the merriment. With eyes on the altimeter (it was reading less than 100 feet), the turn-and-bank indicator (which told him they were spiraling to the left) and the other instruments, he gingerly moved to tame the bucking bronco. He had no idea of what their altitude was, nor where they were, because of the fog—nor, in fact, did the instruments tell him everything. He brought the rudder under control first, gradually damping out the oscillating rudder bar, then pulled the plane out of its turn. This had to be done during that brief fraction of a moment when the rudder bar's slice through its arc reached the end and was about to sweep back again. Bit by bit Chamberlin managed to slow it up and bring it under control.

Then it was a matter of pulling the nose up and centering various instruments to assure himself they were in normal level flight. The speed dropped accordingly and he found they were actually at 4,000 feet—they had dropped three miles into the soup. If they were over Germany, and Chamberlin guessed they were, they would have to give thought to the presence of the Hartz Mountains, with peaks rising as high as 4,000 feet. They would still have to descend to learn where on earth they were.

The clouds diminished as the *Columbia* nosed through; at a height between 500 and 1,000 feet they broke through the ceiling into a drizzly daylight. It was June 6, 1927—the third day since leaving New York. In the near distance they spotted a glow against the ceiling's low-hanging clouds and flew on till they found themselves over a manufacturing town with its blast furnaces operating. They had come down, obviously, over Germany's industrial Ruhr. Chamberlin thought it was Essen where Krupp had a factory and Levine thought it was Bremerhaven, "because he had been in Bremerhaven once." It was Dortmund—as they learned upon flying to a position from which a flare had been shot into the air. There they found an airport and a cheering throng which, once Chamberlin cut the engine and swooped down, helped them by pointing the way to Berlin. They had come down after a blind night of flying nearly on course and 350 miles from their objective.

Though their fuel supply was becoming critically meager, Chamberlin turned the plane for Berlin. After an hour and a half of flying the indicator pointed to zero and he realized they would have to land for more fuel. There were still the Hartz Mountains to contend with—luck had brought them down into a valley near Dortmund, but eventually they would have to fly over the range; no point in running out of gas over the mountains. He hoped to land with fuel still in the tank in order to come in on the engine; but Levine wished to go on until they ran out and come in "dead stick," trusting a bit more to luck on the landing.

"You're the doctor," Chamberlin answered. "It's your airplane, but it's brought us a long way and I'd hate to bend it up trying to make four or five extra miles."

But they went on until the sputtering of the Whirlwind told them they had come as far as they could. Chamberlin ordered Levine aft to balance the plane should they come into a soft field. He selected a likely field and came in with a still propeller. It was a wheat field, rather bumpy—but not so bumpy as the road they bounced over—with a fence on one boundary. Chamberlin ground-looped the *Columbia* to avoid tangling with the fence and there they were: in the middle of a German wheat field forty-three hours after having taken off from Roosevelt Field.

Obviously they had not quite made Berlin; even so, they had broken Lindbergh's distance mark by around 300 miles. They had, in fact, come down at Mansfeldt (near Eisleben) about 108 miles short of their goal. It was a little disappointing, but nothing compared to the disappointment of the farmer whose wheat crop the *Columbia* had harvested prematurely. "They were not highly pleased," Chamberlin admitted. Nor was their initial reception very warm (as they learned later) because they were thought to be members of a band of kidnappers that had been terrorizing the area. With a two-day beard growth Chamberlin could understand that they "probably looked the part and I suppose she [their first German receptionist] thought the airplane was just a new and up-to-date method of carrying off our victims."

There was also a formidable language problem, despite Levine's claim that he could speak "well enough to get by," but eventually they made it understood that it was fuel they needed to continue to Berlin. This arrived at last and, unable to use a funnel, they poured the twenty gallons into the cabin tank a quart at a time by teapot (this historic implement, Chamberlin learned later, was preserved in a museum in Holland).

In keeping with the general antic quality of their flight, as fate would have it, the acquisition of more fuel did not get them to their strangely elusive goal. Neither Chamberlin nor Levine could say with any accuracy just what compass setting would bring them to Berlin, so that as each took his turn at the controls, each flew in the direction he believed would take them to Berlin. "We didn't see how we could miss a city the size of Berlin, so we flew on and on, expecting momentarily to sight the capital in the distance. As it happened his [Levine's] guess was much nearer right than mine. . . ."

But they did manage to miss Berlin, despite its magnitude. Flying on and on they passed over an airfield which was marked "Cottbus" in large letters for them to see. But it meant nothing to them and they continued onward (they were then *beyond* Berlin and to the south, heading for Poland). More flying did not help, so with the fuel again in short supply Chamberlin decided it would be better to settle for Cottbus than a swampy piece of ground over which they were flying. But before they reached the airport their luck, and gas, ran out again.

The engine died, Levine clambered back behind the main tank and

Chamberlin brought the *Columbia* down onto the most convenient clear ground—a pasture this time. Their flight had begun to raise hell with German agriculture, for when the plane set down, again with the stick dead—starkly vertical on the second landing—the wheels sank into the mud and plowed a deep double furrow for several hundred feet. Levine's weight was not enough to hold the tail down and as the plane skidded to a muddy halt, it tipped onto the nose and snapped the end off one of the propeller blades.

All objects not fastened down behind him in the cabin came flying in on Chamberlin; a ration box ripped open and he was soon engulfed in a cloud of white powdered milk, followed by powdered chocolate. His appearance was anything but prepossessing. He was also angry with himself, after days of exceptional flying, to place them in such a tyro's predicament. But neither man was hurt, and they soon found that they had descended near the village of Klinge, not far from Cottbus (but still sixty miles from Berlin).

By this time word had begun to spread that the American *Ozean-flieger* had been wandering over the German landscape and many hands came round to help them. They were taken to a hotel in Cottbus to rest and clean up and for Chamberlin to divest himself of the ingredients of a chocolate shake. A new wooden propeller was sent for—for they were anxious to make it all the way to Berlin. They were offered transportation to Berlin by officials of Lufthansa, the great German national airline, but rejected that.

There was some somber discussion over the wisdom of attempting to take off from the pasture at Klinge (which was rather sticky) with an untested propeller flown in from Berlin. Chamberlin suggested that the plane be towed to a nearby football field out of which he believed he could get off; this shocked the German aviation officials, who hoped to take the *Columbia* apart and transport it to the airfield at Cottbus. Chamberlin did not wish to do that and for a time it appeared that the Germans might invoke certain aviation regulations to prevent what they believed to be a foolhardy attempt. But Chamberlin prevailed and convinced them that he knew what the Bellanca could do.

All was agreed upon, finally, and the plane was hauled over to the football field to await the arrival of the propeller. Chamberlin and Levine fought through the crowds, plus newsmen (including a number of Americans), to their hotel for a bath and a night's sleep—their first in three nights. In fact, as Chamberlin bathed he did so in the presence of a member of the American Embassy who remained on hand lest Chamberlin fall asleep in the tub and drown. After which Chamberlin sank blissfully into the motherlike comfort of a German featherbed.

The next day, Tuesday, June 7, 1927, Chamberlin took off from the football field alone, leaving Levine behind. The propeller had been installed and he found that it did not achieve the number of rpm's that the original one had. So, rather than risk taking off with a load, he flew solo to Cottbus airport, where Levine joined him. They took time out for some local celebrations, wired their wives of their safe arrival and then left for Berlin, where they arrived—early, as it eventuated—in the early evening and spent a little time cruising over the city before coming down at Tempelhof Airdrome.

The reception was as massive and frenetic (but controlled by the police with what Chamberlin called "true German efficiency") as Lindbergh's had been in Paris and London. No one questioned the flight, which had been made in bits and pieces, nor alluded to some of the rather comic overtones. Chamberlin and Levine were air heroes and were treated accordingly. And they had succeeded, even by the time of their initial unscheduled landing at Mansfeldt, in staying aloft longer (42 hours, 45 minutes) and flying farther nonstop (3,911 miles) than anyone else.

Nor was their diplomatic gesture lost upon the Germans, who showed their appreciation with enthusiastic receptions, dinners and luncheons (fortunate especially for Chamberlin, who had arrived with $11.14), meetings with high German officials (President von Hindenburg among them), celebrities, aviation enthusiasts and the usual mobs of autograph collectors. They were showered with gifts and given the keys to the cities which they visited, although the American Embassy officials watched over them like two potential naughty boys and steered them away from the livelier aspects of German *kultur*.

To assure this further, both Mrs. Chamberlin and Mrs. Levine arrived to accompany them on their triumphal visits to various cities in Germany. It was all very exciting and on occasion led to curious sequels. For example, one day they received a letter from America's most famous First World War draft dodger ("slacker" was the contemporary term), Grover Cleveland Bergdoll, who offered to buy the *Columbia*. He hoped to make a return flight to the United States, assuming that so heroic an effort would consequently cancel out all hard feelings over his defection during the war. On another occasion they received a complaint from the sausage venders of Vienna, to which they had to cancel a flying visit because of engine trouble. The venders actually put in a claim for $1,500 to have, in Chamberlin's phrase, "the Government pay for the weenies that went to waste." This crisis appears to have been settled before they finally did arrive in the Austrian city for another tumultuous reception; and so it went through much of Eastern Europe: Hungary, Czechoslovakia, Poland and Switzerland.

In all the hubbub, it came almost as an anticlimax when Byrd, in company with pilots Bernt Balchen, Bert Acosta and navigator George Noville, got off in the *America* from Roosevelt Field on June 29, 1927. Although Byrd had been biding his time while others made the more dashing flights, his got under way prematurely when the rope which held the *America* at the top of its fifteen-foot inclined plane runway snapped. The idea was to run up the engines, cut the rope and take off. As usual with transatlantic planes, the *America* was heavily loaded, but under the skilled hand of Balchen took off without mishap.

Balchen was, in fact, the second pilot. Acosta, who had quit Levine's project, had come in to replace Bennett, who had not fully recovered from the crackup of the *America* on its test flight.

Byrd, on his part, was not interested in racing across the Atlantic, nor in any prize money—nor, for that matter, fame and fortune. He hoped to prove that a multi-engined plane, carrying passengers, could fly the Atlantic as a harbinger of a future air age. This was not readily understood by Fokker, who was eager for someone to make a name for his trimotor, or by the general public caught up in the "Great 1927 New York-to-Paris Air Derby." Byrd's mail overflowed with unwholesome crank letters during the period of waiting: "Coward, I'm sick of seeing your name. You are a disgrace to America. You never had any idea of flying across the Atlantic." When Lindbergh took off Byrd received a telegram from North Carolina which read: "I just want you to know that you may not realize that you are the world's prize boob to get left at the switch as you did."

The flight, once begun with the snapping of a strand of rope, was no easy one. As had his predecessors, Byrd suffered through Atlantic storms —during which it was learned that although Acosta was a noted aerobatic pilot and instructor, he had little knowledge of flying blind. Balchen, who had become an American citizen in compliance with sponsor Wanamaker's rule that only American citizens would make the flight, proved his mettle and pulled them out of a fog-induced spin.

But their flight, seemingly ill-fated from the beginning, ended in keeping with the general pattern. Having battled through the nearly two days of uncertainty (with the compasses none too reliable), they arrived over the coast of France some 250 miles off course. And as Byrd noted, the "worst that we had anticipated—fog at our destination—had happened."

Even so, Byrd hoped that they might proceed on to Paris. But as they approached closer to the capital the weather worsened. Byrd had Acosta

OPPOSITE, TOP   The *Columbia*, with Chamberlin in cockpit, taxiing in (this photo was taken after the flight to Europe had been made). (*U.S. Air Force*)

CENTER   Chamberlin, with engine of *Columbia* directly behind, surrounded by officialdom and the curious, after one of his many landings en route to Berlin. (*U.S. Air Force*)

BOTTOM   Levine (center) and Chamberlin being greeted by the president of Thun, Switzerland, during their good-will flight around Europe. (*U.S. Air Force*)

follow the coastline until they found the Seine River at Le Havre, thence to trace the ribbon to Paris. When rain over Cherbourg (at least, they surmised it was over Cherbourg) interferred with visibility, Acosta turned over the controls to Balchen. The fact was that all compasses they carried were off and they were lost.

When they saw a revolving light Byrd was certain that it was Le Bourget, for their compass reading and flying time should have placed them in the vicinity of Paris. When they dropped lower (they were ever conscious of the thousand-foot tip of the Eiffel Tower) it was surprising to discover that the revolving light was a lighthouse on the water and not an airport with a welcome runway. This stage of the flight is obscured in enigma. Anxious crowds at Le Bourget, it was reported, heard the sound of engines in the vicinity of the field; so did residents of a distant town—at the same moment. Byrd thought they were over Le Bourget, but Balchen, who was flying the *America*, later said he had made a turn and deliberately headed away from Paris, hoping to find better visibility on the coast.

Wherever they were, they were lost and running low on fuel. It would be suicide to attempt a landing in the dark; even the beach was undoubtedly filled with obstacles. Byrd elected to ditch the plane offshore. He approached the unknown adventure with typical scientific curiosity; he and Bennett had often pondered "what would happen to a great three-engine plane landing in the water." It had simply never

Byrd's flight crew: Bernt Balchen (left) and Bert Acosta; both fine pilots. The flight of the *America* itself, however, proved that Balchen was an outstanding pilot. (*National Air & Space Museum, Smithsonian Institution*)

The *America* poised on its takeoff ramp. It was held fast by a cable attached to the tail-skid to let the engines build up enough power for the takeoff. But the cable snapped, and the *America* set off for Europe prematurely. (*National Air & Space Museum, Smithsonian Institution*)

Lumbering, the *America*, loaded with fuel, pulls itself into the air. (*National Air & Space Museum, Smithsonian Institution*)

The *America* down in the water off the coast of France; unable to find Le Bourget because of the bad weather, Balchen, who was piloting, decided to set the big plane down in the water. His skill saved the lives of all aboard, although there were injuries. (*National Air & Space Museum, Smithsonian Institution*)

The morning after: the wreckage of the *America* has been pulled up onto the beach at Ver-sur-Mer. The end of Byrd's dream of a nonstop transatlantic flight. (*Musée de l'Air, Paris*)

been done before—not intentionally. The fear was that as soon as the landing gear whipped into the waves the plane would flip over onto its back and sink with all hands.

They would very quickly find out. With Balchen at the stick and Acosta beside him, and with Byrd and Noville braced behind, the plane settled down toward the black water. Flares were dropped to ascertain whether or not there were rocks within reach of the shore. Balchen throttled down as much as possible, skimmed the surface of the water; there was a tearing sound, a slight lurch—and the landing gear sheared away neatly. The plane remained on an even keel and then slammed into the water.

Byrd almost instantly found himself "in the water swimming around in pitchy dark and rain." All was silent—the engines they had heard for the past forty-two hours were stilled at last—except for Noville's voice calling out Byrd's name. Byrd shouted back that he was all right, but Noville continued shouting. Byrd swam back to the plane to check the cockpit to look for Balchen and Acosta. Shouting brought no responses, and then there was Balchen, popping out from under water after extricating himself from the wreckage of the cockpit. He did not respond to Byrd's questions. "He talked a blue streak but didn't talk to me."

Acosta remained unaccounted for, so both Byrd and Balchen began diving to see if he was trapped in the cockpit under water. They shouted, but there was no answer. Then suddenly Acosta appeared "apparently from nowhere, swimming toward the wing, the leading edge of which was now down to the water." Like Balchen and Noville, Acosta did not respond to Byrd's inquiries but only seemed to babble on. He was, it was later learned, the worst injured of the crew; in being thrown from the plane he had broken a collarbone. Byrd had taken a blow in the chest near the heart which caused it to beat irregularly "for many months afterward." The other men were dazed by the impact but otherwise uninjured. Noville ripped out the rubber dinghy and the men, seated on the water-logged wing, inflated it. Soon Byrd learned why Balchen, Acosta and Noville had not answered him; they had not protected their ears against the engine sounds and were temporarily deafened.

After the boat was ready they paddled to shore and learned that they had "landed" near Ver-sur-Mer—not their ultimate goal, but France nonetheless. When the tide went out, leaving the *America* out of the water and only a few yards from the beach, Byrd and Balchen returned to their landing site to retrieve the mail and their record of the flight. The villagers helped to haul the plane ashore, after which the souvenir hunters got to work on it. What remained was eventually shipped back to the United States.

As before, successful (if with qualifications) Atlantic fliers were treated to ovational, wild celebrations, as Byrd and his crew were welcomed in Paris and other major French cities. It was in France that Chamberlin joined Byrd to share in some of the plaudits. He and Levine had been enjoying their extended tour of Europe very much. Their flight had undoubtedly quickened the preparations in Germany for transatlantic flights. No less than two German planes, Junkers W-33s, took off from Dessau on the evening of August 14, 1927, on what was hoped would be an east-to-west duo attempt. The first turnback occurred shortly after takeoff when the *Europa* returned because of poor visibility; its crew consisted of Johann Risticz and Cornelius Edzard, with newspaperman H. R. Knickerbocker along for the ride and to record the event for sponsor William Randolph Hearst. The second Junkers pushed on; this was the *Bremen*, which carried pilots Friedrich Loose and Hermann Koehl, with Baron Guenther von Huenefeld as a passenger. The Baron was publicity manager of the North German-Lloyd Steamship Lines, sponsor of the *Bremen*. But like its sister ship, the *Bremen*, though it succeeded in passing over Ireland, accumulating some 1,800 miles of distance, turned back also. The double failure was a galling blow to German air enthusiasts hoping to place German aviation back on its feet after the setback of the First World War and the restrictions of the Versailles Treaty. One lesson had been learned from the *Bremen* and *Europa* abortive flights: the potency of head winds on the east-to-west crossing and the critical impact of weather, fog especially, on any such flights.

With Lindbergh, Chamberlin and Levine, Byrd and his crew, and the two unhappy German attempts, Europe bubbled during the spring and summer of 1927 with aviation excitement. Lindbergh had returned home in style aboard the cruiser *Memphis*, under orders from President Coolidge; by mid-July both Byrd and Chamberlin returned to the United States on the *Leviathan* in time for the classic reception in New York on July 18 (for Byrd it was the unique experience of having been treated to the same triumphant mass greeting twice, the first having been in honor of his and Bennett's polar flight in June of 1926).

Conspicuously absent from this 1927 ticker-tape parade was Charles Levine. Having tasted the fruits of the life of an aerial conqueror of the Atlantic, he lusted for more. If Europe had taken him—Chamberlin, too—to its bosom after their flight, what would his reception be upon making a return flight to America? To Charles Levine, the idea had a lovely ring to it.

Not, however, to Chamberlin. "The fact of the matter was," he said, "that I knew only too well what a hazardous thing a trans-Atlantic flight in a single-motored plane is, and did not care to ride my luck too hard by attempting to fly back."

With Chamberlin out, Levine turned to the French pilot Maurice

Drouhin, who agreed to pilot the *Columbia* provided the proper contract arrangements could be worked out. Drouhin was already more or less committed to an Atlantic flight for Farman in their *L'Oiseau bleu* with Pierre Corbu. It was, of course, tempting to join Levine, for he was a celebrated "airman," had the money with which to finance the flight and, perhaps even more significantly, a plane which had proved itself capable of crossing the ocean (Drouhin was proved correct in this thinking; when the *L'Oiseau bleu*, with Leon Givon as his replacement, set out for New York in September of this same busy 1927, it returned to Le Bourget after only three and a half hours of trying).

Drouhin very soon learned that he had much to learn about Charles Levine. There was a major problem from the start: neither man spoke the other's language. Before he left for the United States, Chamberlin gave Drouhin a little instruction in the handling of the Bellanca by making a flight over the English Channel. Drouhin then flew the plane back. Soon the little frictions that Levine seemed master of began to appear. Through an interpreter Levine made it known to Drouhin that he would like to hop back to London for the King's Cup Races; Drouhin bristled and informed Levine—through an interpreter—that he had not been hired as a ferry pilot but as a transatlantic flier.

Undaunted, Levine boarded a British airliner and rather pointedly became acquainted with its pilot, the colorful, one-eyed Walter Hinchliffe. Word very quickly wafted back to France hinting that perhaps Levine would make the flight with Hinchliffe instead of Drouhin. Misunderstanding, disagreement and just plain ill will led to many a bad moment. Levine was even reported from time to time as settling some of the disaffections with a punch in the nose. Finally, early in August, Levine and Drouhin signed an agreement that Drouhin found good, but a few days later—it was a thirteenth of the month—when Drouhin felt ready to start out, Levine demurred because of the unlucky number. This hardly impressed Drouhin with Levine's airmanship.

Levine then had inklings (none of them founded on fact) that perhaps the frustrated Drouhin would take off without him. So he had certain rather essential parts of the engine removed. Drouhin observed, with unusual Gallic understatement, "Apparently Mr. Levine has no confidence in me."

It was at about this point in the drama (or comedy, depending on one's point of view) that sex reared its lovely head. It came packaged in the blonde, monied person of Mabel "Mibs" Boll, an American heiress then living, as did so many Americans at the time, in Paris. She, too, had a dream: to be the first woman ever to cross the Atlantic by air while wearing a sweater woven of gold. (Scoff not, gentle reader; remember this was during the height of the madcap foolishness of the Jazz Age).

Levine rejected the offer. It was doubled and he rejected that too; money was not one of his concerns. So much, so far, for Mibs Boll. But Mibs and her Golden Fleece served him well as a threat to a disgruntled Drouhin. Like his predecessor Bertaud, Drouhin eventually resorted to the law and slapped an injunction on the *Columbia*, which according to the strictures could not be flown by anyone but Drouhin as per the contract with Levine. The flight was then at an impasse; no one could go anywhere in the *Columbia* which sat at Le Bourget under guard of the *gendarmerie*.

Time dragged on and there was no action forthcoming because of the personal and legal stalemate. Then one day, August 29 (Chamberlin had already returned home), Levine announced to his wife that he would hop over to Le Bourget to have a look at the *Columbia*. There he talked the policeman on guard and a mechanic into assisting him in pushing the idle plane out of the hangar so that Levine could warm up the engine for some harmless taxiing here and there to keep things in working order.

As the two helpers watched, Levine maneuvered the plane with no great expertise around the field; then, upon reaching the distant end of the runway, he turned into the wind, gunned the engine and, to their horror, got the *Columbia* into the air. A couple of Drouhin's friends ran to another plane and took off in intrepid pursuit. They had two strikes on them from the beginning: one was that their plane could not match the Bellanca for speed; the other was Levine's own peculiar brand of intrepidity. As they flew near him, he simply pointed the Whirlwind at them and seemed determined to collide. This was rather discouraging and the two men realized it was best to leave Levine alone.

From his general direction of flight it appeared that he was heading for England and soon the wires crackled. If Levine managed to find England, he might very well also find London, in which case he stood a fair chance also of finding Croydon Aerodrome. That busy center of aerial activity almost instantly became even busier; flights were canceled, passengers were kept away from runways and planes were pushed into shelter and the control tower filled with men searching the sky. Ominously, an ambulance and fire truck stood in readiness.

Blithely, Levine flew across the Channel: he found England; he then set a compass course in a direction he assumed would bring him to London—and it did! He definitely identified landmarks and knew he was in the general vicinity of Croydon and, in time, found that.

So far, so good.

Taking off and flying a plane were reasonably simple matters—landing a ton or so of fabric, wood and metal at a speed of about fifty miles an hour: that took experience and skill, neither of which Charles

Mabel "Mibs" Boll, known as the "Diamond Queen of the Twenties," an American rich girl living in Paris who wished to accompany Levine in an Atlantic crossing. Her only demand: to be permitted to wear a golden sweater on the flight. (*Culver Pictures*)

The *Columbia* in its hangar; this controversial plane, which had tantalized Lindbergh and inspired numerous law suits, was the first aircraft to fly the Atlantic twice. Following Levine's ownership it passed through many hands; finally it was completely destroyed by a hangar fire in 1935. (*National Air & Space Museum, Smithsonian Institution*)

Enter, once again, Levine and company. Chamberlin is being diffidently greeted by an unknown admirer; Levine is dashingly attired in a flying suit. To his left is French airman Maurice Drouhin, who is about to suffer some experiences with the adroit Levine. Photo was taken at Le Bourget, the setting for some further adventures of Charles Levine. (*Musée de l'Air, Paris*)

Levine, however intrepid, had. He brought the *Columbia* in over the nearest runway and was still too high and going too fast for a landing over the halfway mark. There was practically no runway left when Levine, still five feet up, changed his mind. Pulling away he violated every rule in the book, as he made a climbing turn for another approach. According to practically every law of aerodynamics as the wing went down and flying speed lessened the *Columbia* should have wavered, stalled and crashed to the ground. Instead, with engine straining and with the plane itself wobbling through the air, Levine did manage to make his turn, build up speed and return for another match with the runway. He lost again and pulled up for yet another try.

By this time a pilot jumped into a small plane and decided to show Levine the way. He got off the ground, climbed up alongside the *Columbia* and beckoned to Levine to follow him on the proper landing approach to Croydon. Levine followed nicely, judging both his speed and the plane's altitude from that of his benefactor's. The latter's plane landed first and almost immediately was practically ground-looped out of harm's way; the pilot, no admirer of Levine's way with a plane, immediately abandoned ship and sought shelter.

The *Columbia* came in, still a bit too fast and not quite right on the approach—but the best so far. The wheels touched with a crunching shock and the plane bounced high into the air; down again and another bounce resulted and, finally, came down with a lesser impact and stayed there. As rightly reported in the London *Times*, "The arrival and subsequent landing by Mr. Levine on Croydon Aerodrome was the most alarming experience which has happened in the memory of the civil aviation traffic officers, regular pilots and the aerodrome staff."

However, it was reported that one pilot who observed the show was heard to mutter with as much admiration as exasperation, "It takes a jolly good pilot to do that."

Perhaps, but when Levine was greeted by airport officials he was not met by an admiring crowd. He greeted them with a disarming, "Oh, hello." And then, "I think I need a shave, I didn't know I was coming." That was, indeed, a likely tale and the Croydon committee coolly informed Levine of the various international and British air codes he had violated—besides flying a plane without a license. Levine bore these impeachments with wide-eyed innocence and, once the most formidable moments with the Air Ministry were over, Levine was treated as a hero by the English. They admired the underdog who could beat the Establishment, and he had put something over on the French.

If Charles Levine had not been the first man to fly the English Channel, he was undoubtedly one of the first to steal his own plane. The British admired that kind of anomaly; he was a kind of anti-hero, even less photogenic than Chamberlin, with an unusual aptitude for stirring up trouble. One of the first things he did upon arriving in England was to announce that he would drop Drouhin and sign on Walter Hinchliffe as the new pilot. Drouhin reacted to this announcement with Gallic

OPPOSITE Maurice Drouhin, for a brief time an anxious employee of Charles Levine. Following his withdrawal from the partnership, Drouhin planned his own transatlantic flight. (*Musée de l'Air, Paris*)

BELOW The Couzinet *Arc-en-Ciel* in which Drouhin hoped to fly the Atlantic. The aircraft crashed on a test flight killing Drouhin and another passenger. (*Musée de l'Air, Paris*)

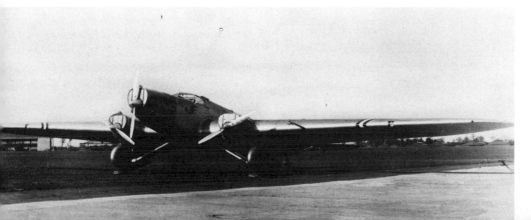

gallantry: he approached golden-haired Mibs Boll with the suggestion that they team up for a round-trip flight to New York and back. Mibs thereupon reacted with unladylike determination. She left for London, where she again talked to Levine, who then made it public that, indeed, Mibs Boll would become the third member of the *Columbia* crew. Captain Hinchliffe, however, had other views and made them known. "There will be no passengers, particularly any woman."

Mibs was, literally, not worth her weight in fuel, whatever she was worth in gold. When this was explained in more or less simple terms, she gracefully bowed out of the flight with the provision, as Levine promised, that once he and Hinchliffe crossed to New York, she would get the *Columbia* and a pilot to make the trip back to Paris.

By this time Drouhin had made new arrangements for an Atlantic attempt with a youthful engineer, René Couzinet, who had designed a trimotored monoplane which was named *Arc-en-Ciel* (*Rainbow*). But fate, clearly, had decided that Drouhin was never to fly the Atlantic, for the *Rainbow* crashed during a test flight (in the following year, August of 1928), injuring two men and killing two, one of them the hapless Drouhin. Around the same time that Drouhin began making alternate plans, the life of being the spouse of a leading nonheroic celebrity palled on Grace Levine, who returned home and, according to reports, suffered a nervous breakdown.

Levine, however, thrived on his notoriety and planned the Atlantic crossing with Hinchliffe until, finally, in late September, still earthbound, he decided to cancel the flight for the simple reason that the weather turned bad. "I am no madcap," he stated, and then he and Hinchliffe embarked on alternate efforts until, they hoped, the next season for Atlantic flights. They wanted to make a nonstop flight to Delhi, India, but that ended in Vienna; later they attended the Schneider Cup races (although not as competitors) in Venice and eventually ended up in Rome, where Levine was introduced to Pope Pius XI—and Benito Mussolini. The latter regarded the cross-Channel flight as Levine's finest hour and told him so.

But time was running out for the doughty Levine. His passage across Europe had left a diplomatic shambles. One attorney, Dudley Field Malone, upon arriving back in the United States after a European trip, mentioned Levine and his exploits and suggested with a straight face that it might not be a bad idea for the United States to send a battleship over to Europe to gather up Levine "in the interest of world peace." While this was not done, Levine was officially summoned back by the government in connection with a claim it had placed against him related to Levine's dealing with scrap surplus materials (this was eventually settled out of court for a healthy $150,000).

So Charles Levine, Atlantic flier, *diplomate extraordinaire*, amateur boxer, nonhero, returned to the United States as did most mortal men by ship after three months of helter-skelter. The *Columbia*, too, returned by ship.

Levine was welcomed back in style upon his arrival in New York; his wife perhaps summed it up best with, "He is a hero in my eyes no matter what anyone else can say." But once he stopped being an aerial primitive (eventually taking serious flying lessons and earning an official pilot's license), Levine's exploits lost some of their astringent color. Not that he abandoned hopes of making another record flight—nor had Mibs Boll.

Her fortunes waned also. History would never preserve her name as that of the first woman to fly the Atlantic; her pilot-to-be Hinchliffe, in fact, abandoned her for another lady flier and went to a watery death in the cold waters of the Atlantic. Another pilot-to-be abandoned her for some social worker from Boston named Earhart. Mabel Boll, finally lent the use of the *Columbia* by Levine, had to settle for the first nonstop flight from New York to Havana, hardly an exciting distinction compared to a transatlantic success.

Levine, friends again with Bert Acosta, wished to make the first nonstop (the Douglas Army planes had made it in stages in 1924) east-to-west crossing in 1928. Mabel Boll, thwarted in her priority race, was willing to settle also for the position of first woman to cross the Atlantic in the more difficult east-to-west flight. She, Levine and Acosta shipped over (the *Columbia* having been eliminated when Levine brought it in for a bad landing into a fence) for France to acquire the craft for the flight. While they shopped, which tour took on some of the old spirit when Levine poked a newspaperman in the face for printing unpleasantries about them, the first east-west flight was successfully accomplished by a German crew in the *Bremen*, which had not been successful the previous year.

Undaunted, Levine then hoped to make the flight, but over a greater distance, flying from Germany to New York (the *Bremen* had flown from Ireland to Labrador). But his old vexations continued to plague Levine. Although he bought a Junkers of the same type as the *Bremen* (of which more later) he could obtain no official permission to take off from a German airfield. They switched to Levine's scene of former triumphs, Croydon, but Acosta insisted that the overloaded Junkers (undoubtedly including Mibs's golden sweater) would never lift off the airdrome. A larger field would not be forthcoming unless Levine were willing to insure his crew rather heavily for a quarter of a million dollars. The trio then decided to start out from Le Bourget, but Levine's financial problems intervened again and he was forced to return to New York for another legal bout and the flight fizzled out in September, 1928.

With the ebb of his fortune Levine could no longer indulge in the luxury of making aviation history. He was content to lease the *Columbia* out for record flights by others. In 1930, piloted by a Canadian, J. Errol Boyd, and an American, Harry P. Connor, and renamed the *Maple Leaf*, it became the first aircraft to make the Atlantic crossing twice. Following this achievement the *Columbia-Maple Leaf* was sold by Levine in 1931; but soon afterward the plane was grounded as unsafe—it had taken a good deal of battering, especially with Levine at the controls.

But the Depression caught up with Levine also, and like the *Columbia* he faded from the aviation scene. For a brief moment of near glory he had splashed some unique colors across the pages of aviation history; that he had never splashed himself and his plane across the landscape, or into the ever-hungry Atlantic, was one of the merry wonders of the Jazz Age. His solo flight from Paris to London, with all its concomitant international misdemeanors, its ultimate kangaroo landing and his warm reception from the staid English (who, indeed, are noted for a curious sense of humor) was a classic. The only question: a classic of what? But it was a triumph of the human spirit, and Charles Levine had that in abundance.

7

South Atlantic
Interlude

Lindbergh's flight in the spring of 1927 led to a quickening of aviation activity and a full share of side effects. Not only did it enliven the air over the route he had selected but over the generally neglected South Atlantic as well.

As a less important body of water because of its smaller width (thus supposedly requiring less intrepidity to cross) and a not very bustling economic significance, the South Atlantic simply did not entice airmen as did the more glamorous North Atlantic. Its aerial crossing attempts were generally fitful; after the first try in 1922 by Coutinho and Cabral-Sacadura, in numerous stages as well as aircraft, its skyways remained undisturbed for about four years. Then in January of 1926 the Spanish

Pilot Ramón Franco—called the "Columbus of the Air," no doubt because his flight originated at the port from which Columbus had set out for the New World, Palos, Spain—proceeded in the usual stages from Palos to Rio de Janeiro. His aircraft was a Dornier Wal tandem engined flying boat which had been christened *Plus Ultra*. Franco's flight, while not afflicted with the problems of Coutinho's and Cabral-Sacadura's and the first truly successful crossing of the South Atlantic, did not grip the imagination nor attract much attention.

It was not ignored in Italy, however, and may well have inspired the flight of de Pinedo's quite pointedly named *Santa Maria* in the following year. The destruction of the Savoia-Marchetti flying boat by a youthful litter-bug at Roosevelt Dam precluded its return flight across the North Atlantic and its participation in the Orteig prize competition won by Lindbergh on May 21, 1927.

By this time the Atlantic Ocean had claimed its first aerial victims—and this distinction, if that is the apposite word, could be claimed by the slighted South Atlantic. This was preceded by a flurry of attempts of variegated attainment. It all began in the spring of 1927 with the attempt by a Uruguayan, Tadeo Larre-Borges. His try caused some discomfort in the Italian camp, although it need not have. Not only was Larre-Borges grounded in Spain by rain before he could get off, his subsequent adventures introduced yet another hazard into Atlantic flying. Once the weather cleared early in March, Larre-Borges and a three-man crew left Casablanca on the first leg of their journey. Before much time had elapsed, it was obvious that the *Uruguay,* as the plane was named, had come a cropper.

French pilots eventually spotted the wreckage of the plane on the beach of the southern Moroccan coast, just at the point nearly opposite the Canary Islands, which were to have been the first stop of the *Uruguay*. This was a pariculary dangerous area because of Moorish tribesmen who preyed on travelers and caravans passing through. Larre-Borges and his crew were like manna from heaven with their ailing engine. After ditching offshore, the men made their way to the beach and into the eager arms of the Moors. The pilots who found their wrecked plane landed and learned that the airmen were safe and were returnable upon payment of ransom to the Moors. This was done, and Larre-Borges two years later made yet another try—this time in company with a French airman, Léon Challe—but to no avail. Still they *nearly* made it, flying from Spain to the waters off the Brazilian coast before their plane came down. That was enough for Larre-Borges, who gave up his transatlantic attempts.

Not long after Larre-Borges and his crew were ransomed, the South

Atlantic was crossed by a Dornier flying boat, this time with a Portuguese crew led by Sarmento Beires. His plan was an ambitious one and the flight in mid-March was but the first step in a planned round-the-world flight. But after reaching South America Beires was informed by his sponsor, the government of Portugal, that the trip was costing too much money and to abandon the grand plan and return home. Sadly Beires began working his way back up the coast of South America and was forced down at sea—only to have his plane, the *Argus,* sink after he and his crew were rescued by a fishing boat that fortunately happened to be passing by.

March blended into April, when there was yet another hapless try, this time by a Brazilian crew led by Joao de Barros flying from Italy and ending up 200 miles short of Brazil; it was dispiriting for these proud men to arrive in port under tow.

May was the fateful month—climaxed, of course, by Lindbergh's flight. On the fifth a French captain, de Saint-Roman, a navigator named de Mounayres and a mechanic, Petit, left St. Louis, Senegal, for the crossing to South America—hopefully nonstop, which had yet to be done. They were never heard from again, the first men to die while attempting to fly the Atlantic. Their passing went all but unnoticed, for three days later Nungesser and Coli winged off on their east-to-west flight into nowhere. What with all the public grief and consternation over the loss of the two celebrated airmen there was little note taken of the fate of the men in the Farman Goliath, down somewhere between Africa and Brazil. Fleetwinged fame, even in death, eluded Captain de Saint-Roman completely. On the other hand, the darling of fame, Nungesser, shared the captain's fate; in that they were equals.

France had lost heavily in the Atlantic sweepstakes and, while Lindbergh was not denied his due, the French yearned for air heroes of their own. They arrived on the scene late in the same fateful year, 1927. One was former First World War "ace" turned transport pilot, Capt. Dieudonné Costes, who had already accomplished some remarkable flights the previous year in a Breguet XIX, a biplane manufactured by the company for which he served as chief pilot. He was joined in the venture by Lt. Comdr. Joseph Le Brix. Their plane, with its meager lower wing, technically a sesquiplane, was powered by a single Hispano-Suiza engine and was fittingly named the *Nungesser-Coli.*

Originally Costes and Le Brix had hoped to meet the challenge of the North Atlantic, but Lindbergh and the coming of autumn weather eliminated that. However, as that avenue faded an even grander one opened up before them, one that would bring honor to French aviation and which would be a tribute to the men whose names were painted on

TOP Breguet XIX, named *Nungesser-Coli* in honor of the two airmen who had been lost in an Atlantic attempt, in which Dieudonné Costes and Joseph Le Brix hoped to succeed where their predecessors failed. (*Musée d l'Air, Paris*)

ABOVE Costes (left) and Le Brix are greeted with due ceremony as the first airmen to cross the South Atlantic non-stop. (*Musée de l'Air, Paris*)

RIGHT Costes and Le Brix on their good-will tour; here flying over the Panama Canal Zone, January, 1928. (*U.S. Air Force*)

the side of the green Breguet. It could be, also, a silent tribute to
Captain de Saint-Roman and his crew (whose given names seem to have
vanished even from French aviation history).

The two Frenchmen began their flight from Le Bourget on October
10, 1927, making their first stop, the West African port of St. Louis,
Senegal, in a single hop (a distance of nearly 3,000 miles). Four days
later they left St. Louis during a good weather spell and chose to eliminate all the little island stops that their predecessors had found so useful
—and at times a life-saving godsend—to make the flight from Africa to
Natal, Brazil, nonstop. Their twenty-hour crossing, reported regularly
by Le Brix via radio, was remarkably trouble free and when they

brought the *Nungesser-Coli* in for a landing at Natal they became the first men to cross the South Atlantic by air nonstop. But their flying was not finished with that happy landing.

From Natal, Costes and Le Brix proceeded down the Atlantic coast of South America, dropping down to visit several capital cities en route: Rio de Janeiro, Montevideo and Buenos Aires. They then crossed over the Andes to Santiago, Chile, and flew northward along the South American Pacific coast, again making several good-will stops, and arriving in Panama (where they met Lindbergh, himself on a good-will tour south of the border) and eventually Washington, D.C., where they were treated to lunch at the White House.

Upon arriving in New York their plane was given a new engine and speculation arose over the chances of returning to Paris over the northern route; but this apparently was discouraged by both the French Air Ministry and the Breguet company, who were willing to settle for triumphs already safely accomplished. The winter weather over that treacherous stretch of water was not particularly inviting either.

By the spring of 1928 Costes and Le Brix were ready to ship out from San Francisco, taking their plane with them. Upon arrival in Tokyo the two men set out for a return flight to Paris, making long jumps to Hanoi, Calcutta, Karachi and, finally, to Paris, where they arrived (having covered some 35,000 air miles) on April 14, 1928. They had not quite flown around the world, but their achievement was no small one—and they had won for French airmen the distinction of being the first across the South Atlantic nonstop.

The French, having captured pre-eminence in the Africa to South America race, took the edge off that one. So obviously another route would have to be selected if any new laurels were to be won. Thus in the summer of 1928 two Italian airmen, Arturo Ferrarin and Carlo del Prete, hoped to make a flight directly from Europe to South America. Their starting point was Rome and their goal was Natal—a distance of well over 4,000 miles, which, if they made it, would be better than the distance record held by Chamberlin and Levine.

Their plane was the old reliable Savoia-Marchetti flying boat, so dear to the Italian aviator's heart during this period of aviation activity. They took off from Rome on July 3, 1928, and, except for the tendency of an engine to overheat, had little trouble in the crossing. It was only when, on the next day, they came within sight of the South American coastline that they found that their destination, Natal, was fogged in. Searching for a likely landing place they ran into storms to the south and turned for Natal again. With their fuel running low there was little choice of landing spots and, although they did not arrive precisely on target, they did bring their plane in safely on the beach slightly to the north of Natal. Ferrarin and del Prete (a veteran, actually, who had made the same crossing with de Pinedo in 1927) had set a record for distance with a total of 4,475 miles.

This was a challenge, then, to other European fliers and soon Spain entered the aerial lists in late March of 1929 with an attempt by Francisco Jiminez and Ignacio Iglesias to blaze a sky trail between Seville and Rio de Janeiro, which, if successful, would beat the mark set by Ferrarin and del Prete. It was late March when they set out and actually succeeded in crossing the Atlantic, but Rio de Janeiro was to prove as elusive to them as Natal had to Ferrarin and del Prete. But the Spanish fliers did find Natal (still no record compared to a flight from Rome) and headed southward into trouble. "From Natal," Jiminez told a newsman, "we had to fight the whole time against storms and head winds which at times reduced our speed to fifty miles an hour." After about twenty hours of fatiguing flying the two men were forced to come down short of their destination in the state of Bahia, to the north of Rio. Although a qualified success, they had not broken the distance record as they had originally intended.

The year closed with the reentry of Larre-Borges, once the prisoner of Moorish bandits, in the South Atlantic race. He joined with a French airman, Léon Challe, in an attempt to fly from Spain to Montevideo, Uruguay, in another distance flight. Larre-Borges fared better in his second try, at least. Their Breguet took them across the Atlantic, but upon reaching the coast of Brazil on December 6, 1929, they ran into the usual complication of fog, an out-of-commission radio and other difficulties. Low on fuel, Larre-Borges attempted to set the plane down not too distant from Natal, as it turned out. The landing was a bit rough and the plane flipped over, although neither occupant was seriously injured. They were safe, they had crossed the Atlantic, but they had accomplished no record-breaking feat, so little was made of it. The flight, and the ill-fated Larre-Borges, became absorbed into the lesser archives of aviation.

Also insufficiently known was the great French airman, Jean Mermoz, whose record-breaking flights were directly devoted to the establishment of a regular air-mail route between Africa and South America. A pilot for the French Compagnie Générale Aéropostale, which was very active in South America and a competitor with the Germans there (this was before the establishment of Pan American Airways south of the border), Mermoz hoped to form an air link between the airlines in Europe and Africa and those already established in South America. With such a link, the time it took a business letter to go from Paris to, say, Buenos Aires was cut in half. By carrying the mails across the South Atlantic by plane instead of steamship, it was possible to complete the delivery in eight days instead of the customary sixteen. At the same

Eminent airmen meet at France Field, Canal Zone. In civilian dress are Le Brix (left), Lindbergh and Costes. (*U.S. Air Force*)

time, it took twenty days by ship for a letter to reach Buenos Aires from New York; thus French business men would have their American rivals at a distinct disadvantage. Mermoz wished to demonstrate that such mail deliveries were practical as well as possible.

Selecting a Latécoère 28 seaplane as his craft and Jean Dabry as copilot-navigator and Leopold Gimié as radio operator, Mermoz took off from Dakar, Senegal, on the extreme western bulge of Africa with 270 pounds of mail aboard. It was about 11 o'clock in the morning, May 11, 1930, when the heavily loaded plane, named *Comte de la Vaulx*, lifted its twin floats off the Senegal River. Mermoz intended, as had Costes and Le Brix, to bypass the usual way stations between Africa and South America. But as a measure of caution, two ships were posted along the route, one about 600 miles off each coast. These were a reassuring presence during the flight, which lasted for just twenty-five minutes under twenty hours, especially during the later moments when weather caused some concern. But no emergencies arose and the plane landed safely on the Rio Potengi, Natal, Brazil, carrying the first load of mail to cross the South Atlantic by air.

For a month the event was celebrated in South America with the customary festivities given airmen after a historic flight. But Mermoz hoped to complete the circle—to fly the mail both ways. The west-to-east crossing had not yet been made and Mermoz was determined to be the man to make it. With the same crew and plane he prepared for the return flight, and then for days suffered through as frustrating a time as ever any airman had endured. Getting the heavily loaded plane off the river proved impossible: the wind was from the wrong direction; the river was too narrow and the engine not powerful enough. Morning, noon and night the three men would climb into the Latécoère, get the engine going and try to get the floats unstuck from the Potengi, but in vain. One day as many as twenty-three attempts were made to get away; by July 7, 1930, the count had reached fifty-two. It was obvious that if Mermoz wished to get the plane into the air he would have to lighten the plane—perhaps he would have to leave the mailbags behind.

Providentially, the wind shifted and Mermoz decided to make the fifty-third attempt—and made it. The plane, its engine complaining, struggled off the water and turned out to sea. As they climbed to cruising altitude Mermoz noted some oil spots on the windscreen which he attributed to surplus oil being cleared by the wind from the engine. So far so good; when night came and the moon rose, they were surprised to find that they were about thirty miles off course, having been led slightly astray by the radio operator on the island of Fernando de Noronha. Their takeoff, they would learn later, had coincided with a convict revolt on the island, which rather distracted the radio operator.

As he guided the *Comte de la Vaulx* through the night, Mermoz himself became disconcerted; the oil he had noted dotting the windscreen had not stopped splashing and had, in fact, begun to soak the fuselage and to splatter across the lower wing. Mermoz checked the oil gauge and saw its needle fluttering—there was, clearly, a leak somewhere. Checking their location with Dabry (they were still about 500 miles from the African coast and in the general vicinity of one of the emergency ships, the *Phocée*), he asked Gimié to begin to keep in close touch with their now single hope of safety. With an eye on the engine for the first wisp of smoke and the first flicker of flame, Mermoz searched the waters for a sign of the *Phocée*.

Within minutes the ship was spotted bobbing on the rather rough sea and Mermoz, with the plane's engine already very hot, passed over the ship, then brought the plane down as gently as possible on the water. A lifeboat was already launched and headed their way, visible one minute then lost to sight the next as the waves tossed it in their general direction.

When the boat pulled alongside the *Comte de la Vaulx* the first objects taken from the plane were the mailbags; then, with some difficulty in the swelling water, the three men left the aircraft and jumped into the lifeboat. Once aboard, Mermoz made plans to save his plane from the Atlantic also, but even as he spoke a wave crashed into the plane, ripped off a float, turned it on its side, filled it with water and sank it.

The lesson Mermoz had learned from his adventure was that the Latécoère 28 was not the plane for an Atlantic crossing. Floats had proved as much a hindrance as an aid, adding drag as well as frontal resistance and weight while in flight. Aéropostale then initiated plans for larger aircraft, multi-engined and designed as flying boats for their transatlantic routes. Meanwhile, Mermoz had found another plane, a trimotored land plane, which he believed could do the job also. It was a design by the young (thirty-year-old) aero-engineer, René Couzinet, a Couzinet 70 named *Arc-en-Ciel (Rainbow)*. With himself, Couzinet and three others aboard, Mermoz set out once again from St. Louis and crossed the South Atlantic in record time, arriving safely in Natal after 14 hours, 27 minutes, on January 16, 1933. After the usual good-will tour, Mermoz was ready to try again for a return flight.

On May 15, 1933, he left Natal before dawn determined to succeed with the *Arc-en-Ciel* where the *Comte de la Vaulx* had failed. With three engines it seemed logical that the chances were good; but as the flight progressed the chances appeared to lessen considerably. One engine had sprung a leak, but luckily that had been caught in time. But when they were roughly in the area where the *Comte de la Vaulx* had

Latécoère 28 seaplane, *Comte de la Vaulx* (in honor of the early French air enthusiast and one of the founders of the *Fédération Aéronautique Internationale*), in which Mermoz crossed the South Atlantic from Africa to South America with a cargo of mail. The plane was lost, although the crew was not, on the attempt to make a return flight. (*Musée de l'Air, Paris*)

gone down, another engine began to overheat. Mermoz's engineer Collenot inspected the engine and came back with the diagnosis: nothing could be done about it. Mermoz cut the engine, throttled down the still running port engine and continued also on the center engine. The aircraft lost speed and altitude, but did remain airborne.

Mermoz simply could not accept a second defeat so close to home. While close contact was kept with ships in the area, he carefully eased the big plane through the sky. In the night he could see the distant lights of Dakar, but they were not yet there. The engines—the two still turning—looked good and he relaxed a little. Within minutes he knew they were home, flashed a reassuring smile to the crew and set the wheels of the *Arc-en-Ciel* on the runway at Dakar. For Mermoz, it was victory at last; he had flown the Atlantic both ways—and proved the practicality of an air-mail route.

By the following year Aéropostale planes had made a dozen crossings of the South Atlantic over the trail blazed by Jean Mermoz—a year later, 1935, there were three times as many flights. The only competition was presented by the German airships, specifically the *Graf Zeppelin* (which had made its maiden voyage as early as 1928 and continued with remarkable regularity to make some 144 flights across the Atlantic over the years).

Shortly after his 1933 round-trip flight, Mermoz became an official of Air France, which had taken over the floundering (financially, that is)

OPPOSITE Jean Mermoz, France's great airman who devoted his life to the conquest of the Atlantic in a pioneering effort to establish regular commercial air traffic over the ocean. (*Musée de l'Air, Paris*)

Aéropostale. Not a man to fly a desk, and despite his position, Mermoz continued with his pioneer flying. One of the planes that had come out of his 1930 failure was a four-engined flying boat, the Latécoère 300, named *Croix du Sud (Southern Cross)*. This flying giant (with a wingspan of 144 feet) had established several records before, on December 7, 1936, Mermoz himself decided to make what for him was a fairly regular flight—the crossing from Dakar to Natal. What should have been a routine crossing went wrong somewhere, for word was flashed from the plane that an engine had failed—and then, no further word.

An extensive search was made, but no sign of the *Croix du Sud* or its crew was ever found. Jean Mermoz had finally been conquered by the ocean he had challenged so often, and France lost one of its outstanding airmen.

The South Atlantic, though slighted generally because for some unknown reason it seemed to lack glamour, took its toll and resisted conquest as tenaciously as the more newsworthy stretch of water to the north. Although Lindbergh had succeeded in crossing the North Atlantic alone in 1927, it was not until 1931 that the South Atlantic was flown by a lone pilot, who at the same time was the first to fly it from west to east.

Everything about that flight was most unlikely, beginning with the small person of Australian Squadron Leader H. J. L. "Bert" Hinkler. Hinkler's particular passion was the tiny plane, which no doubt neatly enclosed his own diminutive frame. In February of 1928 Bert Hinkler first made headlines (at least in Australia and Britain) when he piloted a tiny Avro Avian from London to Darwin. In 1931 Hinkler arrived in New York during October with another small plane, a de Havilland Puss Moth, and began working his way southward through Central America, finally arriving at Natal on the east coast of Brazil by late November. His progress was little noticed by the newspapers; in fact about the only attention Hinkler received in Brazil was from irate immigration officials, who found his papers not quite in order.

Hinkler himself proffered little information about his reasons for flitting about South America in a little Puss Moth. His wife, in the dark as much as anyone, one day received in London a succinct cable which, in its entirety, read: *Here's hoping,* whatever that meant.

What it meant to Hinkler, on November 26, 1931, was that he cranked up the little four-cylinder engine of his small craft and headed out over the Atlantic. For the next twenty-five hours and five minutes no further word was heard from or about Bert Hinkler. Only he knew what a venture he had embarked upon—"one of the wildest nights I have ever spent"—the highlight of which was a six-hour electrical storm which tossed him and his plane around the heavens like a paper glider.

The Puss Moth, with its 36-foot wingspan, was even smaller than the *Spirit of St. Louis,* weighed about half as much and functioned with a good deal less power. The Gypsy engine, however, did not fail, nor did the structure of the plane, despite the six-hour battering.

Even more miraculously, neither did Hinkler's navigation fail, for on November 27, he gently set the Puss Moth down upon the runway at Bathurst, West Africa, the first man to fly the South Atlantic west to east, the first to fly it solo and the second man to succeed in conquering the Atlantic Ocean alone. Hinkler was greeted enthusiastically at Bathurst (complete with being carried about on the shoulders of his greeters) and then flew on to London, where he arrived on December 7, 1931, to be reunited with his mystified wife and to be treated to further welcoming. What Hinkler had accomplished in fact was a flight from New York to London, the long way.

Pleased with the performance of the Puss Moth, Hinkler hoped to use it to recapture the London to Darwin competition (his old record had been broken by Charles Kingsford-Smith in 1929). In January of 1933 he set out in his little plane with the first scheduled stop Brindisi, Italy, but he never arrived. A search did not immediately locate the plane and it was spring before the charred wreckage of the Puss Moth was found on a deserted mountainside; little Bert Hinkler's body was sprawled nearby.

Even as search parties sought him in vain in the forests of France and the wintry Alps, Hinkler's record-breaking South Atlantic flight was diminished somewhat. An English pilot, also an advocate of the small light plane, James Mollison, made the first solo east-to-west crossing in a Puss Moth on February 8/9, 1933 (he had already done the same over the North Atlantic in August of the previous year).

After the flights of Hinkler and Mollison the South Atlantic resumed its secondary position among the oceans so far as aviation was concerned. The *Graf Zeppelin* crossed it with reasonable regularity during the gentler seasons; the Germans were especially active over the South Atlantic route, employing a system of ship and aircraft to deliver the mails. The flight was accomplished by the Dornier Wal, with refueling ships stationed along the route for servicing and catapulting. With a more or less scheduled service across the stretch of water between Africa and South America, practically all the glamour and challenge had evaporated from the South Atlantic. It had produced its almost anonymous heroes, it had taken its toll, but, for real newsworthy excitement, it was no match for the treacherous skies to the north.

8

Flights
to Nowhere:
Matters Melancholy
and Almost
Triumphant

Having innocently ushered in the "Lindbergh Era," the creator him-self sought to elude the limelight and to promote aviation rather than himself or to seek new laurels in further daring ventures. But once the era had been created, there were others eager and willing, even fatally so, to fill the void that Lindbergh so readily vacated.

The year 1927 bristled with aviation events; after Lindbergh there were Chamberlin and Levine, followed by Byrd and his crew. At the end of August another crossing was accomplished with a remarkable lack of fanfare when two Detroiters, one a successful businessman, William Brock, and the other a pilot, Edward Schlee, took off from Harbour Grace, Newfoundland, and landed the next day at Croydon, near Lon-don. They landed with hardly a fuss, since they had not taken the usual steps of advising the press—and, besides, they were aiming at a more impressive record: a flight around the world. In stages, they did fly eastward from Croydon in their Stinson plane, named *Pride of Detroit*, and got as far as Tokyo, where they ran into cautious officialdom. Ready, confident and poised for a cross-Pacific flight to round out their circumnavigation of the globe, Brock and Schlee came up against a general revulsion which followed a suicidal race across the Pacific from the United States to Hawaii which had been sponsored by the pineapple king, James D. Dole.

Even this travesty had been inspired by the Lindbergh flight, but the outcome was deadly in the extreme. No less than ten lives were lost in connection with the Dole Derby, including that of a young school teacher, Mildred Doran of Caro, Michigan. (Had the *Miss Doran* made it, the teacher would have been the first woman ever to have flown an ocean.)

This feminist desire would lead to a series of losses. It was, of course, the golden dream of Mibs Boll, but one she failed to see through to fulfillment, despite the curious alliance with Charles Levine. In a better position to carry through such a plan was an aviation pioneer, Princess Anne Lowenstein-Wertheim. She had the money, could purchase a plane and could hire a pilot and navigator—and she had the will, despite her more than sixty years. The plane selected was a single-engined Fokker named the *St. Raphael* and blessed, along with the crew, by no less a personage than the Bishop of Cardiff.

The Princess Anne (the title had been acquired through a marriage to a German prince) had hired two experienced English fliers, Lt. Col. F. F. Minchin (veteran of the London-Paris run of Imperial Airways) and Leslie Hamilton, an instructor and test pilot. Despite family objections the Princess was determined to make the flight. Shortly after Brock and Schlee had arrived from Newfoundland, the *St. Raphael* started out in the opposite direction on August 31, 1927, bound for Ottawa. With Minchin at the controls, the heavily laden Fokker took a long time to lift off the runway at Upavon, England. It had all but raced to the end of the strip when it lumbered into the air and headed west. The plane was glimpsed a few times over Ireland and for an instant over the mid-Atlantic by the crew of a tanker, the *Josiah Macey*. The time was noted as 9:44 P.M. It was the last ever seen of the *St. Raphael* and its crew.

Princess Anne, at ultimate cost, had achieved a double distinction: she had been the first woman to get off successfully on an Atlantic flight and also the first woman to be lost in such an attempt.

It was the beginning of a series of hard-luck flights which were either abandoned or ended disastrously. Atlantic Fever had burgeoned forth to such an extent that the first three days of September, 1927, saw the

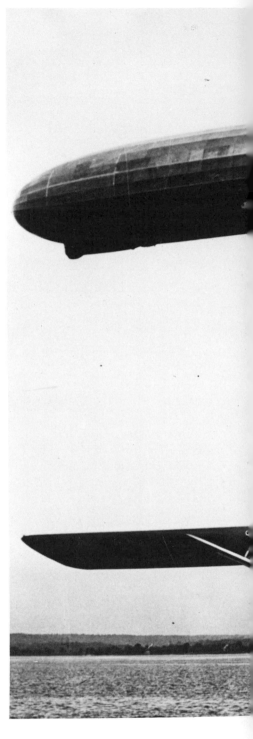

Symbol of Germany's growing aviation
industry. The *Graf Zeppelin* hovers over
a Dornier Superwal. The *Graf* accomplished many a safe Atlantic crossing and
the early Dornier flying boats were often
used in Atlantic attempts and completed
crossings. (*Lufthansa-Archiv*)

beginning of three flights, all of them aborted. The first was to have connected Windsor, Ontario, with its sister city in England. This was, in a sense, a grudge flight, for it was organized in competition with another which, for a prize of $25,000, was to join Ontario's London with England's London. Initially it had been the London flight that had been the cause of all the excitement, but when a Detroiter, Phil Wood, was informed that the competition was limited to Britons he decided he would make a cross-Atlantic flight joining the two Windsors. As a pilot he hired the experienced C. A. "Duke" Schiller; for the flight he arranged for a Detroit-built Stinson which was named the *Royal Windsor*.

This was the same type of aircraft that had been acquired by the London fliers Terrance Bernard Tully and James Victor Medcalf, both veterans. Their craft was named in honor of the founder of the brewery that was sponsoring the flight, Sir John Carling. The two rival planes, as well as the two Canadian cities, generated excitement as they became the focus of newspaper attention, and the race was on.

Both planes took off within hours of each other on September 1, 1927, and both encountered the same abysmal weather which forced the *Carling* down at Caribou, Maine, and the *Windsor* down at St. John, just south of Montreal. Both were weatherbound for several days, with the *Carling* first off on the fifth for the flight to Harbour Grace, from which the Atlantic flight proper was to begin. The *Windsor* managed to get off a day later and, after a stopover at Old Orchard, Maine, continued on to Newfoundland. Upon arrival, Schiller and Wood learned that Tully and Medcalf had taken off about five hours earlier—it was now September 7. Although the *Sir John Carling* carried a radio, no further word was heard from the plane, nor was it ever seen again. Obviously, the *Sir John Carling* was lost at sea. Word soon came from Ontario that the sponsors of the *Royal Windsor* wished Schiller and Wood to abandon their flight; they did, but not before attempting a search over the gloomy waters which might have already swallowed up their friendly rivals.

The loss of the *Sir John Carling* was not the only one of that fateful first week in September. On the second, Givon and Corbu had set out from Le Bourget, only to abandon their flight when they ran into fog; on the third a flight led by Englishman Capt. Frank T. Courtney began at Calshot in a Dornier Wal; it too was abandoned after a bout with Atlantic head winds. On the sixth another flight originated in the United States, headed by the ex-Levine pilot Lloyd Bertaud. Sponsor of the flight was William Randolph Hearst, whose aviation editor of the New York *Daily Mirror*, Philip Payne, was to go along as a passenger. Co-pilot-navigator was Bertaud's friend James D. Hill. The aircraft was a single-engined Fokker similar to the one in which the Princess Lowen-stein-Wertheim made her last flight about a week before. Bertaud's Fokker was named *Old Glory* and carried some of the finest radio equipment then available; it also carried a wreath which was to be dropped in honor of the first airmen lost at sea:

> *Nungesser and Coli*
> *You showed the way.*
> *We followed.*
> *Bertaud and Payne and Hill.*

The flight got under way from Old Orchard Beach, Maine, obviously under a weight handicap (named Payne) and, because of it, a little less fuel; it was September 6, 1927. The weather was anything but perfect over most of the Atlantic (it held Captain Courtney down on the water in Spain, where he finally abandoned his attempt; it kept Medcalf and Tully in *Sir John Carling* grounded for another day). But Bertaud managed to get *Old Glory* off the sand and staggering into the stormy Atlantic air.

By early morning of the seventh, with its radio beyond the reach of land stations on either side of the ocean, ships in mid-Atlantic began picking up SOS signals from *Old Glory*. The plane was in trouble and a position was given, but no sign was found of the plane there. Six days later the wreckage of a plane was found some 500 miles off the coast of Newfoundland—and at least 100 miles from the spot that the crew had thought was their position. But the foundered *Old Glory* contained no human beings. Bertaud and Payne and Hill had, ironically, followed Nungesser and Coli all the way.

So it was that both *Old Glory* and *Sir John Carling* were lost on the same day; it took very little persuasion to convince Schiller and Wood to abandon their flight to Windsor. The loss of the *Carling* had certain political repercussions, for the Canadian government was seriously considering passage of legislation that would prohibit transatlantic flights from originating in Canada. (This would not, of course, apply to Newfoundland, since it was then a Crown Colony and could handle the problem in its own way.) While the law was not passed, it did discourage such flights from Canada for several years.

The losses of the *St. Raphael, Old Glory* and *Sir John Carling* and a toll of eight lives might have distressed concerned officials but it hardly discouraged carriers of Atlantic Fever. One other aborted attempt rounded out September. This was made by an Irish airman, Comdr. James Fitzmaurice, in company with a Scot, Capt. Robert McIntosh, flying another single-engined Fokker, this one being named *Princess Xenia* in honor of the wife of their sponsor, W. R. Leed. The latter had made his money in tin, had married a Russian princess and now longed for some additional glory. For Fitzmaurice and McIntosh it would have been a glory flight, for they were attempting the rough westward crossing, which had been abandoned the previous August by the two German Junkers, the *Bremen* and *Europa*.

They took off from Baldonnel Airport (near Dublin) and hoped to reach New York. Once out at sea they encountered the usual buffeting head winds and found it difficult to fly in a straight line let alone maintain any kind of speed that might get them to New York before their fuel ran out. A few hapless hours of battling invisible monsters

Crew, and ladies, interested in the flight of the *Royal Windsor*: Phil Wood, Mrs. Wood, Ada Greer and C. A. "Duke" Schiller. (*Courtesy of National Museum of Science & Technology, Ottawa, Canada*)

The Stinson Detroiter named *Royal Windsor*, taking off on its race with the *Sir John Carling*. (*Courtesy of National Museum of Science & Technology, Ottawa, Canada*)

Crew of the Stinson Detroiter named *Sir John Carling*: Terrance Tulley (left) and James Medcalf, photographed just before their ill-fated flight. (*Courtesy of National Museum of Science & Technology, Ottawa, Canada*)

The *Sir John Carling* poised on its strip at Harbour Grace, Newfoundland, before take-off. (*Courtesy of National Museum of Science & Technology, Ottawa, Canada*)

Takeoff into oblivion: the *Carling* leaves Harbour Grace for the Atlantic. (*Courtesy of National Museum of Science & Technology, Ottawa, Canada*)

convinced the two men that to continue with the odds so much against them was pure foolishness. They turned around and headed back for Ireland. That haven was spotted in the gloom just as the rain came to complicate visibility by beating on the windscreen. All thought of making it back to Dublin was given up as they approached the ground seeking any port in the storm. They spotted the River Shannon on the coast, then followed the coastline a bit to find what appeared to be a

The Fokker *Old Glory* in which Bertaud, Hill and Payne flew to their deaths; it was in this type of craft, a single-engined Fokker VII, that the Princess Lowenstein-Wertheim flew to hers also. Lindbergh had hoped early in his planning to acquire a similar type for his flight but was turned down by the Fokker salesman. (*National Air & Space Museum, Smithsonian Institution*)

smooth piece of beach. With the wet wind whipping them and the wings dancing in the gloom, Fitzmaurice set the *Princess Xenia* down safely on the sand; they had landed near the little village of Ballybunion, where they spent a hospitable night. In the morning they boarded the plane again to return to Baldonnel Airport, where they postponed, then finally abandoned the flight altogether.

Fitzmaurice, however, had not been discouraged as far as Atlantic flying was concerned. His takeoff from Ireland had had its effect in Germany and would, in time, bring an odd assortment of airmen together for a future aerial spectacular.

Meanwhile, the parade of aerial misadventures continued. And so did the lure of the Atlantic for women. Of the five failures which followed that of the *Princess Xenia,* four involved women—two fatally. However, two of the unsuccessful flights brought a touch of show biz glamor to the Atlantic aerial sweepstakes and, happily, concluded without serious damage to the participants.

The American representative was a very pretty young lady named Ruth Elder (actually Mrs. Lyle Womack of Lakeland, Florida) who suggested to her flying instructor, George W. Haldeman, that they make an attempt at an Atlantic hop. Haldeman had been impressed with his pupil's flying ability, but revealed scant knowledge of the Atlantic. In agreeing to make the flight he also assented to making it quite late in the season: October. With the help of some Florida and West Virginia businessmen, Miss Elder and Haldeman were supplied with a Stinson monoplane which was appropriately named *The American Girl.* This was the period during which the showman Florenz Ziegfeld was "glorifying the American girl" and the news that Ruth Elder was about to make an attempt to become the first woman to fly the Atlantic fetched forth broad hints that she was really more concerned with a career in show business and wished to use aviation as a mere stepping stone.

Some degree of wisdom was demonstrated by Haldeman when he decided to cross directly over the Atlantic instead of following the shorter, but in October especially stormy, Great Circle route. This decision no doubt saved the lives of both of them. The more southern route also coincided with the shipping lanes which, in their case, was to make all the difference (as it had, by nearly pure chance, for Hawker and Mackenzie-Grieve).

With some difficulty Haldeman managed to get *The American Girl* off the runway at Roosevelt Field in the early morning of October 11, 1927; it was barely dawn and the weather ahead was not at all promising. But that usual scourge was not to prove their undoing, for they actually had covered practically enough ocean to have arrived either over England or France when trouble struck. Oil pressure dropped alarmingly because of a break in the system; within minutes their engine threatened to seize up or burst into flame. Haldeman's SOS was picked up by a British ship and was relayed to a Dutch vessel, the *Barendrecht,* which happened to be close by. Haldeman had by this time ditched *The American Girl* and he and Ruth Elder awaited the arrival of rescue.

They had come down about 360 miles north of the Azores—and way off course (their original goal was Paris). A lifeboat from the *Barendrecht* was lowered into a rough, swelling sea and, following a struggle, the two occupants were taken from the plane, its wings awash and its nose deep in the water. The captain of the *Barendrecht* was especially impressed with Ruth Elder's aplomb. When she stepped to the deck of the ship, bedraggled, wet and with her hair plastered to her head, she thanked the captain graciously, then reached into a bag for a mirror and a lipstick to repair the damage that had been done to her makeup by an inconsiderate sea.

The attempt to salvage *The American Girl*, complicated by the high waves, failed. As it was being taken from the water it struck the side of the ship, the wing crumpled and then the plane burst inexplicably into flame. To prevent any damage to the ship, the plane was immediately cut loose and it sank sizzling into the Atlantic. Then the *Barendrecht* set course for Horta in the Azores. There Ruth Elder would meet her German counterpart.

She was the already established Viennese actress, Lilli Dillenz, who had flown over from Lisbon in a Junkers flying boat piloted by Fritz Loose (who had been pilot of the unsuccessful *Bremen*) with Rolf Starke as copilot. Their plane was in good-natured competition with another German craft, a Heinkel seaplane with a crew of three: Horst Merz, Friedrich Rode and William Boch. Neither plane got any farther than the Azores, the Heinkel flipped over in a takeoff attempt and the Junkers returned after bumping into very heavy weather. So it was that when Ruth Elder arrived in the Azores she met another disappointed lady aviator-actress. Both persisted for a while, although Lilli Dillenz quickly returned to her greasepaint and Ruth Elder, after visiting Paris, returned to the United States for a career in vaudeville, signing up for a twenty-five-week tour at a handsome pre-Depression figure of $5,000 a week. She continued to dabble in aviation, even flew in the first National Women's Air Derby (she came in fourth) in 1929, but eventually she faded out of aviation in favor of a movie career in the Thirties.

The radiant year—1927—in aviation ended, as the new would begin, on a grim note, especially so because the flight which marked it began on Christmas Eve and was over by the next day. Actually the flight was initiated in October, around the time of the futile attempts of Ruth Elder and Lilli Dillenz, but a series of misfortunes delayed the final takeoff till December.

The ambitious lady who wished to be the first to fly the Atlantic was one Mrs. Frances Grayson of Forest Hills, New York, where she had a successful real estate business. Determined, rather square of jaw, Mrs. Grayson was a divorcee and a feminist—although her chief claim to fame was that she was the niece of the late President Wilson. Her sponsor was a Mrs. Aage Ancker, a North Carolinian of Danish extraction, who helped Mrs. Grayson acquire a new Sikorsky twin-engined amphibian, an S-38, which was rather poetically named the *Dawn*. Nor did

LEFT Ruth Elder being assisted into her bulky flying suit before boarding *The American Girl* (a Stinson similar to the *Windsor* and the *Carling*) for her try at becoming the first woman to cross the Atlantic by air. (*National Air & Space Museum, Smithsonian Institution*)

BELOW Ruth Elder aboard the *Barendrecht* after being plucked out of the Atlantic Ocean. Her plane, *The American Girl*, fell into the water 360 miles short of the Azores with a malfunctioning engine. (*National Air & Space Museum, Smithsonian Institution*) they stint in crewing the plane; as pilot they hired Wilmer Stultz, well known as an expert pilot, and as navigator, Brice Goldsborough, the instrument expert who had contributed so much to Lindbergh's flight, among others. In honor of their sponsor, the city of Copenhagen was selected as the *Dawn*'s destination.

But not all was well. The first two attempts to get off ended ludicrously: the little Sikorsky was so heavily loaded that it could not rise off the water. A third try, with less of a fuel load, on October 17 (by which time both Ruth Elder and Lilli Dillenz were safe in the Azores, thinking twice about the delights of Atlantic flying), was successful—at first. They left New York and headed northward; but when they were about 500 miles out, the port engine began sputtering and finally conked out entirely. Stultz, no stuntman, kicked rudder and headed for home, although some reports say that Mrs. Grayson—whose knowledge of aircraft was rudimentary, to say the least—insisted that they proceed.

As far as Stultz was concerned it was three strikes and out; he had had enough of the *Dawn* and Mrs. Grayson. Besides, the weather would not get any better for several months. Wilmer Stultz withdrew from Mrs. Grayson's rather mad project and she was left without a pilot (Stultz later took a similar job with another lady flier the following summer with completely different results).

Stranded, Mrs. Grayson spent the time while the engine of the *Dawn* was being checked searching for another pilot. Neither Chamberlin nor Balchen were interested, but a friend of Balchen's, Oskar Omdahl, who according to Balchen was always "ready for the first wild adventure," was. He chose not to listen to Balchen, who dismissed the flight, particularly at that time of the year, as a "useless stunt flight." Omdahl may also have been restless, working as he was at the time in the Fokker plant instead of flying. He had come over from Norway, at Balchen's request, to join with a new Byrd Antarctic expedition, and was merely marking time. Mrs. Grayson presented the opportunity to make some money, freedom from the monotony of the Fokker works and, best of all, to fly.

Goldsborough remained faithful and would come along; as an added precaution, in view of the engine trouble they had suffered in October, another member was added to the crew: engineer Fred Schroeder. All three men, it would appear, should have known better, for the delay had stretched into December and the weather was abysmal (although Goldsborough thought he had that licked after studying the problem). Their greatest enemy was the fever that raged over getting the first woman across the Atlantic. As the temperatures over, and on, the Atlantic plummeted, the rashness over Being First and Female elevated alarmingly. Mrs. Grayson just had to be First!

It was Christmas Eve, 1927, before the *Dawn* left Roosevelt Field bound for Newfoundland on the first leg of its flight. They never arrived; they had simply flown into what was then murderous weather and disappeared. A search, complicated by rough weather, was begun on Christmas Day and abandoned at the year's end. One report from a ship far out at sea on December 24 mentioned hearing the sound of aircraft engines and then an explosion, but no confirmation of that ever came. Two years later a bottle of questionable authenticity drifted ashore at Salem, Massachusetts, with a message: "1928. We are freezing. Gas leaked and we are drifting off Grand Banks. Grayson." The date, unless Mrs. Grayson was particularly distracted, was of course wrong. It was highly unlikely that she and her crew could have drifted—and remained alive—for a week in the killing weather of the Atlantic that December of 1927; nor would their plane have remained intact long enough to float into the New Year. But it could have been merely a mistake on the part of Mrs. Grayson in her last pathetic moments.

Just before takeoff it was noted that she had put a small revolver in her handbag—an unladylike piece of equipment. Perhaps she used it; Frances Wilson Grayson went out in a blaze of senseless glory.

So it was with the loss of the *Dawn* and its crew that the Atlantic death toll reached an even dozen from May, when Lindbergh made his flight, until the December flight of Mrs. Grayson. This does not take into account the number lost in the South Atlantic (three), in takeoff accidents (four) and in an attempt before Lindbergh (two). This would make a total of twenty-one lives sacrificed (all but two during that frenetic year 1927) to the urge to be "First," to win Fame and Fortune, or to the even more mysterious urge simply to do it because you thought it should be done.

If there was any moral to be drawn from the grim roster of fatalities, few were prepared to heed it. Obviously a successful—and above all safe—transatlantic flight took much preparation, nearly superhuman skill, a worthy aircraft and an incalculable quantity of pure luck, even if you were not superstitious. While it had been proved that, indeed, an aircraft could fly the Atlantic, it was obvious that not every aircraft could achieve this; nor were engines, though improving every day, always reliable. As for navigation, so essential to happy landings in long-distance flights, there was much that was yet to be learned about that science. Few pilots, motivated by a taste for adventure and emboldened by courage, had the inclination to learn navigation. And all too many were all but ignorant of the winds, clouds and weathers over the Atlantic until it was too late.

But it was the challenge that could not be ignored, so certain truths were disregarded also. And the two still remaining primary challenges

Frances Grayson, Igor Sikorsky and Mrs. Aage Ancker (who sponsored the flight) are photographed before the hull of the Sikorsky amphibian being built for Mrs. Grayson's transatlantic flight. (*Sikorsky Aircraft*)

The completed Sikorsky S-36, *Dawn*, which was lost with all hands, including the headstrong Mrs. Grayson, in an attempt to conquer the Atlantic in December, 1927. (*Sikorsky Aircraft*)

were: to make the first nonstop crossing from east to west, from Europe to America, and to be the first woman Atlantic flier. Certain other questionable "firsts" would remain operative for a long time: after Paris and London had been used up as links with New York (as of the first of January, 1928, no one had yet flown from Paris to New York, however), it was only a matter of selecting some new terminal. Since no one had flown to many places, it was possible for a long time to make some sort of name by being the first to fly from Somewhere to Somewhere Else, a dubious contribution to aviation, commerce or common sense.

If 1927 ended on a lamentable note, 1928 opened on the same grim tone. After Charles Levine returned to the United States to discuss a matter of some $150,000 with his government, he left his new flying ally, Capt. Walter R. Hinchliffe, disgruntled as well as determined to make the Atlantic crossing. Hinchliffe had rejected Mibs Boll as a possible passenger and rather mysteriously showed up late in 1927 in the United States to arrange for the purchase of a Stinson Detroiter. This being done he had it shipped back to England, where he made his preparations and announced that these were aimed at an Atlantic flight in March. He was terribly reticent about revealing the name of his copilot-cum-navigator-cum-companion.

With word coming out of Germany of another attempt brewing there, Hinchliffe was rather anxious to get off first. There was an air of

mystery about the entire undertaking, for although a civilian, Hinchliffe had somehow acquired the use of Cranwell, a military installation in Lincolnshire. The customary winds held Hinchliffe down and the military authorities became restive, especially after Hinchliffe and his plane, named *Endeavor*, overstayed their access by a week. It was by then the second week in March and word had leaked out that Hinchliffe's copilot would be a Capt. Gordon Sinclair. But the weather did not improve for a couple more days; finally on March 12 Hinchliffe stated that they would be off the next morning, despite some unlovely weather promised for the Atlantic.

Early on the thirteenth the two fliers climbed into the *Endeavor* and left Cranwell. The wheels had barely left the runway when to the surprise of the large gathering that had witnessed the takeoff, Sinclair appeared out of nowhere. It was then revealed that Hinchliffe's companion was the handsome daughter of Lord Inchcape, the Honorable Elsie Mackay, well known for her devotion to flying, an accomplished pilot and a former actress. Because Hinchliffe had not announced his intended destination (it was widely believed that it was New York) it was not known where to expect him and his attractive copilot. Wherever that had been, it was obvious after the passage of a number of hours and then days that the *Endeavor* had not arrived anywhere.

Eventually a glimmer of their fate was revealed when a part of their plane was washed ashore at Donegal on the northwest coast of Ireland. They had barely left home before something had happened to the plane, to the engine or to them.

Finally, after what had begun to seem to be an unrelenting succession of disasters, a new Atlantic triumph was achieved; it was a qualified victory with tragic overtones, however, quite in keeping with what had happened before. The inception of this flight had its roots in two previous failures: the August, 1927, attempt of the German Junkers *Bremen*, two of whose veterans, the Baron von Huenefeld and pilot Hermann Koehl, persisted in a dream of transatlantic adventure; the other failure was that of Capt. James Fitzmaurice, of the Irish Free State Army Air Corps, who had suffered his failure in the *Princess Xenia* about a month after the crew of the *Bremen*.

This unlikely alliance between the Irish and the German crews had, in turn, its roots in the fact that Koehl believed that they could succeed in crossing the Atlantic flying from east to west if, as had Fitzmaurice, they took off from Baldonnel, near Dublin. Thus the *Bremen*, with von Huenefeld aboard, Koehl at the controls and Arthur Spindler along as copilot, arrived late in March at Baldonnel. Theirs was a private venture—the earlier one had been sponsored by von Huenefeld's firm, North German-Lloyd Lines. Their new flight was backed by the Baron

Elsie Mackay engaged in preflight preparations in a happier time of her flying career, prior to her Atlantic attempt. One of Britain's most celebrated lady fliers, she was lost in March, 1928, along with pilot Walter Hinchliffe. (*National Archives*)

himself; because of the flight, which was regarded as premature and risky by his employers, Koehl was dismissed as Night Flight Manager of Lufthansa.

For its time, although it was not a new design, the Junkers W-33L *Bremen* was a remarkably advanced plane, particularly if compared with the previous transatlantic aircraft. One of its major distinctions was that it was of all-metal construction, including its "skin," which was corrugated Duralumin. It was a low-wing (the first of that type to be employed over the Atlantic) monoplane with a span of 58 feet, 3 inches; fuselage length was 34 feet, 10 inches. It was a land plane and was powered by a single six-cylinder Junkers engine. Although the standard Junkers W-33 could achieve a top speed of close to 120 miles an hour, the addition of fuel tanks added to the weight and cut the top speed to about a hundred.

Koehl learned of his dismissal by Lufthansa after he had flown to Ireland, the news of which he received with a shrug, saying, "If I don't make it, I won't need a job. . . ." On his part, the aristocratic von Huenefeld appeared to be ravaged, which he was because of an illness which would snuff out his life within a year. It was at Baldonnel that the German airmen were entertained by their brother Irish airmen while awaiting the proper weather conditions for a start. During this period Fitzmaurice took the Junkers up for a hop or two and perhaps, with a touch of blarney, talked himself into the flight. Whatever happened, for there may also have been an argument as is generally reported, Spindler quit and returned to Germany. Fitzmaurice was taken on as co-pilot, and since he spoke no German, von Huenefeld served as interpreter for the two pilots.

Early on the morning of April 12, 1928, the *Bremen* was made ready for the takeoff and by 5:30 A.M. the extremely heavy craft, wheels sinking in the turf, began moving into the wind. There was not a great deal of optimism displayed by the airdrome officials for, as the *Bremen* lumbered bumpily and ever so slowly across the runway, two ambulances "suddenly darted out from behind the hangars," Koehl noted. The vehicles made better time than the plane and "at the time it almost looked to me [Koehl] as if they would reach America before we did."

Gaining air speed in the heavy craft was complicated by the fact that for some stretches of the runway they were confronted with an uphill climb. "Now we began to win the race," Koehl later recorded. "The last third [of the runway] sloped gently downward. I hoped that here we would make up the speed we had not initially reached, since we needed to achieve 75 mph in order to leave the ground and our speed indicator was already hovering round 68 mph. I felt triumph in my grasp when Fitz suddenly shouted something in my ear. The next moment I saw him snatch the elevator control.

"A sheep had walked from the right, straight onto the runway. Fitz had noticed it and at the very last minute got the aircraft higher, but it lacked sufficient speed and stalled, and because of the landing gear suspension bumped several times along the ground. I thought it was all over and that we would certainly crash.

"Ahead of us the exhaust pipe was red hot and spewing flames, behind us 440 gallons of fuel were stored. If a spark brought the two of them together, we were done for. I wondered if it might not be better to switch off the ignition.

"Then the propeller would stop. We couldn't have that! So I left the ignition on and kept the plane very steady. Ahead of us lay a further 1300 feet of flat meadowland." This was small comfort for, according to proper procedure, they should have already been, in Koehl's sardonic

phrase, "proudly airborne." But they were not and continued to head
for the runway's end at which they would have to contend with a thir-
teen-foot hill covered with grasping trees. Their speed was not yet sufficient for a safe takeoff, so Koehl kept the nose down as long as safely
possible—perhaps a little beyond. Then the "plane soared up, the landing gear whipping through the tops of the trees. Later the machine
stalled heavily more than once but remained airborne. Takeoff had
been satisfactorily completed, as things worked out, but we were heading straight for a mountain. To the left, to the right, and ahead, its sides
rose more speedily than we could climb. Only on the right behind us
stretched a flat valley.

"I didn't think it possible that an aircraft so heavily loaded, at such
low height and slow ·speed, could undertake a turn to the right. But as
the wheels were almost touching the ground we had to take this final
risk. We started to make the turn. The right wing dipped low; it
skimmed the grass surface, struck a hedge, but thanks to the aircraft's
excellent aerodynamic qualities we got it through, had the valley ahead
and passed straight on. Immediately afterward the *Bremen* was traveling
at 75 mph and 90 seconds later was flying at 500 feet. We were off to a
successful start."

That was certainly one way of looking at what must have been a
harrowing ten minutes or so. They climbed higher, accompanied by a
small biplane of the Irish Free State Air Corps, crossed over Ireland—
about halfway their escort was forced to return to Baldonnel. The
Bremen passed over Clifden, where Alcock and Brown had started it all,
and then headed out into the inhospitable sky over the Atlantic. It was
then about 7:30 in the morning and the three men in their plane were
lost to the world for the next dozens of hours, for they had decided to
sacrifice a radio for additional fuel.

Koehl and Fitzmaurice spelled each other at the controls. Von
Huenefeld attended to the navigation, kept the log and, when required,
translated the conversations of the two pilots. For quite some time the
flight was reasonably uneventful. By day they generally plotted their
course by the sun, by night they shot the stars. Every few hours a smoke
bomb was dropped to check the drift. With the coming of night the first
of the problems arose. First, the lights on the instrument panel went out
and the pilots could read them only when the Baron used his pocket
flashlight to indicate the essential instrument.

Then the reek of fuel suffused through the cockpit when a fuel pipe
snapped. "Fitzmaurice took the flashlight from Huenefeld and crawled
back to the point where the pipe came out of the fuel tanks. We had no
dividing wall between the tanks and the pilot's cabin. The pipes ran
along the floor and that's where the leak was. Fitzmaurice found it and

The Junkers *Bremen* being prepared for its second Atlantic try at Baldonnel, Ireland. (*National Air & Space Museum, Smithsonian Institution*)

The *Bremen*, with the redoubtable Koehl at the controls, in flight. (*National Air & Space Museum, Smithsonian Institution*)

The Junkers *Bremen* being put back together after its unscheduled landing on Greenly Island after it had become the first aircraft to cross the Atlantic flying from east to west, the most difficult direction. (*Courtesy of National Museum of Science & Technology, Ottawa, Canada*)

repaired it with insulating tape, I believe. It all took place very quickly. The engine didn't even begin to miss." Nor, the taciturn Koehl might have added, did the plane even begin to burn.

With the coming of daybreak, Friday, April 13, 1928, the three men found themselves in a spot that Charles Levine would never have experienced. He simply would not have been up on a Friday the thirteenth; but they were and the day began with the demise of their compass and a

OPPOSITE Floyd Bennett and Bernt Balchen, who were sent on a pointless mission to "rescue" the crew of the *Bremen* from Greenly Island. Both pilots were ill with influenza, but proceeded nonetheless at the cost of Bennett's life. (*National Air & Space Museum, Smithsonian Institution*)

Bennett died afterward autographed this but

Balchen

thickening of the overcast. In a word or two: they did not have the slightest idea of where they were. Koehl began to consider the realities. Although they had started with sufficient fuel, they had been flying for nearly a day and a half buffeted by a strong head wind which cut down their air speed to barely sixty miles an hour. What with their rather imprecise navigation it was unlikely that they were anywhere near Mitchel Field, New York, their destination. But they must be near land somewhere. He decided, "We'll keep on flying till we reach land."

With the cloud cover thick they hardly realized that they were already over land—way off course, perhaps, but over land nonetheless. Then through a rift in the clouds they spotted a coastline and a ship, apparently frozen in the ice. That, at least, was a welcome sign of life in a barren landscape.

Taking over from Fitzmaurice, Koehl brought the Junkers down lower to inspect the terrain. As they dipped around again the "ship" emerged from the mists as a lighthouse. The area around it was not inviting, a jumble of snow drifts, ice and, no doubt, snow and ice-covered boulders. They had no idea of their whereabouts but it was a definite port in the storm—and they had to alight somewhere soon. Circling the snow-incrusted rubble, Koehl spotted a small, reasonably smooth area, obviously a frozen-over pond. This would have to serve, so he set the plane down onto it as gently as possible. The wheels touched the surface, the plane settled down and suddenly there was a lurching crunch as the landing gear ripped away when it struck an outcropping of ice. The *Bremen* skidded, tipped onto the nose, damaging the propeller, and then ground to a stop in a flurry of snow. None of the men aboard the Junkers was injured and—wherever they were—they were safe after thirty-six and one-half hours of grueling, blind and confusing flying.

The keeper of the lighthouse quickly arrived and the fliers learned that they had pancaked onto tiny Greenly Island, just off the northern tip of Newfoundland (which they had not been able to see in the driving snow) in the Strait of Belle Isle. They had missed the United States completely and were nearly a thousand miles off course. Greenly Island's total population of fourteen very quickly attended to the comfort of the three intrepid airmen and sent word out (via a telegraph station twenty miles distant at Port Armour) that the *Bremen* had safely (more or less) succeeded (more or less) in making the first crossing from Europe to America nonstop.

This was an achievement on par though in reverse to Lindbergh's and the wires sparkled with the news of the arrival of Koehl, Fitzmaurice and von Huenefeld. And following so soon after an unrelenting series of failures and disasters, what they had done (especially since for some hours they had been given up for lost) inspired jubilation and a round of quite frenetic "rescue" activities.

The spirit of the fraternity of the air soon revealed itself in the dispatching of Canadian bush pilots, including C. A. "Duke" Schiller of the failed *Royal Windsor* flight of the previous September. Another plane carried a full load of newsmen. Schiller's plane, a ski-fitted Fairchild, was to get the airmen out of their predicament (actually they were comfortable and safe) and back to civilization for the celebrations already being formulated.

Getting into the tiny island was no simple project and it took Schiller two attempts before he skidded in safely for a landing. He then took Fitzmaurice aboard for the flight back to Lake Sainte Agnes, Quebec. Koehl and von Huenefeld remained behind hoping to receive some parts with which to repair the lightly damaged Junkers and to finish off their flight by flying to New York.

The parts were shipped by plane from New York to Murray Bay, Quebec, and then to Greenly Island. The landing gear was repaired and a new propeller fitted and the *Bremen* was ready to fly. Koehl and von Huenefeld climbed aboard, ready to continue their journey. The engine warmed up and the plane moved over the uneven ground. Within minutes it had depleted the nearly level surface, a wheel caught on a rock or some ice and swerved onto a rough area and once again lost the landing gear and bent the propeller. The two German fliers decided to get out of Greenly in a lighter plane.

Excitement over their fate had grown to great proportions. Not only had Clarence Chamberlin flown up to Quebec to be on hand should he be needed, but Herbert Bayard Swope, editor of the bustling New York *World,* suffered a brainstorm. He knew that Byrd was getting ready for a new polar flight and had a Ford trimotor fitted with skis. Floyd Bennett, not quite fully recovered from the injuries he had received in the *America* crackup, and Bernt Balchen were the pilots and had just returned from Canada where they had been practicing landing and takeoffs on skis. They had also returned with bad influenza cases.

In spite of this Swope was able to convince Byrd to release the plane and pilots for use in the dramatic "rescue" of the transatlantic fliers stranded in Canada. His argument was that this would bring valuable pre-expedition publicity to Byrd's South Pole venture. When the agreement was reached Bennett was already down in bed with a temperature and a bad cough, but willingly left it to make the flight. The plane, by then, was in Detroit and the two men flew there to pick it up, but both immediately were placed in a hospital by the expedition sponsor, Edsel

OVERLEAF President Calvin Coolidge (left) welcomes the *Bremen* crew to Washington. To the President's left are Koehl, von Huenefeld and Fitzmaurice. Following the medal-pinning ceremony the airmen attended the funeral of Floyd Bennett. (*National Archives*)

Ford. Within a couple of days the trimotor was ready and the two men, still weak, left Detroit for Lake Sainte Agnes. The nine-hour flight was sheer misery for both men, but worse for Bennett, who was in no condition to continue once they had arrived. He was in fact seriously ill with pneumonia, had to leave the flight and was rushed to a hospital in Quebec.

When word of this new development was flashed to the world, Lindbergh made a dramatic night flight through a raging snow storm from Detroit to Quebec with a serum. It had been hopeless from the beginning, for the weakened Bennett was so ill he never recovered and died in the hospital in Quebec.

Meanwhile, Balchen, taking Fitzmaurice with him, flew up to Greenly Island and set the big Ford down on the ice near the shore and lifted Koehl and von Huenefeld off the island. The *Bremen* was eventually hauled across the ice by dog team and later shipped to the United States.

The death of Bennett took the edge off the entire "rescue," although Balchen went through with the original idea. He flew the crew of the *Bremen* to New York; the Ford was now named the *Floyd Bennett*. There were, of course, receptions and medal-pinnings and meetings with officials. Fitzmaurice, for example, was promoted to Major in the Irish Free State Air Corps and Koehl was re-embraced by Lufthansa, which offered him his job back at a higher salary and the position of a director of the company. Koehl rejected the offer. For von Huenefeld it was a final glow in a rapidly ebbing life, for in less than a year he would die of cancer.

The oddly assorted airmen were welcomed in Washington by President Coolidge and decorated by him; after which they attended Bennett's funeral at Arlington Cemetery and placed offerings on the grave. Except for this one nagging, lamentable aspect their reception in the United States was an unalloyed triumph, especially for Koehl and von Huenefeld, representatives of a once hostile nation in a recent unpopular war. The trio then returned to Europe, where they were exultantly received in Ireland, England and Germany. They had, after all, been the First to have crossed the Atlantic nonstop from east to west; they had completed the circle begun by Lindbergh. In too many ways the flight had not gone as they would have liked it—that hair-raising takeoff, for example—and then the small vexations of the flight itself, which might have led to catastrophe. There was, too, their faulty navigation thanks to compass failure and the ever confounding fog. The landing, however skillfully carried off by Koehl, left something to be desired—and there was, tragically, Floyd Bennett.

In other words, it had been a scarifying, remarkable adventure, and in spite of its Firstness, was not any way to run an airline. It had proved that It Could Be Done, but who would want to do it regularly? Besides there really wasn't much traffic running between Baldonnel and Greenly Island.

9

Lady
Lindy

With the Atlantic having been crossed in both directions, the one really outstanding remaining First belonged to the ladies. There was still that challenge to be met, despite the fate of Princess Anne, Elsie Mackay and Mrs. Grayson.

Wilmer Stultz had reason to be thankful for having withdrawn from Mrs. Grayson's doomed venture. He was not out of work long, for Byrd hired him to break in a new Fokker trimotor which he intended using for an Antarctic expedition. He also, more or less, was committed to ferrying the indefatigable Mibs Boll across the Atlantic for a consideration of $25,000 (he had already made her the First Woman to Be Flown Nonstop to Havana in Levine's *Columbia*, for whatever that was worth).

But Stultz was in no rush to fly the lady in a golden sweater across the pond and he leisurely spent his time breaking in the Fokker in the Boston neighborhood while Mibs made plans for getting off to Europe. It was about this time, in the spring of 1928, that two nearly simultaneous developments converged. Byrd had changed his mind about taking the Fokker with him to the South Pole, choosing instead a Ford trimotor (the one that would be named *Floyd Bennett*), and was looking for a likely purchaser. She was found in the matronly person of Mrs. Frederick Guest (formerly Amy Phipps of Pittsburgh), wife of a former member of the British Air Ministry and a force in British aviation. It was Mrs. Guest's fervent desire to be First.

The plane was duly purchased from Byrd, the wheels removed and pontoons added as a safety precaution. Mrs. Guest, in spite of the airmindedness of her family, was a center of controversy in her own home. High objections were raised to her making an Atlantic flight and the pontoons were the first concession. The final one was that she withdrew as an active member of the flight, insisting however that a woman be aboard when the plane, which she had named the *Friendship* (namely British and American), made the flight.

Preparations for the flight were obscured in much cloak-and-dagger activity. Wilmer—better known as Bill—Stultz continued flying the plane around, only now in company with an ex-Texan, Louis Gordon. As far as the world knew they were still working for Byrd. The problem now was to find the girl to fly in place of Mrs. Guest. This was done *sub rosa* mostly, perhaps to avoid a great deal of newspaper attention. A committee was formed to accomplish this, consisting of George Palmer Putnam, of the publishing house, and his friend, Hilton H. Railey, a former U.S. Army captain and a skilled public relations man who specialized in aviation. It was Railey who finally traced the project to Mrs. Guest and learned from her attorney that she had withdrawn and was seeking "the right sort of girl" as her replacement.

Soon Railey found himself involved in the *Friendship* venture and while in Boston one day mentioned the idea—off the record—to a friend, Rear Adm. Reginald K. Belknap, who answered, "I know a young social worker who flies. I'm not sure how many hours she's had, but I do know she's deeply interested in aviation and a thoroughly fine person. Call Denison House and ask for Amelia Earhart."

Railey called Denison House and guardedly asked the young woman to come to his office that afternoon. She was apparently an outspoken, forthright young woman and she refused to talk with him unless he gave her some idea of the reason for the call; she was then busy preparing for summer classes at Denison House as she was to be in charge of summer school that year. When she arrived at Railey's office she was accompanied by Marion Perkins, the head worker of the settlement house. Railey was immediately impressed: he saw a slender girl with short cropped hair, attractive though no beauty in the conventional sense; she had grace and poise and piercing gray eyes. She was not quite a girl, for on that April afternoon she was just three months short of her thirtieth birthday. Railey liked what he saw—and his public relations mind quickened when he realized how much Amelia Earhart resembled Charles Lindbergh. He could see it immediately, headlines beginning with "Lady Lindy. . . ."

His first words, according to his own version of the story of that meeting, were, "How would you like to be the first woman to fly the Atlantic?"

She would, of course, but there were a few details that would need working out. Railey was still playing it close to the vest and gave her only the barest of details. One of them which she did not care for was that she was merely a substitute for Mrs. Guest; Stultz and Gordon would attend to the flying. She did have some 500 hours of flying time, but it was true that she was not acquainted with instrument (or "blind") flying and had no experience with a multi-engined plane. Still there was the chance of being the first woman to fly over the Atlantic and Amelia Earhart agreed. She then had to submit to the judgment of the committee in New York consisting of Putnam, David T. Layman, Jr., Mrs. Guest's attorney and her brother, John S. Phipps. Apparently they liked what they saw also and what she said, for following that meeting she was officially selected to be First Lady Over the Atlantic.

The air of conspiracy continued to befog the enterprise and, besides being sworn to secrecy (as was her superior at Denison House, the only outsider who knew about the proposed flight), she was advised to keep away from the *Friendship* lest the show be given away prematurely. Thus she saw the plane only twice before the Fokker left Boston. "When I first saw *Friendship* she was jacked up in the shadows of a hangar in East Boston. Mechanics and welders worked nearby on the struts of the pontoons that were shortly to replace the wheels. The ship's golden wings, with their spread of seventy-two feet, were strong and exquisitely fashioned. The red orange of the fuselage, though blending with the gold, was chosen not for artistry but for practical use. If we had come down orange could be seen further than any other color."

The reason for the secrecy was in fact good. Once word leaked out it would have been impossible to have proceeded with the preparations without much unhealthy attention, which in turn might very well instigate an equally unhealthy competition.

By mid-May the plane was ready and all weather data had been gathered by the faithful Doc Kimball in New York. But there, as usual, was the rub. Three weeks were to go by during which the three participants grew restive. Miss Earhart, at least, kept busy by driving in her small open touring car (which she called "The Yellow Peril"), squired either by Railey or Putnam, dining exotically in various restaurants and seeing the plays. Louis Gordon was ill with food poisoning (thanks to Boston clams) and the more restless Stultz, grounded as he was, took to nipping at the brandy. And so it went with the weather alternating: when it was good over Boston, it was poor over the Atlantic and vice versa. Two attempted takeoffs had not worked out and the three fliers became more anxious and more tense.

Finally in the predawn of Sunday, June 3, 1928, the three climbed into the *Friendship* without fanfare or ceremony and Stultz, slightly hung over but in good form, lifted the plane off the water and headed the plane for Trepassey, Newfoundland. Originally another pilot, Lou Gower, was to have come along to spell Stultz "in case of sickness or accident," but the extra weight would have canceled out the takeoff again; as it was, six of the eight 5-gallon cans of fuel that were to have been carried in the fuselage were jettisoned to lighten the *Friendship* enough to get it off the water.

Although she referred to the flight as a "grand adventure" (this in a light-hearted though grim note to her father in the event that things did not work out), Amelia Earhart had little more to do than gaze in wonder at the sights and keep the log.

Once they were off the veil of secrecy was lifted, of course. Then about halfway on the flight to Trepassey they were forced down at Halifax by dense fog. That did it: "When we were forced down in Halifax our difficulties of maintaining secrecy increased. Publicity, we feared, was probably inescapable. But at all events, escape seemed worth an effort. And especially, so far as possible, we thought it wise to conceal the presence of a woman on the *Friendship*. The Sergeant [a Flight Sergeant at Halifax who helped moor the plane] had the surprise of his life when he came aboard the plane to look over the equipment and found me part of it."

Word eventually leaked out and newsmen descended on Halifax and the news swiftly went out to the world. "We have a sheaf of Halifax newspapers with strange assertions about us all," Amelia Earhart noted in the log. "They will make strange reading matter if we ever have opportunity to re-read them." One person who got the full import of the message was Mabel Boll, who had all the time assumed that Stultz would pilot her across the Atlantic in the *Columbia*. According to *The New York Times* she had expected Stultz to visit her that very day and "now he has gone and taken off with this other woman. . . ." Considering that Stultz was married, such "strange assertions" made interesting reading matter indeed. It also galvanized Mibs Boll into action. She hired Oliver LeBoutillier (who had been Stultz's copilot on the flight to Havana) and Arthur Argles as navigator and clambered aboard the *Columbia* and headed for Newfoundland.

When she arrived in Harbour Grace, at the other end of the oddly shaped peninsula on the southeastern end of Newfoundland from Trepassey, Miss Boll's first question was about the state of the *Friendship* flight. It was June 12 and all was well as far as Mibs was concerned: the *Friendship* had arrived from Halifax a week before and was still sitting in the harbor at Trepassey. The winds blew and the waters chopped and the *Friendship* bounced dangerously in the bay. There was little to do and there were endless rummy games, spontaneous diversions (such as sightseeing in Trepassey, where little was to be seen in the barren landscape) and Stultz entertained all with something called a "guitar harp," on which, self-taught, he could produce a recognizable version of "Jingle Bells." He also kept a wary eye on the weather and a ready hand on his brandy, the latter fact giving AE, as she was by then becoming known, some cause for alarm. Gordon, nursing his ptomaine by not eating local food and subsisting mainly on candy (thereby exhausting the complete supply of the local merchant), was unperturbed; he knew Bill Stultz would straighten out as soon as they were airborne.

But when would that be? They received messages of encouragement from friends, some of them hopefully humorous. One came from Putnam, who, knowing how little clothing AE had brought with her, wired: "Suggest you turn in and have your laundry done." The reply, collect, came: "Thanks fatherly Telegram. No washing necessary. Socks underwear worn out. Lost shirt to Slim [Gordon] at rummy. Cheerio." The communique was signed "AE."

In her log on June 12 she wrote:

> This has been the worst day.
> We tried for four hours to get away in a wind we have been praying for. The most unexpected and disappointing circumstance ruined the take-off. The receding tide made the sea so heavy that the spray was thrown so high that it drowned the outboard motors. As we gathered speed the motors would cut and we'd lose the precious pull necessary.

It was on this day also that Mibs Boll arrived at Harbour Grace to the north of them. The race was on.

Their enforced stay, now further aggravated by the presence of Mabel Boll, stretched into fifteen days. There were a couple of bright glimmers: the first was the arrival of Capt. Charles Kingsford-Smith in Brisbane, Australia, after taking off from Oakland, California, and stopping in Honolulu and Fiji. It was the first flight from the United States to Australia—and it had been made in a Fokker trimotor, the *Southern Cross*, which was similar to their *Friendship*. "They made it; so could we. Their accomplishment was a challenge."

The real challenger however (one never mentioned in AE's accounts) was to the north in the *Columbia*. That provided the second glimmer, for Mibs Boll was socked in also by the weather (later she would accuse the incorruptible Doc Kimball of supplying her with one set of weather reports and the *Friendship* crew with another. This was, of course, nonsense).

Then on Sunday, June 17, 1928, Trepassey opened up and the three piled into the *Friendship*; hopefully, before she left, AE prepared a simple telegram which read, "Violet." This was the code word meaning that they had taken off—and after three tries they finally did after discarding the final cans of extra fuel. The message was then sent, a half hour after the Fokker left the water.

From that moment on and for the next 20 hours and 40 minutes Amelia Earhart spent her time as a passenger in the aircraft, contributing nothing more than her log, filled with poetic descriptions of clouds and fog.

> . . . Marvelous shapes in white stand out, some trailing shimmering veils. The clouds look like icebergs. It seemed almost impossible to believe that one couldn't bounce forever on the packed fog we are leaving. The highest peaks of the fog mountains (oh, we didn't get out) are tinted pink, with the setting sun. The hollows are grey and shadowy. Bill just got the time. O.K. sez he. 10:20 London time my watch. Pemmican is being passed or just has been. What stuff! . . . I am getting housemaid's knee kneeling here at the table gulping beauty.

So she spent her time delighting in the wonders of the air, or marveling at the very idea of the flight and the machine and men who made it possible. She moved around the small space of the cabin, found a bottle of whisky, wondered about that, too, and tossed it out of one of the side windows. Stultz, apparently too busy with controlling the plane, never missed it; or, at least, he never mentioned missing it.

The burden fell upon Stultz, for the fog and clouds necessitated flying on instruments to keep on course; then the radio went out and there was no means of checking their position or direction. And so it went until the next day. Stultz shifted the plane down through the soup and from 3,000 feet: "Himmel! The sea! . . . We have been jazzing from 1000 to 3000 where we now are, to get out of clouds. At present there are sights of blue and sunshine, but everlasting clouds always in the offing. The radio is dead."

Later, at a lower altitude they sighted a large ocean liner but they were still not in good shape. The radio was out, they had only about an hour's supply of fuel and their flight path cut *across* that of the ship—it should have been parallel. Hoping to get their bearings they circled the ship (it was the *America*, although they did not know it). Unable to communicate by radio, Stultz "scribbled a note. The note and an orange to weight it, I tied in a bag with an absurd silver cord. As we circled the *America*, the bag was dropped through the hatch. But the combination of our speed, the movement of the vessel, the wind and the lightness of the missile was too much for our marksmanship. We tried another shot, using our remaining orange. No luck."

They considered landing beside the ship and letting it all go at that, but the water was rough and it seemed safer to continue on their original course, conserve fuel, and pray for land. What they did not know

At the reception in New York for the crew of the *Friendship*: Louis Gordon, Amelia Earhart and Wilmer Stultz. Although she was the center of attraction—as the first woman to cross the Atlantic by air—Amelia Earhart insisted Stultz and Gordon deserved the real credit, that she had been no more help to the flight than "a sack of potatoes." (*Culver Pictures*)

was that they were actually already over the Irish Sea—they had missed Ireland completely in the fog—and were about seventy miles from land. They continued on their way and within a half hour were rewarded with the welcome sight of, first, a fishing boat, then a few little boats and finally, out of the mist, the indistinct form of solid landscape.

Visibility was poor and they were flying at an altitude of about 500 feet. "With the gas remaining, we worked along as far as safety allowed. Bill decided to land. After circling a factory town he picked out the likeliest looking stretch [of water] and brought the *Friendship* down in it. The only thing to tie to was a buoy some distance away and to it we taxied."

They hadn't the slightest inkling of where they were and the natives of their locale exhibited only the slightest curiosity. They were marooned in the Middle of Carmarthen Bay, off the town of Burry Port, Wales. They waved to attract attention and three men working on a strip of railroad on shore stopped a moment, took a look and went back to work. It was as if an aircraft dropped into the bay every day.

AE decided to use her womanly wiles and waved a white towel to a small group of people that had gathered on the shore after a while. A gentleman took off his coat and waved it back. It was nearly an hour before a boat was finally launched from shore and the word went out. Phlegmatic Welshmen and women encircled the plane, which was eventually taken to a safe harbor. All thoughts of continuing on to Southampton, where Railey and Mrs. Guest were anxiously awaiting word of the *Friendship*, were abandoned. The tide was rushing out, and that would have complicated a takeoff, and besides the three were hungry and tired.

The greeting they received ashore was hectic. "There were six policemen to handle the crowd. That they got us through was remarkable. In the enthusiasm of their greeting those hospitable Welsh people nearly tore our clothes off."

Not the least of the enthusiasm was owed to the fact that the *Friendship* had carried the first woman across the Atlantic. "I tried to make them realize that all the credit belonged to the boys, who did the work. But from the beginning it was evident that the accident of sex—the fact that I happened to be the first woman to have made the Atlantic flight —made me the chief performer in our particular sideshow."

It was not a role that AE relished. Railey had been flown from Southampton as soon as he had word of their arrival and landed close to the *Friendship*. His first glimpse of AE was as she sat almost forlornly in the door of the *Friendship*. While he could understand her being fatigued, Railey imagined she should have exhibited some sign of excitement. She did admit it had been "a grand experience," but she had been little more than baggage, "like a sack of potatoes."

"Oh, well," she added, "maybe someday I'll try it alone."

Soon after, she was swept up in the round of receptions, and attracted a following of newsmen—who told her she was already known as "Lady Lindy"—both in England and later in the United States. Most of the fuss centered around Amelia Earhart, which made her uneasy. She was uncertain as to her future: "I still had no plan for myself. Should I return to social work, or find something to do in aviation? I didn't know— nor care. For the moment all I wished to do in the world was to be a vagabond—in the air." She did have a plan after all; like Lindbergh she wished to promote aviation.

As for Stultz, who had carried off most of the flight, he spent most of the trip home on the ship in a haze of brandy. "Drunkenness," he was heard to say, "is the only true form of happiness." For his part in the flight he was given $20,000 (Gordon earned $5,000 and AE nothing), but money apparently did not bring him happiness. A little over a year after the *Friendship* flight, on July 1, 1929, Stultz died, along with two passengers in his plane, when he crashed near Roosevelt Field.

Although she had gained nothing from the flight but the distinction of a First, Amelia Earhart did not suffer financially. Putnam commissioned a book on the flight, she began writing for magazines, she lectured, and literally became a "vagabond of the air," crossing the country from coast to coast and back in a little plane she had bought in Britain from Lady Mary Heath, one of that nation's lady fliers.

In her writings and speeches AE made a great point of the potential contribution by women to aviation; second only to flying was her determination to prove that women could hold their own in any field, but especially aviation. The year after the *Friendship* crossing she participated in the first Women's Air Derby (in which she came in third, one place ahead of another Atlantic hopeful, Ruth Elder). The year 1929 also saw the formation of the "Ninety-nines," an organization of women pilots (the name came from the number of original members). In 1930 Amelia Earhart held the women's speed record and the next year the altitude record for autogiros. By this time, also, she had married George Palmer Putnam. It was a curious match and, while Putnam was the driving extrovert to her unassuming introvert, Amelia Earhart was no shrinking violet. She maintained her own proud independence, admitted that she married with "reluctance," and did so only on her own terms. In short, she remained Amelia Earhart and never was Mrs. George Putnam.

Putnam, who thrived on action and excitement, not only was active in his publishing firm, but also produced films (one was the aviation epic *Wings*), dabbled in public relations and, in fact, served in that capacity for his wife. Eventually he gave up publishing to give his full time to films and to his wife's career. He was a controversial figure and unpopular with many people, among them hard-bitten newsmen who often referred to him as a "lens louse" because of his penchant for managing to appear in most pictures taken of Amelia Earhart.

One of the main points of the agreement AE exacted from Putnam before their marriage was "let us not interfere with the other's work or play." (She had also said, "I shall not hold you to any medieval code of faithfulness to me, nor shall I consider myself bound to you similarly. . . .") She was a fascinating woman and a strong-minded one, and made it clear that she was her own master; that a man as driven as Putnam could have accepted her on her terms was a tribute to her strength of character and charm. He even went so far as to refer to himself (others maliciously did it often) as "Mr. Earhart." Meanwhile he spent his time promoting her and soon she was endorsing coffee, automobiles, luggage. She did refuse to lend her name to a hat she did not like and ordered the hat off the market. Putnam tried to explain that he had already made the deal and thousands of hats had already been made. AE wanted them unmade. Since she could not sue the hat company (Putnam had full power of attorney) she threatened to sue him if the silly hats ever appeared on the market. Needless to say they did not.

So it was that in the winter of 1931, at breakfast, when Amelia Earhart looked up at her husband and asked, "Would you mind if I flew the Atlantic?" he knew her mind was made up and there was nothing he could do, even if he did mind. Besides, he could see the beauty of such an enterprise in terms of publicity, renown and other benefits that would occur to a business manager.

One aspect of the old race was still open: to be the first woman Atlantic soloist. The previous summer her friendly rival, Ruth Nichols, had gotten as far as St. John (New Brunswick), where she cracked up in making a landing, wrecking her Lockheed Vega and suffering a bad back injury. That year, too, had opened with a sad event: the loss of Beryl Hart, who, with copilot-navigator William S. MacLaren, had attempted to become the first woman to pilot a plane across the Atlantic. Mrs. Hart, widow of a New York advertising man, actually held a transport pilot's license, but to no avail. She and MacLaren were lost somewhere between Bermuda and the Azores in January, 1931. Ruth Nichols made her try in June, then returned to the United States in a stretcher and a cumbersome plaster cast in a plane piloted by Clarence Chamberlin—and vowing publicly to make another attempt the following year. So were two others, Laura Ingalls and Elinor Smith, both fine pilots. And there was also, but saying nothing, Amelia Earhart.

She went about her preparations quietly; the plane she had chosen for the flight was her faithful Lockheed Vega which she had been flying for about two years on her lecture tours. She had in fact flipped over in it while making a landing at Norfolk, Virginia. This had happened because, as she was pulling back on the stick for the landing, the cabin door unaccountably opened behind her and she sprawled back into the cabin. In her attempts to regain equilibrium she stepped hard on the brakes and the plane, its wheels locked, was carried by momentum onto its back. Neither Amelia Earhart nor her passenger was injured, but the plane required attention and was shipped to the Detroit branch of Lockheed. There it was put in good shape again, with the most drastic alteration being a change of fuselage.

When she decided to fly the Atlantic she had the plane put in the hands of Bernt Balchen, who strengthened the fuselage, added fuel tanks and instruments; a new Pratt & Whitney Wasp engine was installed. Since Balchen was known to be preparing for an Antarctic flight with Lincoln Ellsworth, his preparations at Teterboro Airport in New Jersey were assumed to be connected with that flight and not Amelia Earhart. Thus was she able to avoid publicity during the early phases.

To prepare herself for the solo flight, Amelia Earhart spent a great deal of time in the Lockheed practicing instrument flying and, to a limited extent, navigation. With Balchen serving as chief adviser, confidant and smoke screen for the press, she was able to prepare for the flight without fanfare. "For several reasons it seemed wise not to talk about the proposed flight in advance," she stated. "After all, there was nothing to talk about until it became an actuality, and from the start I definitely planned that I might abandon it at any time." Only Putnam, Balchen and her cousin, Lucy Challis, were aware of Amelia Earhart's plan. Not one let a word out to anyone. Miss Challis, however, wondered why, as would others once they knew. After all, the Atlantic *had* been flown time and again (even if not by a woman alone).

"It was clear in my mind that I was undertaking the flight merely for the fun of it," was her answer. "I chose to fly the Atlantic because I wanted to. It was, in a measure, a self-justification—a proving to me, and to anyone interested, that a woman with adequate experience could do it." Her agreement with Balchen, no daredevil ace, was that if at any moment he felt that neither she nor the Lockheed was capable of the flight "I would quit, and no harm done."

Balchen had no doubts and the sole remaining unanswered question lay with the weather. While Balchen attended to the plane at Teterboro and Amelia Earhart awaited word either at her home in Rye, New York, or at the airport, her husband spent his time haunting the office of Doc

Another outstanding lady flier of the Thirties, and friend of Amelia's, Ruth Nichols, who also wished to make an Atlantic flight. Her hopes ended with the crash of her plane at St. John, New Brunswick, in June, 1931. (*National Air & Space Museum, Smithsonian Institution*)

Kimball. The more favorable weather would begin to appear in May so that the triangle—New York, Rye, Teterboro—grew tense.

On the morning of the nineteenth, the weather not having proved cooperative over the past few days and not promising much for the future, Amelia Earhart drove over to Teterboro while her husband took his post at Dr. Kimball's office. When she arrived she was informed that a call had come from New York and, calling Kimball's office, she was informed by Putnam that finally they had a break in the weather, particularly from New York to Harbour Grace, Newfoundland, from which she intended to begin the hop.

It was then about noon; she made up her mind on the spot that the flight would begin at three that afternoon. There was only time to dash back to Rye (without lunch), where "I changed into jodhpurs and windbreaker, gathered up my leather flying suit, maps and a few odds and ends and raced back to the field."

To enable her to rest for the Atlantic flight Balchen flew the plane,

Mechanic Eddie Gorski, Amelia Earhart and Bernt Balchen, her technical advisor on the Atlantic flight, at Teterboro Airport, New Jersey, before her Atlantic flight in the spring of 1932. (*National Air & Space Museum, Smithsonian Institution*)

aboard which also was Eddie Gorski, the mechanic. They left Teterboro at 3:15 P.M. and landed at St. John, New Brunswick, three hours and forty minutes later. The next morning, which happened to be May 20 (exactly five years since Lindbergh's flight), they continued on to Harbour Grace, arriving there shortly after two in the afternoon. Putnam had already dispatched the weather reports: "The outlook wasn't perfect but it was promising."

While Balchen and Gorski made final checks AE took a little nap; by seven she was in the cockpit ready to go, after shaking hands with Balchen and Gorski. "The southwest wind was nearly right for the runway. At twelve minutes after seven, I gave her the gun. The plane gathered speed, and despite the heavy load rose easily. A minute later I was headed out to sea."

For several hours, with the sky a spectacular spectrum of colors as she flew away from the setting sun, there were no problems. She centered her various instruments, adjusted controls and thoroughly enjoyed the view

Amelia Earhart, alone, climbs into the cockpit of her Lockheed Vega. (*National Air & Space Museum, Smithsonian Institution*)

from about 12,000 feet. "And then something happened that has never occurred in my twelve years of flying. The altimeter . . . failed. Suddenly the hands swung around the dial uselessly and I knew the instrument was out of commission for the rest of the flight."

That was the first thing that went wrong. As long as she could see, all would be fairly well. But if and when the weather souped up she would never really be certain of the altitude. "About 11:30, the moon disappeared behind some clouds, and I ran into rather a severe storm with lightning, and I was considerably buffeted about. . . ." This ordeal, with the rain lashing against the windshield and with the cockpit echoing to the sound of the rain's diminutive hammers, continued for an hour before she caught a glimpse of the moon again.

Certain which way was up, she decided to climb out of the clouds to avoid further storminess, if possible. Steadily the Vega rose through the dark, bulbous clouds. It was gratifying to see that it was clearer at the higher altitude; on the other hand it was not especially comforting to realize that she had probably gotten off course in the storm. Then she noticed that the plane was climbing sluggishly and little chunks of something began forming on the windshield. This could only be ice. The motor began to complain of the extra weight it carried as the ice formed on the wings. Then her tachometer (which measured the rpm's of the propeller) became clogged with ice "and spun around the dial."

She had to get back down to the warmer air before her plane became too heavy and the wing too misshapen to fly. It would then stall and dive into the ocean. The problem was further aggravated because of the failed altimeter—in the darkness she would never know how high she was above the water. She selected a more or less neutral middle ground, "that is, to fly under the altitude at which I picked up ice and over the water by a sufficient margin. This would have been much easier to do had I been able to know my height."

She kept her eyes on the instruments, holding the plane to its course, level and at the right speed. One thing that did unnerve her somewhat was the flame. About four hours after she had left Newfoundland she noticed a break in the manifold ring which carried the exhaust from the engine. Flames shot out of the break but since the manifold was constructed of very heavy metal she was reasonably certain it would hold for the flight. However, as the darkness deepened, "I was indeed sorry that I had looked at the break at all because the flames appeared so much worse at night than they did in the daytime."

But there was plenty to occupy her in the cockpit to distract her attention from the crack in the manifold. When daylight came—she had been flying for about ten hours—she found herself sandwiched between two cloud layers. Beneath the lower ones, "little puffy white clouds," she saw the Atlantic. Soon the clouds below, gathered by a northwest wind, resembled a field of snow, and the ocean again vanished. The sun broke through the upper layer and dazzled her so that even dark glasses would not help. She decided to descend through the cloudy "snow field" to see what could be seen, hoping to spot a ship or boat to assure her. It was breakfast time but she was strangely unhungry; her total ration for the entire flight was a can of tomato juice.

Flying close to the water she wondered where precisely she was. Despite her close attention to the gyro-compass through the night, there was still the chance of having strayed during the trip's many vicissitudes. She glanced at the manifold and noted that the break had become larger although the flames were not as pronounced. But then the manifold began vibrating, striking the fuselage, which was no happy sound.

She had been flying for more than ten hours and it was about time to switch to the reserve fuel tanks, the wing tanks being fairly depleted. But then came one final misadventure: the cockpit filled with the smell of fuel—there was a leak in the gauge. She then "decided I should come down at the very nearest place, wherever that was."

With a manifold rattling and fuel leaking into the cockpit it was a wise decision. Doc Kimball had informed her that she could encounter rain should she get too far south of her course, which is where she thought she had wandered in the storm. She set compass due east for Ireland. (Curiously in her own account she never mentions her intended destination, which is sometimes given as Paris. Her entire purpose was "to fly the Atlantic," not to duplicate Lindbergh's flight to Paris. Had that been true she should have begun the flight, as he did, from Roosevelt Field in New York. In her own story she does not mention the fact that she set out on the same date, plus five years, that Lindbergh had. This congruity must be attributed to the weather, not to her desire to compete with Lindbergh in any way.)

She flew on and then imagined she saw land, but she had imagined that before and it had all too often turned out to be low-lying clouds. But as she approached it did not change form and finally solidified into real land. She passed over the coastline searching for a place to land; thundershowers in the foothills farther inland obscured the ceiling. "Not having the altimeter and not knowing the country, I was afraid to plow through those lest I hit one of the mountains, so I turned north where the weather seemed to be better and soon came across a railroad which I followed hoping it would lead me to a city, where there might be an airport."

She came upon a settlement, but it was so thoroughly rural that there were no airports to be found; she "found lovely pastures instead." She later admitted that she had succeeded "in frightening all the cattle

AE (*U.S. Air Force*)

in the county," as she swooped in low to select a likely place on which to alight. She spotted a nice sloping meadow and gently eased the Vega into it with scarcely a bump. She switched off the engine for the first time in 15 hours, 18 minutes. The silence was unreal, for she had become accustomed to the engine's roar, the rattle of the manifold—not to mention the reek of fuel. Wherever she was, she had made it.

She had landed on the farm of Patrick Gallagher, near the town of Culmore, Londonderry, Ireland. It was Gallagher who first approached the plane and was astonished to see a woman poking a touseled head out of the cockpit. "Hello," she announced, "I'm from America."

The nearest phone was five miles distant and she was taken there by her bemused "host." Amelia Earhart placed a call to George Putnam, her first words being a triumphant, "I did it!" Later she would publicly try to place her feat in some perspective with her customary candor. "This trip," she said, "was simply a personal gesture. My flight has added nothing to aviation but I hope it has meant something to women in aviation. If it has, I shall feel justified, but I can't claim anything else."

Except that she was the first woman to fly the Atlantic alone and only the second pilot up to that time to make it solo. In addition, it had been the speediest crossing to that time and she had also captured the women's distance record. But in the fullest sense, it had not contributed anything to aviation; one New York newsman even went so far as to point out, rather ungallantly, that "Amelia Earhart has given us a magnificent display of useless courage. . . ." But then, she had never claimed any more than that for the flight. In fact, when she was awarded the Gold Medal of the National Geographic Society by President Herbert Hoover on June 21, after her triumphant return to the United States, she graciously accepted the medal and then said, "I think that the appreciation of the deed is out of proportion to the deed itself. . . . I shall be happy if my small exploit has drawn attention to the fact that women, too, are flying."

She had become the most celebrated woman flier in the world and quickly found herself enmeshed in the celebrity net. She had fully proved herself and could readily with a clear conscience discard her own description of herself as a "sack of potatoes," but at the same time she was driven to seek new conquests, to break new records. She did this because she sincerely believed that there was a niche for women in aviation and that her own accomplishments would vindicate this and promote the concept at the same time. This was often the theme of her speeches and her courses at Purdue University, where she taught briefly. Another favorite topic was the important contribution that youth could make to all aspects of living, including aviation. She was a remarkable person, at least a generation ahead of her time—and she solidly refused to be lumped with a "lost generation," as were so many of her contemporaries.

But she was, in a sense, lost. She continued to make random flights which broke established records but contributed little beyond a touch of public relations to her causes. She broke various transcontinental speed records, including her own; she made the first solo flight from Honolulu to California in 1935; she made the first solo flight between Los Angeles and Mexico City and so on. Only one avenue remained to her, since she had flown the Atlantic, the Pacific and across the country, besides the various inter-city flights, and that was a flight around the world.

This too had already been accomplished, but not by a woman, and she wanted to be that woman. After one false start in March, 1937, which ended prematurely when the plane veered off a runway and crashed at Honolulu, she set out again in July and made it as far as New Guinea. Somewhere between Lae and Howland Island in the Pacific Amelia Earhart and her navigator, Fred Noonan, disappeared. Aviation lost one of its most attractive figures on that day, one who had, despite her denials, contributed much to aviation.

Both she and Lindbergh, following their transatlantic flights, had returned from Europe highly impressed with the passenger airlines there, while the United States continued to sputter along with mail routes. Both made solid contributions to the growth of passenger flying in the United States. Amelia Earhart's was a bit more subtle, for she had shown that women were not congenitally afraid of flying. She had proved that commercial flying was safe and no doubt encouraged more women to fly, even if not in the adventurous style she herself loved. That she ultimately lost was, to her at least, a part of the game during an adventurous, risky time. Her attitude toward the odds was best expressed in the letter she wrote to her mother just prior to her *Friendship* Atlantic crossing (to be read tearfully should the flight fail and to be laughed over if it should, as it did, succeed); it certainly summed up the credo of a remarkable human being.

"Even though I have lost," she wrote, "the adventure was worth while . . . My life has been very happy, and I didn't mind contemplating its end in the midst of it."

10

*The Last
of the Firsts
and Flights to
Anywhere*

The Thirties, with their sobering Depression, did not curtail Atlantic flying. But they did bring the flights under closer scrutiny, criticisms, questioning of motives and even attempts at governmental control. Where once the newspapers anxiously swarmed around the intrepid pilot who jauntily announced he—or she—would hop the pond, they now editorially questioned the point of the enterprise. Newsmen had become blasé about a succession of events that had become monotonous and *The Saturday Evening Post*, a weekly magazine which had almost religiously and exhaustively covered aviation in the past, spoke out in 1932 intimating that people were "bored to death with oceanic flights and the pilots who make them."

Just about everything that could be had been done. Flying exploits simply no longer merited the front pages as they had during the exciting latter Twenties. Unless the pilot happened not to make it—then he would achieve a brief front-page flurry, luridly illustrated with shots of his smashed plane, before he was "forgotten like the rest."

Obviously, some fliers were not motivated by whatever ephemeral glory they might gain through the press. Many were driven by a simple love of flying, by an adventurous desire to accomplish an ineffable something, whatever that was, without regard to its "contribution to science" or to aviation. It was little more than a form of self-expression (as so gracefully admitted by Amelia Earhart), a deadly one at times, but exhilarating, venturesome and just plain fun.

Still, considering that so many of the early flights did contribute to the improvement of aircraft, engines, flying and navigational techniques, these very advancements, in turn, inspired further proving flights. The refinements led to greater effort and, sometimes, to greater risks. But certain deductions could be made from the fact that aircraft were capable of flying longer distances at greater speeds and, with sad exceptions now and then, more safely. Much depended upon the professionalism of the pilot, how much preparation went into the flight and the intelligent measurement of risk and its diminution by using dependable engines, radio and navigation instruments. What the flights pointed to, of course, was the eventual establishment of regular transatlantic air travel.

But when the decade began that denouement was still nearly ten years away. However, the Atlantic continued to be crossed with surprising regularity.

The first flight of the year was not purely an Atlantic flight, but part of a greater enterprise. This was the crossing in June, 1930, of the old *Southern Cross*, veteran of the 1928 Pacific flight, on its way around the world. At the stick was Charles Kingsford-Smith, a veteran himself, accompanied by a fine pick-up crew. Evert van Dyck, on leave from Holland's KLM, was copilot; he was also an experienced man in blind flying. The radio operator was a New Zealander, John W. Stannage, and the navigator, picked up in Ireland, was Capt. J. Patrick Saul of the Irish Free State Army Air Corps.

Kingsford-Smith's plan was to fly from Ireland directly to New York, but it was found that when fully loaded with fuel, it was impossible to get the *Southern Cross* off the runway at Baldonnel. So the Fokker was flown to nearby Portmarnock, a strip of beach, fueled up, and it took off from there. The usual westward flight problem confronted Kingsford-Smith: the head winds which cut air speed considerably and gorged the fuel. The fog came tripping in on elephant feet and navigation became a scientific guessing game. Obviously New York was out and all three men voted to land at the first possible strip, which turned out to be Harbour Grace, Newfoundland.

This haven was found by merest luck, for although Saul was certain they were near or over land, he had no real conception of where they were. They circled for hours, consuming fuel and waiting for a break in the fog. When they passed over the coastline heading inland they had no idea they had done it, thanks to the thick fog. But for an instant there was a break and Kingsford-Smith tipped the wing through it and to his delight (and surprise) found Harbour Grace below. The *Southern Cross* was the second plane to make the east-to-west crossing, but unlike its predecessor, the *Bremen*, was capable of proceeding the next day (June 26, 1930) to its announced destination for a gala reception, after which the crew of the *Southern Cross* continued on its world-girdling flight.

Following Kingsford-Smith's feat the Atlantic air began churning again to the reverbation of engines and the whirr of wings. Three of the attempts got practically nowhere, although happily without serious damage, before being abandoned. One flight from Germany to New York, in stages, was successfully completed in a Dornier Wal, under the command of ambitious flying instructor Wolfgang von Gronau—although his pilot was Eduard Zimmer. But the flight hardly broke any

The history-making *Southern Cross*, the Fokker trimotor in which Charles Kingsford-Smith not only flew the Atlantic but the Pacific too. (*National Air & Space Museum, Smithsonian Institution*)

Costes and Bellonte, first airmen to fly from Paris to New York, thus completing the circle initiated by Lindbergh. (*Musée de l'Air, Paris*)

The Breguet XIX of Costes and Bellonte flying over New York City after crossing the Atlantic. (*Musée de l'Air, Paris*)

new ground; it was the mixture as before, with the same problems, the same—luckily—happy ending and the same warm reception in New York.

The year's epochal flight, however, originated in France. The moving force behind it was Dieudonné Costes (veteran of the first South Atlantic crossing, with Joseph Le Brix, in 1927); his navigator was Maurice Bellonte. Their aim was to do a reverse-Lindbergh, to succeed where Nungesser and Coli had failed, to fly nonstop from Paris to New York. In the summer of 1929 they had started out in a Breguet, but returned in disappointment when fuel problems and weather turned against them. The mileage accumulated, however, proved their plane could, indeed, remain airborne long enough to make the New York to Paris flight.

The plane, named *Point d'Interrogation (Question Mark)* for some mysterious reason or other, was the same Breguet with which they had accumulated many records. The cost of the plane had been borne to a generous extent by perfumer François Coty. It was a great handsome plane with fabric-covered wings and fuselage (except for the nose section). It was finished in a bright red, except for the metallic nose and decorations of stripes on the fuselage and rondels on the wings in the French national colors. A large question mark was painted on the fuselage, just fore of the front cockpit. A stork in flight, symbol of a famed *Cigogne Escadrille* (Spa. 3) to which Costes belonged during the war, was affixed to the fuselage sides aft of the rear cockpit. The cockpits were not enclosed, although the forward (pilot's) one was partially protected by a windshield and adjustable sidescreens. A more modern touch was the fixed landing gear with streamlining "pants" over the wheels.

At nearly eleven o'clock on the morning of September 1, 1930, Costes and Bellonte took their respective posts in the *Question Mark* and took off from Le Bourget. The weather they had been waiting for was finally promised by France's Dr. Kimball, André Viaut. No roaring crowd was on hand to speed the two men on their way; their flight, it was supposed, was just another test hop. Although they had discarded the auxiliary fuel tanks which were carried under the wings, there was still enough fuel in the Breguet's fuselage and upper wing tanks to keep it aloft for some fifty hours. About four hours later, when the plane was sighted over southern Ireland, it was obvious that Costes and Bellonte meant business. They were on no test hop.

The flight was remarkably trouble free, though not without some expected difficulties. Bellonte kept in constant touch with ships along their route—the radio worked beautifully. So did Bellonte as navigator and Costes as pilot, both of whom had to contend in his individual manner with head winds and side winds. Head winds, which had so contributed to the cancellation of their earlier attempt, were reckoned with, but side winds, which caused them to drift southward, were troublesome. This made it necessary to point the plane in one direction in order to be certain they were traveling in another, on course, much like tacking a sailboat across the wind.

By six in the morning (now September 2) word was flashed from Newfoundland that they had been sighted over St. Pierre Island; four hours later they passed over Nova Scotia. This gave plenty of time for excitement to begin mounting in New York (not to mention Paris and all of France), so that when Costes came in to land at Curtiss Field, Long Island, escorted by a squadron of fighter planes, thousands of people were waiting for the two French fliers. Among the first to greet them when they struggled out of their cockpits, stiff after 37 hours and 18 minutes in the air, was Charles Lindbergh. It was fitting, for Costes and Bellonte had at that moment completed the complementary flight to his, and had made the first Europe to America crossing of the Atlantic by air.

Costes and Bellonte were treated to the full honors of a New York ticker-tape parade and reception; as a little special touch they presented Byrd with the altimeter from the *America* which had been recovered from the beach where the plane had crash-landed. But there was not much time for ceremony. On September 4 the two men took off again headed for Dallas, Texas, to make a bid for a prize offered by Col. W. E. Easterwood. The Colonel had offered $25,000 to the first man who could fly from Paris to Dallas (with an allowance for a stopover at New York), thus bringing the Texas city into the aerial sweepstakes and incidental fame.

After a jubilant tour of the United States, Costes and Bellonte returned to France by ship and were given an even greater reception by their own countrymen, besides the usual honors that such occasions merit.

The flight of Costes and Bellonte exhausted, or so it seemed, all the Atlantic Firsts. But that was not to be. A Canadian pilot, J. Errol Boyd, dusted off Levine's old *Columbia*, renamed it *Maple Leaf* and took off in the company of an American, Harry P. Connor, headed for London on October 9, 1930. A clogged fuel line forced them down, considerably short of their goal, in the Scilly Islands, off the extreme western tip of England. They had not really proved anything, but the Bellanca became the first plane to cross the Atlantic twice.

This same kind of nonconclusive flight continued to be made with the usual endings, some fatal. The Atlantic was crossed also as part of a greater plan, such as Kingsford-Smith's flight in the *Southern Cross* (1930). And there were others which were not intended as mere Atlantic flights, among them the crossing of Wiley Post and Harold Gatty in their round-the-world flight in 1931; Jimmy Mattern and Bennett Griffen followed in 1932, but cracked in Russia; a German crew, led by the ever active Wolfgang von Gronau, passed over the Atlantic in their successful world flight. In 1933 Italo Balbo led a fleet of Savoia-Marchetti flying boats as part of a good-will flight to Chicago; that same year Wiley Post made history when he flew solo around the world (and incidentally over the Atlantic). In 1933 also Charles and Anne Lindbergh rather casually flew the Atlantic on a survey flight for Pan American Airways; finally, in 1938, Howard Hughes and a crew of four crossed over on their epochal flight around the world.

These flights underscored the fact that the Atlantic was by then relegated to a secondary place in the plans of airmen. True, it was not crossed regularly, and continued to be a challenge, but just about everything had been done. What else was there?

Leave it to the human imagination to think of something, even if it rather begs the issue. In the same summer in which Amelia Earhart succeeded in making her solo crossing, a young Scot (he was then twenty-seven) named James Mollison dreamed up an idea for a flight.

No tyro, Mollison had been flying since his eighteenth year when he was commissioned in the Royal Air Force. Following this stretch of service he became an instructor, later an airline pilot in Australia; in 1931 he first attracted attention with a record-making flight from Australia to England in a small de Havilland Gypsy Moth in the (then) remarkable time of 8 days, 19 hours. The next year he made a record dash from Lympne, England, to Cape Town, South Africa, taking 4 days, 17 hours to do it. This, too, was accomplished in a diminutive de Havilland, for Mollison became a staunch advocate of the light plane.

Handsome, quiet-spoken, with a flair for dashing attire, Jim Mollison was the perfect image of the popular conception of the "intrepid" airman. To round off the picture, Mollison married in the summer of 1932 a young woman pilot, Amy Johnson (who herself had already accumulated a few flying records). They were, next perhaps to the Lindberghs, the world's most celebrated flying couple.

About the time he was considering marriage, Mollison also had an idea that he could fly the Atlantic in a tiny de Havilland Puss Moth, a popular light plane of the period. Small, light and comparatively low-powered, the Puss Moth was hardly the plane anyone would have selected for an Atlantic crossing—especially in the east-to-west route. Mollison went even further: the idea was to fly over, refuel and fly back. While the enterprise was frowned upon by the British authorities, Mollison managed to get permission and immediately got to work.

He discussed the weather and navigation with Kingsford-Smith's navigator, J. P. Saul, and, in fact, selected the same stretch of sand at Portmarnock, near Dublin, from which the Southern Cross had taken off, for his takeoff. The plane, named rather obviously (since the Mollisons had only recently married) The Heart's Content, was stripped of all equipment to make room for fuel and the few navigational aids that Mollison chose to carry. In his tiny craft, Mollison was literally hemmed in by fuel containers.

Pilot and plane were ready on August 18, 1932, when at around 11:35 in the morning the fragile-looking but heavily loaded little Puss Moth took off from the sandy beach after a run of nearly a mile and headed out over the Atlantic. Flying westward was none too difficult at first; the weather was clear, head winds not too strong and now and then he would sight a ship, which he could circle and watch the steam of the whistle toot him good speed. But by morning of the next day, Friday the nineteenth, the weather thickened and the wind strengthened. During a moment of clear sky, Mollison identified the coast of Nova Scotia, and soon after was flying over Halifax, which he could not see because of the fog.

For the next six grueling hours Mollison flew through fog and mist, lost. His navigation across the Atlantic had been flawless; he had made landfall right on target, but from then on he simply could not find New York. He wandered in the misty air until his once ample supply of fuel dwindled and he had no choice: he had to land. Landing the little Puss Moth through the soup, at least, was fairly simple and when he could see the ground, Mollison saw plenty of open fields near a cluster of farm buildings. He set the plane down gracefully and soon learned, to his chagrin, that he had landed at Pennfield Ridge, near St. John, New Brunswick, Canada. He had missed the United States completely. Despite this frustration he was safe on the ground and had made the first solo westward crossing, and he was the first ever to use a light plane over the North Atlantic (Comdr. H. C. MacDonald had attempted such a

Wolfgang von Gronau (center) who made no less than three Atlantic crossings (1930, 1931, 1932—the last as a leg in an around-the-world flight). To von Gronau's left are Fritz Albrecht and Edward Zimmer, two members of his crew; a third, Franz Hack, is not shown. (*U.S. Air Force*)

flight in 1928 and simply disappeared in his Gypsy Moth; in 1930 Squadron Leader C. S. Wynn-Eaton tried an east-west flight which was cut short when his Puss Moth crashed on takeoff).

Exhausted after a trip of nearly thirty hours, Mollison rested while de Havilland engineers came up to inspect the plane, which was in perfect shape. He then continued on to New York, where he was treated to a gala reception, and made plans for a return flight. Although, late in August, Mollison started out, he encountered heavy fog again over New Brunswick and came down in a strip of pasture for the second time. Although not injured, Mollison was obviously in a poor state and was told by a doctor to cancel the flight, for he was obviously suffering from nervous exhaustion. The flight over the Atlantic, the last wracking six hours over Pennfield Ridge, the New York reception—all these had taken their toll. Mollison was in no shape for a return match with the Atlantic air; wisely, he decided to return home by ship while he was still ahead of the game.

Not that he was through with the Atlantic; in February of 1933 he soloed across the South Atlantic and had an even grander scheme in mind. He and Amy Johnson would fly the North Atlantic to become the first husband-and-wife team to accomplish this feat—and more: they would then turn around and fly back with Baghdad as their objective to establish a new nonstop distance record. The plane would be another de Havilland, this time, however, a somewhat larger Dragon cabin biplane which they named *Seafarer*.

The first attempt to take off on June 8, 1933, from London's Croydon Airport was a failure. The runway proved too short for their Atlantic-equipped plane; still earth-bound when it ran out of concrete the plane ran into rough ground which ripped away the landing gear. That it did not burst into a burning funeral pyre for the Mollisons was a miracle, for the plane had a full load of fuel. They were not even injured and the repair job, which included a change of propellers, took a few weeks. By that time the Mollisons had selected a new jumping-off point, a clean strip of beach in Carmarthenshire, Wales.

At noon, July 22, 1933, Amy and Jim Mollison took off in the *Seafarer* and pointed its nose toward New York. Despite their spelling one another at the controls, the flight proved to be exhausting. Although fair weather had been predicted, it turned against them over the Atlantic and head winds reduced their speed. On the morning of the twenty-third some clearing made it possible to see icebergs and finally land, which they could identify as the coast of Newfoundland. Pushing on they continued southward for New York.

Darkness and low fuel supply overtook them before they sighted their objective and they decided that they would set down in the first

Amy Johnson Mollison wishing her husband Jimmy well as he prepares to take off in *The Heart's Content* to fly the Atlantic. (*National Archives*)

The de Havilland Puss Moth in which James Mollison crossed the Atlantic in 1932. (*National Air & Space Museum, Smithsonian Institution*)

The Bellanca, originally owned by James Fitzmaurice, later taken over by James Mollison and in which he made a record solo crossing of the Atlantic in 1936—his fourth flight over the Atlantic. Mollison renamed *The Irish Swoop* simply *Dorothy*. (*National Archives*)

Jimmy Mollison and Amy Johnson Mollison visiting President Franklin D. Roosevelt shortly after their joint Atlantic flight in 1933. (*National Archives*)

airport they saw. It turned out to be one at Bridgeport, Connecticut (just twenty minutes flying time from New York). Tired, again disappointed in being thwarted, Mollison had trouble landing on the strange runway. He made several passes before actually setting the plane down (he had been in the air for 39 hours), and overshot the runway. He also came in downwind—all of which carried the *Seafarer* out of the airport into a swamp, where it flipped over onto its back.

Realizing that a crash was inevitable Mollison luckily cut the engine so that they did not burn, but they were in bad enough shape. Even so, neither Mollison nor Amy Johnson was seriously injured, although he suffered a crack on the head that required thirty stitches to close. Both pilots were quickly taken to a nearby hospital; as for the plane, what the crash did not damage souvenir hunters completed, so that barely more than a skeleton and parts too heavy to carry remained.

Bandaged and free of the hospital, the Mollisons continued on to New York and to Washington where, accompanied by Amelia Earhart, they visited with President and Mrs. Franklin D. Roosevelt. While Amy Mollison remained as a guest with Amelia Earhart, Mollison returned to England by ship to acquire another plane, a similar de Havilland named *Seafarer II*. The Mollisons were determined to proceed with their original plan of returning to Europe, and farther, by air.

Finally in October they felt themselves ready for the return trip and had their plane poised again on a sandy beach, this time at Wasaga Beach near Ontario, Canada. But a combination of weight and the wrong wind defeated them; after several attempts to get off, the landing gear of *Seafarer II* collapsed and the Mollisons elected to forget the whole enterprise. They returned to England by ship; within three years the storybook aerial romance was over and the Mollisons went their separate ways. Mollison flew the Atlantic again in 1936, in a Bellanca named *Dorothy* (for his "very dear friend," the actress Dorothy Ward). This made him a four-time Atlantic crosser.

Amy Johnson (again) remained England's favorite lady flier. Although she did not make any further spectacular flights, she continued flying and, with the coming of the Second World War, served as a ferry pilot in the Air Transport Auxiliary. On one of her flights, in January, 1941, she was forced to parachute from a plane near London, landed in the Thames River and was drowned.

Mollison, too, drowned in a sense; though he survived the war he had become a serious drinker, which prevented him from making any further contributions to aviation.

The *Seafarer II*, however, did make the overwater flight; after the Mollisons had abandoned their attempt in October, 1933, the plane was bought by two Canadians, Capt. James Ayling and Leonard Reid. In

Italo Balbo, leader of a mass flight of Italian flying boats across the Atlantic in 1933. (*National Air & Space Museum, Smithsonian Institution*)

Savoia-Marchetti S-55s of Balbo's flying fleet winging over the Chicago World's Fair ("A Century of Progress") after completing a good-will flight that began in Italy. (*U.S. Air Force*)

August of 1934 they took off from Wasaga Beach and landed nearly
thirty-one hours later near London. They had hoped, as had the Mollisons, to set a distance record, but fuel. consumption brought them
down far short of their goal. They had to be content with having made
the first nonstop flight between Canada and England.

Shortly after the Mollisons sailed into a bad landing at Bridgeport
another record-breaking Atlantic flight was made, setting a distance
record of 5,657 miles (which would have been the mark for the Mollisons to beat had they ever gotten off in *Seafarer II*). The pilots were
Paul Codos (who doubled also as navigator) and Maurice Rossi, two
experienced French airmen with a number of records already to their
credit. Codos had flown with Costes in the *Question Mark* to establish
closed-course records; Rossi had participated in previous distance and
duration flights. The two men, though they hardly looked the part (they
were definitely not lean and raw-boned), were suited ideally for the
flight they hoped to make.

Their plane was a Blériot-Zappata 110 named *Joseph Le Brix* (to
honor the memory of the flier who, with Costes, had made the first

Paul Codos (left) and Maurice Rossi, French airmen who collected a great
number of records for France in their plane the *Joseph Le Brix. (Musée de
l'Air, Paris)*

nonstop South Atlantic crossing in 1927), and was designed specifically for distance flying. In some ways, with its high-aspect ratio wing—that is, narrow in chord width as compared with the span—and slender fuselage, it resembled a sailplane with an engine and propeller.

The two airmen, with a crated *Joseph Le Brix* aboard, left for the United States in June of 1933. For some reason, they encountered their first tribulations at the American Customs, which pothered over the crated aircraft. Not until the French Ambassador himself intervened could the parts of the plane be taken off the *Champlain* and carted to Floyd Bennett Field for assembly. As a touch of nostalgia, a mechanic named Paragot, who had assisted Blériot on his 1909 English Channel flight, had accompanied the Blériot-Zappata to assist in the assembly. What followed thereafter was a wait of more than a month as the weather went its own way.

The air was rife with international rivalry. As the two Frenchmen waited for the right weather, Wiley Post flew in and took off on his solo round-the-world flight. They met the hapless Marchese de Pinedo, fallen from grace with Il Duce, waiting with his Bellanca the *Santa Lucia* for a

The Blériot 110, *Joseph Le Brix*, in which Codos and Rossi broke the world's distance record—New York to Rayak, Syria, a distance of 5,657 miles—in the summer of 1933. (*Musée de l'Air, Paris*)

weather break also (when it did come early in September, de Pinedo died in the crash of the plane during the takeoff). Another Italian, Gen. Italo Balbo (who had displaced de Pinedo in Mussolini's good graces), was winging westward with an armada of flying boats for Chicago's World's Fair and on to what would become a round trip, the first for an entire formation of aircraft. It did not amuse Codos and Rossi at all, after the Balbo armada had arrived, to be asked by an Italian representative to cancel their distance attempt in order to fly the films of Balbo's flight back to England and Europe.

Fuming, the duo awaited the break in the weather which did not come until early August. The plane was fueled up with a special mixture of gas and benzol, and food and water were placed aboard. To discourage the formation of ice, various critical parts of the plane were lathered with a mixture of lard and wax. There were those who were certain that with a load of nearly 1,400 gallons of fuel in the plane, it could not possibly take off. Early on the morning of August 5, 1933 (with Balbo already preparing for his return trip), Codos and Rossi demonstrated that it was possible to get the heavy *Joseph Le Brix* out of Bennett Field, although not before traversing practically all of the runway before lifting off. And then they had to skim the surface of the Atlantic while building up speed for a climb, nearly colliding with fishing boats on the way. But, persevering, they remained airborne and climbing and were actually on their way.

Beyond Boston they ran into the rough weather that Doc Kimball had promised them. They fought turbulence and hail, spelling one another every few minutes at the controls. But, despite that, they managed to keep on course and once enough fuel had been consumed to lighten the load they were able to climb to a quieter layer of sky. And so they flew through the night. But the next day, August 6, brought its share of weather: clouds, which forced them to fly blind, and icing, which froze the carburetor. The latter problem was solved, engine sputtering, by dropping down to a lower, warmer altitude (about 1,000 feet). By early evening they had crossed over the French coast, where they were met by a formation of French aircraft and escorted to Paris. Theirs was the second plane which had flown directly from New York to Le Bourget, although they did not land. Instead, they circled the field for a while, dropping messages to their families and friends, and even their own account of the trip so far for a French newspaper. Then they pushed on and eastward for, they hoped, Baghdad, to make a new distance record. To avoid some poor weather in their path as well as the rough terrain of the Balkans, they ascended to an altitude of 15,000 feet. But the long flight, the high-altitude flying, which robbed them of oxygen, the very fumes of their fuel were taking their toll.

By the afternoon of August 7, well over the Mediterranean Sea and certain that they had already broken the world's distance record (held by Britishers O. R. Gayford and G. E. Nicholetts), they decided to land somewhat short of their goal. They selected a small airfield at Rayak, Syria, and landed there after fifty-five hours in the air and flying 5,657 miles, bettering Gayford and Nicholetts' mark by 316 miles.

Codos and Rossi returned to France three days later to receive a magnificent reception and a shower of French honors, but there was a sequel to their flight. The next year, hoping to break their own record, they set out from Le Bourget on May 27, 1934, with California—nonstop —as their destination. Their craft was the faithful *Joseph Le Brix*. The flight went well, despite the usual hazards of the westward crossing, until they sighted Newfoundland the next morning. Suddenly and inexplicably the wings began vibrating and worsened as they flew on. Nothing they did seemed to help—lessening the speed, speeding up. So nursing the plane along with a bad case of tremors, they limped into New York. Before landing at Floyd Bennett Field they jettisoned a large load of fuel and came in, without further incident, after making a nonstop flight between Paris and New York. They were then the first airmen to have flown both directions nonstop.

Their flight to California was, of course, off, and then they learned that their troubles which had canceled it had been caused by the propeller, which had been damaged slightly and thrown out of balance. Although they had failed in their original design, Codos and Rossi were welcomed as conquerors of the air in the United States, Canada and France.

This done, what else was there?

The answer, again, came from England, specifically in the person of wife and mother, Beryl Markham. A veteran pilot of six years' flying experience, which added up to an impressive 2,000 hours flying time, Beryl Markham had gained most of it in flying between England and South Africa and as an aerial game spotter over the wilds of Tanganyika and Uganda. She was one of the few women in the world who held a commercial pilot's license.

For some reason, in 1936 Mrs. Markham was bitten by the Atlantic bug. All possible kinds of flights had been made by that time except one: the east-to-west solo by a woman. For this hop she selected as her plane a small Percival Vega Gull which belonged to a friend, one Lord Carbery, who loaned it with misgivings. It was not exactly the type of aircraft for a flight into the head winds of the Atlantic. But the tiny blonde's mind was set and she even went so far as to get expert advice and help from Jim Mollison himself. The Percival was a somewhat sturdier plane than the Puss Moth in which Mollison had made the westward crossing; no reason then why Beryl Markham couldn't make it also.

The *Messenger*, as the plane was named, was prepared for the crossing by a change of engine and the installation of a large fuel tank in the rear of the cockpit (this brought the total amount of fuel carried up to a mere 185 gallons—compared, say, with the 1,225 gallons carried by Costes and Bellonte). In order to make room for the tank no radio was carried. Sandwiched in by fuel containers—always a deadly situation in the event of trouble—Beryl Markham was most certainly on her own once she stepped into the cockpit of the *Messenger*.

The plane was readied at an RAF station at Abingdon, west of London. James Mollison flew Mrs. Markham from London to Abingdon, from which she took off in the early evening of September 4, 1936, with New York, she hoped, as her next stop. Through the night she encountered the customary head winds and whatever wild thoughts came to anyone flying alone in a tiny plane over the dark Atlantic. It seemed to her that she was flying interminably—and when the early streaks of day began to appear and there was no land in sight, she fretted over the possibility of having flown in the wrong direction somehow. Instead of flying toward land, she could very well be flying at right angles to it into the open sea.

Long after she assumed she should have spotted landfall, and with her fuel supply dwindling, there was still no land to be seen. Then, with welcome suddenness, solid strips of earth began to materialize on the horizon. As she passed over, she picked out details from her map and found she was directly on course over Newfoundland. Although she was headed for New York a glance at the fuel gauges told her she would never make it. The wiser decision was to find a nice soft spot and land.

She soon found a likely place, smooth, uncluttered with man-made obstacles, and brought the plane in with a deft hand. All seemed fine and she knew she was somewhere over Nova Scotia. The plane touched down, skimmed along the ground for about forty feet and then just seemed to run out of good solid ground; the nose suddenly whipped into the turf and buried itself in the muck. Beryl Markham was whipped around inside the cockpit but, except for a smack on the forehead, was uninjured. Her flight had ended somewhat like that of Alcock and Brown's—the nice, smooth landing field she had selected was a bog. Shaken, though otherwise in good form, Mrs. Markham learned that she had landed at Baleine Cove on Cape Breton Island, Nova Scotia, after 24 hours, 40 minutes of grueling flying.

Even if she had come down short of her goal she was the first woman to have soloed on the westward Atlantic crossing. Once she had accomplished what all must have realized was the Final First, Beryl Markham was content and attempted no further such exploits.

Not that the fact that just about every possible First had been exhausted stopped Atlantic flights. Someone always managed to think of something. Late in 1936, for example, word came from France that in commemoration of the tenth anniversary of Lindbergh's flight an international air derby would be held the following year. That it also happened to coincide with the Paris International Exposition planned for 1937 was more than pure accident. The race was to be run on May 21, 1937, from Roosevelt Field, New York, and would end at Le Bourget. An attractive money prize awaited the victor—or survivor, depending on how one regarded the idea. It was not greeted with any degree of warmth in the United States, whose Bureau of Air Commerce saw little merit in such a competition; likewise various aeronautical organizations saw little more in the Lindbergh Derby than a promotional stunt replete with deadly dangers. Even Doc Kimball spoke out against it. So for that matter did Lindbergh, then living in near seclusion in England after the tragic kidnap-murder of an infant son. He wished no attention brought to him and his family, nor could he see that the Lindbergh Derby would benefit aviation in the least.

The French promotors were disappointed; their newspapers jeered American chicken-heartedness and went on with their plans, although these suffered many a change as time went by. A number of well-known fliers filed entries, among them both Amy Johnson and Jim Mollison flying in separate planes. May 21, 1937, came and went and, while there were appropriate ceremonies (which Lindbergh shunned), there was no Lindbergh Derby. The date was pushed back a couple of months, but American opposition stiffened and to that was added the force of official Canadian resistance. No international air derby could begin either in the United States or Canada. The Lindbergh Derby thus petered out, although not without a few words of recrimination from, among others, Amy Johnson, who before she left New York for England told newsmen that she considered the Bureau of Air Commerce "very far behind the times and the only reason they made the ruling was to protect Pan American Airways, which is going to start a transatlantic line. The ruling is as good as saying that flying is not safe."

Although not a participant in the Lindbergh Derby, a worthy commemorative flight with overtones of things to come was made in May of 1937. At the controls was Henry T. "Dick" Merrill, who had successfully made his first transatlantic flight the previous year. The plan then (as was the plan in 1937) was to make a round-trip crossing within a span of a few days. The 1936 flight was made in a Vultee monoplane, *Lady Peace*, owned by Broadway singer Harry Richman. For the flight Merrill obtained leave of absence as a pilot for Eastern Airlines and, with Richman as copilot, took off for London on September 3, 1936.

Although an exceptionally well-planned undertaking, with a good deal of aid from Eastern Airlines, its famed president Ace Captain Eddie Rickenbacker and the latest devices, the trip did not quite work out as hoped. One of the most publicized facts about the flight was that ping-pong balls had been stuffed into the wings to provide buoyancy should the *Lady Peace* come down at sea. This happily did not occur, but practically everything else did, including the missing of London and a landing in Wales, where they had a language problem (mistaking Welsh for Scottish). Eventually they proceeded on to Croydon, then to Paris. But time drifted away and they did not set off on the return flight until September 14, which rather took the edge off the impact of the round-trip aspect of the flight. Also, when they did arrive over Newfoundland and were anxious to alight after a bad night over the Atlantic, they pulled an Alcock and Brown and set the *Lady Peace* landing gear deep in a bog, 150 miles short of their goal, St. John's.

Merrill and Richman had almost succeeded in making a dramatic round-trip Atlantic crossing to show that it could be done. So with all the talk of the Lindbergh celebration in the air, Merrill once again revived the round-trip idea. He hoped to demonstrate the feasibility of such crossings as a preview of the future dawn of an air age for the Atlantic. The stunt aspect of such flying would eventually be eliminated with the use of the latest equipment, aircraft and engines. Merrill teamed up with another Eastern Airlines flier, John S. Lambie, to fly to London nonstop to pick up the pictures of the coronation of King George VI and Queen Elizabeth, which was to take place on May 12, 1937. The financial backing for the flight was furnished by International Photo Service, which would then have the photo scoop on all rival picture agencies on the coronation films.

As history had it, the flight was advanced a few days by an aviation disaster, the destruction of the German airship *Hindenburg* during a landing at Lakehurst, New Jersey, on May 6. That event, well covered by news photographers, produced a cargo for Merrill and Lambie to carry on their flight to London. Two days later, with the film aboard their Lockheed Electra, they set out on their delivery and pickup. The next morning they set down briefly at a RAF base at North Weald, got their bearings, and took off again, landing within a few more minutes at Croydon. Their cargo duly delivered they waited around for the coronation and its pictorial documentation.

In the morning of May 13, 1937, they set off again, landing at Floyd Bennett Field 24 hours and 22 minutes later. Not only had they demonstrated a commercial use of the airplane in speedy delivery over a great distance, Merrill had also proved that round-trip Atlantic flying was no mere dream. At the same time he became the first airman who had crossed the Atlantic nonstop no less than four times. Since the flight was almost as well covered in the papers as the two events whose photos the Lockheed had carried, Merrill was criticized for the dramatic quality of it. He insisted that the flight had involved no risk and that "I dislike having this trip characterized as a stunt . . . It was a pioneering commercial venture in aviation." This was, in a sense, true but it would be some

Vultee *Lady Peace* in which Broadway entertainer Harry Richman and Eastern Air Lines pilot Dick Merrill hoped to make a fast round-trip Atlantic crossing in 1936. Although the flight did not work out, Merrill succeeded the next year with another plane and copilot. (*National Air & Space Museum, Smithsonian Institution*)

time before such flights became the convention rather than an isolated news event.

Even so, the greater number of flights that followed Merrill and Lambie's were directly connected with the establishment of commercial flying over the Atlantic. One final First actually occurred as late as the spring of 1939, the last peacetime spring the world would know for several years. This one originated in Moscow, of all places. Russian airmen had been pioneering long-distance flights, many of them over the North Pole, so that it seemed logical that an attempt to fly from Moscow to New York might not be a bad idea.

The aircraft, a ZKB 26 standard medium bomber named *Moskva*, had been converted into a long-distance plane, a twin-engined monoplane. It was to be flown by Gen. Vladimir Kokkinaki, holder of several

The German airship *Hindenburg*, which
entered regular transatlantic service in the
summer of 1936; its destruction, while mooring at Lakehurst, New Jersey, on May 6,
1937, closed the era of the dirigible. (*National Air & Space Museum, Smithsonian
Institution*)

distance records in Russia, and Maj. Mikhail Gordienko. Their flight plan would carry them over the Great Circle route from Moscow over Iceland and Greenland and down to New York. The Atlantic was only incidental to this route, although technically Russia did lie across the Atlantic. The flight, in fact, dramatized the global nature of the aerial world. On April 28, 1939, the *Moskva* took off from Tshelkovo Airfield and ascended gradually to an altitude of 18,000 feet (where, besides the extreme low temperatures, they encountered tremendous head winds). Although their plane was fitted with practically all of the most modern equipment, one thing they did not have was an automatic heating system. They were dependent for warmth only on their flight clothes. At lunchtime it was not a little disconcerting to find their chicken sandwiches frozen solid.

Soon after they headed out to sea there was an even more disconcerting development: their automatic pilot broke down, which meant that, if they wished to continue the flight, Kokkinaki would have to fly it all the rest of the way. They pressed onward, steering by their precise radio compass and fighting the wind which subtracted at least thirty miles from their air speed. Not until they were over Cape Farewell, Greenland, and cruising at 28,000 feet did they enjoy the benefits of a tail wind which brought their air speed up to more than 300 miles an hour. But this was no sign that their luck had turned good.

The weather piled up on them, with clouds packed tightly from the water up to as high as 30,000 feet; their oxygen supply was running low and word had come from New York that the entire eastern seaboard of the United States was blanketed with fog. Ceiling was zero for miles inland and every airport in the general vicinity of New York was impossible to find from the air—it was, in fact, hard to find anything from the ground. One other fact gleamed out at Kokkinaki from the instrument panel—they were getting low on fuel also.

He pointed the nose of the *Moskva* down through the clouds, eventually breaking through the overcast to find themselves over nothing but icy water—the Gulf of St. Lawrence. There was no point in continuing, so Gordienko indicated a westward turn, where they were bound to find land. Soon they were barely 1,000 feet over the water. The air was murky and visibility was poor when they crossed a coastline and saw signs of human habitation. Then out of the fog loomed a feebly glowing beam of a lighthouse. Using the lighthouse as a point of reference, Kokkinaki circled around seeking a likely place to land. Not knowing the terrain and realizing what appeared to be a smooth patch could very well be little more than icy swampland, he did not lower the wheels for the landing.

By this time the two men stationed in the lighthouse had come out, having heard engines in the sky. Because of the fog they did not see the plane; then they heard the engines die out and the sound of a heavy machine hammering along the earth.

Kokkinaki brought the plane into the bog, and belly-whopped it down; soon he and Gordienko were roughly handled by the impact of the landing, as they bumped and bounced. Kokkinaki received a terrific blow in the chest from the control column, then the life raft was flung loose, neatly packed in a metal case, and struck him in the head. Then all motion stopped and, except for incidental aches and bruises, the two men stepped out onto solid ground. They had covered a distance of 5,000 miles in 22 hours, 56 minutes. The only problem was that they did not quite know where they were.

They had landed, guided by the Goose Lake Lighthouse, on Miscou Island, off the northern tip of New Brunswick—something they learned when joined by a rescue party from the lighthouse and the nearby fishing settlements. Since neither party spoke the language of the other, the tiny pinpoint was indicated on a map for the airmen. Upon learning this, both men took time out to sleep, Gordienko inside the plane and Kokkinaki in the now inflated life raft out in the open. Before this however he mailed off a letter which he had carried from Moscow for President Roosevelt (a well-known stamp collector), which was graciously received and acknowledged. While their plane was dismantled and shipped back to Russia, the two fliers were flown to New York for a hero's welcome. They had not quite succeeded, but they had not failed either. Their accomplishment brought a touch of international good will in a world rapidly disintegrating.

Sadly, Atlantic air crossings by individuals in 1939, in which the first transatlantic commercial crossings were made, finished tragically for all three of the private flights which ended the year's flying. All three were attempted in light planes, as if their pilots wished to flaunt the need for big airliners for Atlantic flying, as if it had become a commonplace. The first was an attempt by a young Swede, Carl Backman, who wished to make a sentimental journey to Stockholm. His was the last in a series of such homeward-bound flights attempted, with varying success, by several nationals who had succeeded in the United States and succumbed to a longing to return to their homelands by air.

By the time Backman made his try the U.S. Department of Commerce, following the great outcry over the aborted Lindbergh Derby, did all it could to discourage and prevent what Col. Monroe Johnson, assistant secretary in the Bureau of Air Commerce, called "freak flights." Backman had acquired a little Monocoupe monoplane, popular with weekend sporting fliers, which he hoped to "deliver" to a "purchaser" in Stockholm (the plane was then technically under Swedish registry and

jurisdiction). Thus legally equipped, Backman took off in the Monocoupe on May 16, 1939, and flew into oblivion. He was followed nearly
two weeks later, on May 28, by Thomas H. Smith, a Californian and a
former air-mail pilot. His plane was a little Aeronca which he had
dubbed *Baby Clipper*, a satirical nod in the direction of Pan American.
He was never found either.

Two young men from Brooklyn just barely in their twenties, Alex

Bellanca *Liberty* in which Otto Hillig, with pilot Holger Hoiriis doing the
flying, returned more or less indirectly to his native Germany. This initiated a
series of flights by one-time Europeans who longed to fly to their homelands
from America. Not all made it. (*National Air & Space Museum, Smithsonian
Institution*)

Loeb and Richard Decker, in a plane wishfully named *Shalom*, though
thwarted in any ambitious adventure by American authorities, did fly
their plane up to Nova Scotia. It was a small Ryan plane, not particularly suited for a transatlantic flight. They took off on August 11, 1939,
and, like Backman and Smith, vanished from the face of the earth.

A final fillip was contributed by one Pat Johns, young son of a
Wisconsin senator. He arrived on the scene with an Aeronca similar to
Smith's, which was rather appropriately named *Screwball*. Johns's arrival in the Atlantic environs in a tiny plane fitted out with enormous
fuel tanks aroused the suspicions of the authorities, who seized the plane

and ended the student pilot's ambitions, which vaguely had something to do, according to his statement to newsmen, with helping to bring peace to Europe. How, he did not venture to say, but since he planned a takeoff on September 6, peace had already fled from Europe. The only peace he might have found would have been deep in the Atlantic.

Backman's fatal attempt to return to his homeland from the United States by air introduced a category of transatlantic flights which dated back to 1931. Even those that ended happily contributed very little besides an element of foolhardy homesickness to the narrative. They also introduced a number of flights between various unlikely spots on the globe and were, in their way, firsts of a kind, however haphazard.

The first in the cycle of the "Goin' Home" flights—for want of a better term—got the series off to a reasonably successful and light-hearted start. The initiator, or perpetrator, was one Otto Hillig, a German-born photographer of about fifty-five years of age, living in Liberty, New York. Hillig, apparently, was air-minded, for he bought the plane for his flight with the money won in an out-of-court settlement in a suit against the *Graf Zeppelin* operators, Deutsche Zeppelin Reederei. Hillig had purchased a ticket for the *Graf Zeppelin's* round-the-world flight in 1929 and was unaccountably omitted from the passenger list and, consequently, from the historic flight itself. Claiming great personal embarrassment, Hillig sued for $100,000 and won enough, eventually, to buy a Bellanca and a few flying lessons.

Hillig then got the idea he would like to visit his home village in Germany, but wisely realized he could not hope to fly nonstop. He found a younger Danish pilot Holger Hoiriis, who had a yearning to visit his old home town in Denmark. Thus they compromised on Copenhagen, from which the home town of each could be readily reached. Blithely they set out from Harbour Grace on June 24, 1931 (the day after Post and Gatty had left there on their world flight) and flew eastward. For Hoiriis, at least, it was no pleasure flight, for he was glued to the controls for thirty-two hours, thanks to a heavy cloud cover, and he set the plane down in the first possible opening. As soon as the Bellanca, named *Liberty* in honor of Hillig's American home town, stopped rolling in a gentle meadow, Hoiriis went to sleep. Hillig then learned they had landed not in Denmark but Germany, near a little town named Krefeld—more than 200 miles from Copenhagen.

Upon learning this Hillig is reported to have been unperturbed, saying, "What's the difference? We arrived all right and, besides, we found Europe!" Hoiriis, having been refreshed by his nap, took the plane to their intended destination and the two native sons were fêted in Copenhagen as well as in their respective home cities.

Within a month two homesick Hungarians who wished to protest the political slashing of their homeland made a flight like Hillig and Hoiriis. The inspiration grew in the mind of Alexander Magyar (original name Sandor Wilczek; Magyar in Hungarian means "Hungarian"), who talked over the idea with fellow Hungarians in the United States and Canada (Magyar was a resident of Ontario). The money for the plane, a low-winged Lockheed Sirius named *Justice for Hungary*, came from a sausagemaker from Flint, Michigan. The copilot came directly from Hungary itself and was Gyorgy Endres, a captain in the Hungarian Air Force. He joined Magyar sometime in the summer of 1931 and on July 15 they took off from Harbour Grace for Budapest. They carried thirty-two pounds of mail—postcards which were sold to help pay for the flight and which read: "The Hungarian American Ocean-flight emphasizes the injustice done to Hungary by the Trianon Peace Treaty."

Their flight, too, ended happily, although a mere twenty miles or so from Budapest, near the hamlet of Bicske. Again there were joyous receptions, the plane was covered with flowers and London newspaper publisher Lord Rothermere, who had encouraged the flight, presented Magyar and Endres with a prize of $10,000. This plus other benefits that followed led to bad blood between the two Hungarians and to Magyar's (or rather Wilczek, for he had reassumed his real name in Hungary) challenging a number of people to duels, including Endres.

The Hungarian Aviation Society managed to intervene and had the duels, particularly the one between the two hero pilots, canceled—although it is notable that Magyar (Wilczek) married the ex-wife of a fencing master in Budapest soon after. But Magyar returned to America with his new wife and, for some reason—perhaps to settle the duel out of the fencing court—Endres retained ownership of the Lockheed. (He and his radio operator, Julius Pittay, were killed in it the following May in Rome, where Endres had flown to attend Balbo's Congress of Trans-atlantic Fliers).

With the advent of the new Atlantic flying season in the spring of 1932 the "Goin' Home" flights, particularly after the success of the Hungarian mission, started up again. First on the line was Polish-born Stanislaus Haussner of Linden, New Jersey, who decided to make a flight to Warsaw. Purchasing a second-hand Bellanca which he christened *S. Rosa Maria*, he started out from Newark, New Jersey, on May 28, 1932, just a week after Amelia Earhart had made her successful solo crossing. Haussner was content to make it the hard way, no short-cutting from Harbour Grace. After a few hours over the Atlantic, with the fog pushing him closer to the sea, he was content to turn around and await better weather conditions.

On June 3 he was off again; he carried no radio, but he did have a horseshoe mounted in the Bellanca's cabin for good luck. Whether this would have any effect upon his fortune, or his compass, for that matter, was open to conjecture. But on this second try Haussner flew onward and was seen over Nova Scotia—over Halifax and Sydney he tossed printed leaflets from the window as he circled the cities. This was his only means of communicating with his family (he had a wife and two children). Onward he flew, the sound of the engine nearly lulling him to sleep in the fleecy nothingness of the sky. Alone with his plane and his horseshoe he flew into the next day (May 4), when he was suddenly snapped to full consciousness by a sharp, characteristic aroma. He glanced at the fuel gauges and at this point of the flight the charm of the horseshoe expired. There was a leak and he was dangerously low on fuel. He flew about hoping to spot a ship, but none was in sight, and even as he did this, the engine consumed precious liquid and the rest dwindled from the break in the line.

With a cough and a sputter the engine died and the Bellanca plowed into the sea. Haussner, battered in the impact, quickly came to himself

Alexander Magyar (left) and Gyorgy Endres pose beside the rudder of their aircraft, *Justice for Hungary*, in which they successfully flew from America to Hungary in the summer of 1930. (*Lockheed Aircraft*)

in the cockpit, neck-deep in cold water. The Bellanca, its fuel tanks full of nothing but air, remained afloat. Unable to open the cabin doors, Haussner tore his way out of the cockpit with a screwdriver and scrambled out. Sitting there on the cabin of the plane he waited for rescue.

He waited and waited and waited. Ships did pass by, but they were too far to see him waving his shirt. He ran out of food very quickly and was unable to catch anything from the sea with improvised fishing tackle. For eight days, from May 4 to May 11, he spent a miserable time on the miraculously still floating plane. Then, it was already the evening of the eleventh, the horseshoe apparently took over again. A British freighter, *Circe Shell*, carrying creosote from New Orleans, happened to be in the vicinity. The Captain, J. W. Wilson, "decided to deviate from the usual seasonal course, the 'Hole in the Wall' (Providence Channel), in consideration of the cargo. I started to pass between the westernmost Azores." This shift in course brought the *Circe Shell* within four miles of the drifting Stanislaus Haussner. What appeared to be a buoy turned out to be on closer inspection the tail section of an airplane. But there also appeared to be no sign of life.

"The *Circe Shell*'s engines were put 'slow' and we approached about one mile. Daylight was falling rapidly. Both the *Circe Shell*'s engines were stopped and we closed on the derelict. I was amazed to see a figure that seemed lashed to the machine. The plane heaved on the increasing sea.

"I blew the siren and the figure moved and waved frantically. Obviously it was not lashed. A life-boat was ordered away with eager volunteers under the second officer. At a distance of fifty feet he called through the megaphone and the reply came in English:

" 'I am Stanley Haussner, save my ship.' It was feared that the plane might submerge at any moment, as the sea was increasing. Haussner literally fell into the life-boat."

Although exhausted, famished and practically incoherent, Haussner had been plucked from the sea and later learned that he had come down about 550 miles off the coast of Portugal, a long distance from Warsaw. His luck, sadly, which held against stiff odds for eight days in 1932, ran out on him three years later when he crashed while stunting near Detroit.

The year 1932 fulminated with home flights, two of which—with Norway as the goal—began almost simultaneously. First to get off was the *Enna Jettick* (named for the flight's sponsor, a shoe company), flown by Thor Solberg and Carl Petersen. The flight began at Floyd Bennett Field, New York, on August 23 and by that evening was over when their Bellanca suffered an engine failure off the coast of Newfoundland and they splashed into the chilly waters of Darby's Harbour. Fishermen saved them from the wing of the plane and the attempt was over, luckily with no damage to either Solberg or Petersen.

The second Oslo-bound flight began at Barre, Vermont, in a Stinson monoplane named *Green Mountain Boy* and carried John Bochkon, a local boy who had obtained local sponsorship but who had originally hailed from Norway, and copilot Clyde A. Lee, a barnstormer and ex-mail pilot from Wisconsin. They started on the same day as Solberg and Petersen and arrived, after an enforced stopover on the beach at Burgeo, Newfoundland, at Harbour Grace on August 24. The weather was not at all pleasant and they rested a day preparing themselves and the plane and took off for Oslo on the twenty-fifth. They never arrived there or anywhere, the first to be lost in the homeland flights.

Although not strictly belonging to the "Goin' Home" category, though with an element or two which was characteristic, the final 1932 Atlantic crossing attempt supposedly was to have been flown for scientific purposes. Behind this flight was Dr. Leon M. Pisculli, a Yonkers and New York City gynecologist whose interest in aviation dated back a few years when he backed a project involving an Italian flier, Cesare Sabelli, in a 1928 flight in a Bellanca named *Roma* that, for many reasons including financial ones, did not come off. Dr. Pisculli had hoped to go along on the flight to Rome to study the effects of a long flight on the pilot.

This was, to some extent, the purpose of the 1932 attempt for which he had acquired another Bellanca, formerly *Miss Veedol* in which Clyde Pangborn and Hugh Herndon, Jr., had crossed the Pacific as well as the Atlantic in 1931. The plane, which had come in rather heavily on its nose when Pangborn landed it (having dropped the landing gear after takeoff in Tokyo), was refurbished and named *The American Nurse*. It was about at this point that Dr. Pisculli's flight to Rome began to take on the smack of showmanship beyond any scientific value. He had engaged as pilot a handsome young man named William Ulrich and as Dr. Pisculli's assistant, a licensed nurse and, it appears, parachutist (a rare combination to say the least), Edna Newcomber. To lend the entire project additional scientific value the doctor also planned to carry a woodchuck named Tailwind, to check the effects of flying on the animal.

As an added attraction Nurse Newcomber was scheduled to drop by parachute into the city of Florence as a tribute to the great nurse, Florence Nightingale (who had been born there, although to British parents). The Italian government could not bring itself to smile on this aspect of the flight.

The American Nurse got under way from Floyd Bennett Field on September 13, 1932, and headed eastward on its curious "scientific expedition." In the early morning of the next day it was sighted from the ship *Ashburton* some 450 miles north of the Azores heading for Spain—but a long distance from Rome. Between that point and landfall *The American Nurse* simply vanished.

Lithuania was next in the succession of home flights, the dream of two men, Stephen Darius and Stanley Girenas. Money for the flight, as it had been in the case of the Hungarian expedition, was raised among the American residents with roots in the Old Country. Various categories of donations assured the donor a certain immortality by having his name inscribed on the fuselage of the plane, a Bellanca named *Lituanica*, as well as in a Book of Honor which, along with the plane, would be placed in a museum after the successful completion of the flight.

But Darius and Girenas were among the first to smack up against the concerned Department of Commerce hoping to discourage random amateur flights. Thus the homesick Lithuanians were not issued authorization for the flight. They were forced to wait around, day after day, as the legalities were argued over—and as they did they saw Wiley Post arrive at Floyd Bennett Field to take off on his round-the-world flight.

On the same day, July 15, 1933, the two men gassed up the Bellanca, climbed into the cockpit and announced they were going to fly to Chicago to test the plane's characteristics with a full load over a long-distance hop. But instead of flying westward, they nosed the plane into the same direction that Wiley Post's *Winnie Mae* had flown earlier—out over the Atlantic. In doing this Darius and Girenas violated several statutes which would lead immediately to the cancellation of their flying licenses.

Their goal, no longer—nor ever—Chicago, was Kaunas, Lithuania. With no radio aboard, there was no means of communicating with the two men; there was no word of them on the sixteenth, although police of Koenigsberg (where Post had been forced to land because of storms) reported seeing an unidentified plane over the city that night. Then on July 17 word came of the fate of Darius and Girenas; the twisted wreckage of the *Lituanica* was found in the forest near Soldin, Germany. The occupants were, of course, dead. They had flown a distance of 4,000 miles, but were about 400 miles from Kaunas.

Soon after the sad conclusion to the *Lituanica*'s flight, two brothers from Brooklyn who owned a profitable soft-drink bottling plant longed for their old homeland, Poland. They were the Adamowiczes, Joseph and Benjamin. They thought it would be fitting to fly to Warsaw and purchased the old *Liberty* (which had carried Hillig and Hoiriis, roundabout, to Copenhagen), renaming it *White Eagle*. No pilots, the Adamowiczes hired Emil Bergin to attend to the flying. They made no public announcement of their intentions, but they did take off one day

(August 8, 1933) on what appeared to be a test flight and no further word was heard from them until a flash came from Harbour Grace that the *White Eagle*'s landing gear had been wiped out in a landing and a wing damaged, although the three occupants suffered no serious injuries. That finished the Adamowiczes' hope for a flight to Warsaw for that year.

However, the next year, after repairs had been made to the plane, which was renamed rather obviously *City of Warsaw*, and a new pilot, none other than Holger Hoiriis himself, was hired, they again felt the urge to fly home. They left Floyd Bennett on June 28, 1934, flew up to Newfoundland, where a landing was made without incident, and then the next day took off for Warsaw. As fate would have it they didn't quite make it, although Hoiriis brought the plane down on solid ground on the thirtieth—it turned out to be France, near the village St. André de Messel. Encouraged, they took off again, making it only as far as Le Bourget, where some small repair was made on the engine. Onward: only

The Lockheed Vega, *Lituanica II*, in which Felix Waitkus attempted to succeed where his predecessors, Darius and Girenas, fatally failed—a flight between the United States and Lithuania. Waitkus also failed, but did fly the Atlantic and landed short of his destination in Ireland. (*Lockheed Aircraft*)

this time as far as Nedlitz-Termendorf, Germany, for some more attention to the engine (had these forced landings occurred a few hours earlier the flight would have been less a comic-operetta than it was). Onward and upward some more, and finally, on July 2, 1933 (a day late according to their own timetable), the Adamowiczes and Hoiriis landed in Warsaw. After a fashion, they had made it and there were polkas in the streets of Warsaw and Brooklyn.

Cesare Sabelli, whose wish to fly from New York to Rome nonstop in 1928 had been thwarted by money problems, never gave up the dream. Around the same time that the Adamowiczes pondered their second attempt at Warsaw, so did Sabelli again look longingly Rome-ward. He planned thoroughly on the second try; he had made a good deal of money in real estate and paid for a new Bellanca in cash (the first plane, the *Roma*, had been repossessed by Bellanca), naming it *Leonardo da Vinci*. As copilot Sabelli took on an ex-U.S. Navy pilot, George Pond. They set out from Floyd Bennett Field on May 14, 1934, and headed directly over the Atlantic, choosing to bypass the stopover at Harbour Grace. When next heard from they were down with a hot engine two miles from the village of Lahich, County Tyrone, Ireland, a rather exotic place should one's destination happen to be Rome.

The hapless airmen had suffered a hard night of engine problems (attributed by some to sabotage: cardboard strips in the oil tank, a bottle cap in the oil line, etc.), plus weather conditions of a dire nature. With their engine overheating they had been, indeed, lucky to make it to Ireland. After repairs they did proceed on to Rome, but by then the point of their flight—the nonstop aspect—was dissipated.

Two brothers, this time two members of Portuguese nobility (or so they claimed), Alfred and George de Monteverde, opened the new season; theirs was the first try since the successful flight of the Adamowiczes. It was, in fact, the first try of the year. With Lisbon as their goal the brothers de Monteverde boarded their Bellanca named the *Magellan* on June 22, 1935. The flight was over before it really began; the heavy plane lifted off the runway of Floyd Bennett Field just as the concrete ended; then it settled back down to the ground. The landing gear buckled, a wheel shot away and the plane swirled over the rough ground, ending up as a tangled jumble of wreckage, dripping and trailing splashes of highly combustible aviation fuel. As the few spectators who had come to observe the takeoff watched breathlessly, the de Monteverdes extricated themselves from the ball of wreckage and miraculously nothing occurred to cause a fire. The de Monteverdes, having had enough of transatlantic flying, returned to Cincinnati and forgot about Lisbon.

Next in line in a year not noted for great flights was Thor Solberg, whose attempt to get to Norway in 1932 ended in the waters of Darby's Harbour, Newfoundland. Goaded by that failure, Solberg planned carefully for three years. Although his goal was Oslo, Norway, as of yore, he had no intentions of making any new mark, no nonstop gaudy flight; his major aim was to get there. He selected as his plane a single-engined Loening amphibian, similar to the type which had seen much use in the U.S. Navy during the latter Twenties. A biplane, it was a good solid craft, reliable but hardly looking like a transatlantic type.

Also flying with Solberg was Paul Oscanyan, who would assist in the navigation and other duties. The Loening was named *Leiv Eiriksson,* in honor of the explorer-seaman generally credited with a pre-Columbian discovery of America. It was Solberg's plan to trace Ericson's route in reverse.

Solberg and Oscanyan left New York on July 18, 1935, and at an unhurried pace proceeded on to Montreal, Quebec, Labrador, Greenland, Iceland, the Faroe Islands and then to Bergen, Norway, on August 16, finally arriving at Oslo on the nineteenth. Solberg took no risks with the weather and thus he and Oscanyan remained as comfortable as possible at all their stops, not fretting, nor motivated by any urgency. Although they were greeted in their former homeland with proper jubilation, their exploit was not exciting enough to merit much more than passing mention in the press. Any flight lasting a full month merely to go from the United States to Norway was more than the attention span any newspaper reader could sustain. Nor was the flight of the *Leiv Eiriksson* accorded much notice in aviation history (Loenings had flown such flights before, as had other aircraft); but the significance might have been noted. The amphibian had arrived safely with Solberg and Oscanyan because of their patience and care, not taking risks and because they were not racing with anyone.

The final flight of 1935 was, like that of Solberg, a kind of return match on the United States to Lithuania flight. After the death of Darius and Girenas in the *Lituanica* in 1933, the American-Lithuanian Trans-Atlantic Flight Association of Chicago had hoped to sponsor a memorial flight in their honor. They purchased a plane, a Lockheed Vega which was named *Lituanica II,* and approached a young U.S. Army Air Corps reserve lieutenant, Felix Waitkus, to fly it. Waitkus was then running a flying school at Kohler, Wisconsin, where he and his father-in-law prepared the Lockheed for an ocean hop. The twenty-eight-year-old pilot had also elected to make the crossing solo.

Although not very promising weather was predicted along his course, Waitkus took off from Floyd Bennett Field in the early morning of September 21, 1935. Carrying only a heavy load of fuel, letters, decorations for the graves of Darius and Girenas, a small rubber raft and a revolver, Waitkus pointed the big nose of the Lockheed into the uncertain dawn.

Had he chosen the worst possible weather deliberately, Waitkus could not have done better (or rather, worse) than he did for the next twenty-two and a half hours of his life. He rammed into rain, fog and head winds which forced him to fly by instrument most of the time. If he attempted to shake the ghostly nothingness by climbing to higher altitudes, then he found icing a serious threat. And so it went, flying blind through what he later described as "the filthiest weather imaginable and unimaginable."

By the next morning Waitkus realized he would never make it to Kaunas, not after so much fuel had been consumed battling the winds. He imagined that land must be somewhere below; he would land, refuel and proceed on to Lithuania. Soon, through scattered patches in the mist, he did see the earth, undoubtedly Ireland. There being no airport in sight, Waitkus selected a likely looking stretch of ground near a small village (it was Ballinrobe, County Mayo). It was not a large clearing, so that he had to sideslip into a landing. After hours of exhausting flying Waitkus was not completely alert and as he sputtered to the ground, the right wingtip scraped something, snagged, twisted the plane roughly, then the landing gear ripped away. The Vega finished the rest of its landing run on its belly.

Waitkus climbed out of the cockpit unhurt, although he realized that as far as the plane was concerned the flight was over. In his disappointment and shaken condition he did not consider one fact: he was the sixth person to successfully cross the Atlantic alone, the others being Charles Lindbergh, James Mollison, Amelia Earhart, James Mattern and Wiley Post (the latter two in round-the-world attempts). What did matter to Waitkus was to proceed on to Kaunas in another plane with which he was provided to make the pilgrimage to the graves of Darius and Girenas.

Following that completion of a mission, Waitkus was happy to leave the Atlantic flying to others and to attend to his flying-school activities. The damaged Lockheed was later shipped from Ireland to Lithuania, where it remained until 1940 when the Russians overran the little country during the Second World War. Conjecture has it that the historic aircraft remains somewhere in Moscow.

One "Goin' Home" flight was attempted in 1936, although not by an American resident, and it had certain interesting qualities that harked back to earlier times. To begin with there was a Swedish baroness, a beauty according to contemporary accounts, Eva von Blixen-Finecke. She contributed a touch of glamour. Swedish airline pilot Kurt Bjorkvall contributed his considerable skill if not a great deal of common sense. The money was contributed by a Swedish paper, hoping, no doubt, to swell its reputation and circulation in reporting the flight firsthand, particularly with the sporty baroness aboard.

The first sour note was that someone had chosen to begin rather late in the year, Bjorkvall arriving in September to purchase a plane—a Bellanca Pacemaker.

A second sour note was the pressure brought to bear on the Stockholm *Tidningen* for encouraging a flight at that time of the year, especially with a beautiful lady aboard. The lady was happy, however, echoing another lady when she said, "We are making the flight for the fun of it and for no other reason."

The third sour note was that the newspaper withdrew its sponsorship —thus the money—and in a pet Bjorkvall paid for the Bellanca out of his own pocket. This put control of the flight completely into his hands and—memories of Mibs Boll—he decided to bounce his lovely passenger and to make the flight solo. By which time it was already early October and not the season for Atlantic flying. Word, too, came back to the baroness of Bjorkvall's decision and she confronted him with tears in her eyes and a flow of language, the most printable of which was, "It is sure a dirty trick refusing to take me."

Bjorkvall finally got under way on October 6, 1936. The baroness was on hand to see him off, refusing to shake his hand or even to wish him luck. Possibly she may even have placed an old Scandinavian curse on him. But Bjorkvall seemed unperturbed; he took off into threatening weather of the very worst kind, secure in the knowledge that the wings were filled with ping-pong balls (as had been the plane of Harry Richman and Dick Merrill which had preceded him by about a month).

A full day went by and Bjorkvall was overdue at Stockholm. The next day, October 8, dawned and still there was no word. Obviously Bjorkvall had come down in the sea.

He had, after fighting the most miserable weather of his flying career. He was about 100 miles from Ireland when engine trouble settled the whole thing and he soon splashed into a rough sea. Despite this the buoyancy of the ping-pong balls in the wings permitted him to bounce around without sinking. During the afternoon of that day, the seventh, a French trawler, the *Imbrin*, came in sight and managed to pluck him out of the sea. The sea was too rough, however, to do the same for the plane, which was still floating when the *Imbrin* headed for La Rochelle, where on October 8, word went out that Bjorkvall had been rescued. When she heard of the fate of the Bellanca and Bjorkvall, the still disgruntled baroness replied, "I wouldn't have minded a little water." Perhaps, but there is no further record of her ever trying again; likewise a wiser Bjorkvall.

Short-Mayo Composite, the ingenious solution to the weight-lifting problem, devised by Maj. R. H. Mayo of Imperial Airways. Upper plane carried a heavy load of fuel and the cargo; lower plane, a Short S-23 flying boat, assisted in the takeoff (with propellers of both planes pulling). Once airborne the upper plane, the Mercury, separated from the lower, the *Maia*, and flew on to America. (*British Overseas Airways Comporation*)

The attempts to fly anywhere merely for the sake of crossing the Atlantic dwindled off, closing with the final tragedies of Backman, Smith and Loeb and Decker in 1939. There was simply no further point to making such flights, partly because they did not prove anything and mainly because commercial airlines, drawing upon all that could be learned from the early flights and applying the latest technical knowledge, proved that all the guesswork, risk and, therefore, adventure could be taken out of Atlantic flying.

As early as 1936 the Germans had begun an Atlantic service of a kind using flying boats and refueling ships, which was neither direct, nor carried passengers. Later they used catapulted planes (to lift a heavy load of fuel and cargo), but this was by no means regular nor especially successful.

In July of 1937 Britain and the United States, whose Imperial Airways and Pan American were contending for commercial supremacy over the Atlantic, achieved a tentative truce by cooperation. In July Imperial dispatched a Short S-23 flying boat, the *Caledonia*, in a westward test flight, while Pan American sent a Sikorsky S-42 flying boat, *Clipper III*, eastward in a joint effort. Imperial followed in July of the

A French contribution to transatlantic commercial flying: the Latécoère 521. (*Musée de l'Air, Paris*)

next year with a curious pickaback arrangement, the Short-Mayo Composite, the upper element of which was the cargo-carrying Short seaplane Mercury and the bottom, weight-lifting element, a Short Empire flying boat. The first flight of this odd hybrid, in which a thousand pounds of mail and newspapers were delivered to America, demonstrated the concept. Both planes took off together and then, once airborne, the Mercury broke away from the larger ship and completed the journey. With a lesser load, the Mercury (manned by Capt. D. C. T. Bennett and Radio Officer A. J. Coster) made a trouble-free return flight to Southampton via Montreal, the Azores and Lisbon.

Within a month Germany and France had accomplished demonstration flights, the former in a land plane, a Focke-Wulf Kondor which, under command of Capt. Alfred Henke, flew nonstop to New York from Berlin—and then turned around to make the return flight. The newly formed Air France-Transatlantique made its crossing in an old Laté-

OVERLEAF Boeing 314, Pan American's most modern clipper of the latter Thirties, which inaugurated the first regular transatlantic mail and passenger service in the spring of 1939 and officially marked the close of private Atlantic flying. (*Pan American Airways*)

coère flying boat, the *Lieutenant de Vaisseau de Paris,* commanded by Henri Guillaumet. This was followed by a series of flights during the next several months.

In May of 1939 Pan American introduced a new flying boat, the Boeing 314, one of the most advanced craft of its type and time, making its first crossing with a cargo of mail. Then in June the first crossing with passengers was completed. This would have marked the beginning of regular transatlantic passenger service, except, of course, it was interrupted by the advent of the Second World War. But the point had been made: should anyone wish to cross the Atlantic it was no longer necessary to acquire a none-too-reliable plane, nor to fly it yourself or—worse—depend on rudimentary navigation. All that, by 1939, belonged to a romantic past.

With the coming of war transatlantic flying did not stop—in fact it increased enormously as American aircraft were flown literally in swarms to Britain. The pilots of these planes, ranging from fighters to heavy bombers, were often as not young men who had never touched a throttle before signing with the Air Corps—and not a few were women members of the Women's Airforce Service Pilots (WASP) and the Women's Auxiliary Ferrying Squadron of Air Transport Command. Flying in the pathway blazed by Lindbergh and Earhart became a daily chore rather than a great new adventure. These commonplace flights further underscored how unnecessary were the once daring "freak flights" of the Thirties and laid the groundwork for the great burgeoning of commercial aviation after the war.

11

"Where
Am I?"

In retrospect, perhaps one of the marvels of transatlantic aerial adventuring during its most romantic years is that there were not more disasters than there were. True, there were in fact too many, but if not for some divine providence there might easily have been more considering the aerial activity, much of an amateurish nature, over the Atlantic circa 1919-1939.

In this period a total of forty-two lives were lost in the North Atlantic. It is interesting that there were no fatalities in the most primitive phase: from the 1919 crossing of the NC-4 up to the start of the race for the Orteig prize, during which eleven attempts were made, four managed to make it but no one was lost. The first loss of life occurred in

271

1926, when Fonck's plane crashed and burned in a takeoff. This, for those who are scientifically superstitious, seems to have initiated a cycle and was followed by two more lost aircraft. Then came Lindbergh.

The year 1927 was the one in which the most transatlantic losses occurred, most of them after Lindbergh's successful crossing. Not all of them happened to eager innocents anxious to follow in Lindbergh's slipstream. There were a number of reasons for the various accidents, some of them mechanical, some because of an unrelenting, quirky weather little understood at the time; some could be attributed to pilot error and many of the reasons will never be known. Even so, even these unknowns are bound to fall into one or the other of the above-mentioned categories.

It was during the Thirties that most of the amateur flights—or "freak flights" as they were often called—took place. The number of attempts lessened and so did the losses. Even so, those losses could have been a great deal higher—and taking into account some of the rather helter-skelter flying done in that period, they *should* have been higher. Some even had comic overtones (*vide* the exploits of Charles Levine); some had no reasonable right to succeed, but did.

Who is so godlike, at this latter day, to decree which of these 120-odd trips (not counting early commercial survey flights) were not necessary? Who could deny them their venturesomeness, their spirit, their ineffable quest for self-expression? Often as not the only life risked was the airman's own; if not, all others aboard the plane were aware, more or less, of the risks involved. That some leaped into a project with a naïveté bordering on stupidity is true, but that was a rarity.

At the same time theirs was a wonderful *esprit*; all who attempted transatlantic flights approached them with a will to win. Fatalism did not figure when the dreams were dreamed and the plans drawn up. When something went wrong this driving force sustained many who managed to survive, despite adversity. Typical of this outlook was a headline which appeared in the Philadelphia *Public Ledger* of August 7, 1928. It read: "Courtney Calls Crash 'A Success.'" This was not one of those landings which could be defined as good merely because the pilot could walk away from it. Captain Frank T. Courtney, an English pilot, was at the controls of a Dornier Wal in what was his second try at an Atlantic crossing; his first, in 1927, had not panned out. Neither did his second, for while over the Atlantic the plane burst into flame. Spreading flames threatened to get at the reserve fuel supply so that Courtney dived the plane toward the ocean, selected a nice wave and smacked into it, dousing the entire plane. This extinguished the fire, saved four lives and, as crashes went, was a total "success." With the radio aboard, distress signals were sent out and the men rescued. To Courtney, though he had failed, this was an indication that with the right plane and proper radio equipment it could succeed. Although he did not accomplish this himself, he was vindicated in 1930 when von Gronau crossed in the same type of plane.

Some flights were successful despite the odds, certain unknown factors which never entered into the planning, despite all reason or common sense. There are several such classic flights, none of which ended fatally. Two were even, after a fashion, successful. All of them, taking everything into consideration, could have ended tragically.

The first was, in fact, a First and, except for its slightly antic character, rightly belongs among the historic firsts of the period. It began on a peculiar Gallic note in France. Armand Lotti, Jr., was an air-minded son of a Paris hotel owner who objected to his son's devotion to flying. The younger Lotti, it seems, had money of his own and with it hoped to sponsor—and go along on—a transatlantic flight. He approached two sergeants in the French Air Force, Jean Assolant and René Lefevre, the former to serve as pilot, the latter as navigator-copilot, with Lotti earning his way as radio operator. They acquired as their "mount" a Bernard 191 monoplane which they decorated in a vivid yellow and named, echoing the name of Nungesser and Coli's lost plane, *L'Oiseau Canari* (*The Yellow Bird*). An aborted attempt was made at a flight in September, 1928, but ended prematurely at Casablanca, getting all three young men in assorted parental and official trouble.

But they were not disheartened, not even when the French Air Ministry put a clamp on Atlantic flying the next year. On April 17 the three aspiring airmen boarded the *Yellow Bird* and took off on what appeared to be a routine test flight and dashed across the Channel out of reach of the French Air Ministry. The plane was dismantled and shipped to the United States, the three then followed three weeks later (no doubt after contending with various passport and customs problems) on the *President Roosevelt*. The plane was then taken to Mitchel Field on Long Island, assembled and issued an American registration number. By the end of May the crew had flown the Bernard up to Old Orchard Beach, Maine, which they had selected as their jumping-off place.

Meanwhile the plane had been tested and proved a worthy craft, speedy and easy to handle. On May 29, 1929, the trio felt their plane and they were ready to go, weather willing. It willed and they took off with a load of 880 gallons of fuel—and that's where they ran into trouble. Their Hispano-Suiza engine did not operate properly on the American-made fuel and after an hour and a half of flying they returned to Old Orchard Beach, after jettisoning most of the fuel. They then proceeded to find the proper blend of fuel and benzol for their cranky engine.

They were ready again by June 13 and, back in the plane, roared down the beach. Despite the fact that they carried a bit less fuel, Assolant could not understand why the plane seemed so little inclined to take off. It had certainly never behaved so before. Finally, after a long run of nearly a mile, the sluggish *Yellow Bird* became airborne, and then continued to resist all attempts to climb, besides moving along with the nose unaccountably high and the tail dragging low. Assolant had little time to worry about that, except that a seawall loomed ahead and he realized he had to lift the plane higher. This was accomplished during anxious moments as the tail barely brushed the top of the wall. Assolant was mystified.

But they were away and climbing, although it took an hour to get to 1,000 feet. Something would have to go, however, if they ever hoped to get to Paris. Lotti began dismantling the radio in order to toss it out and lighten the load, when a head poked into the cockpit.

ABOVE Three intrepid French aviators and an uninvited "friend": Lotti, Assolant, Lefevre—and Arthur Schreiber, who stowed away in the *Yellow Bird* and hugely complicated the flight. (*Musée de l'Air, Paris*)

LEFT Bernard 191, the *Yellow Bird* of French airmen Lotti, Assolant and Lefevre. (*Musée de l'Air, Paris*)

"My name is Arthur Schreiber," said a youth none of them had ever seen before. Assolant, Lefevre and Lotti were stunned; at the same time they realized immediately why the *Yellow Bird* had flown so crazily. Young Schreiber, of Portland, Maine, had stowed away in the tail of the aircraft. Having thrown the plane off balance, he might have caused, as indeed he nearly did, a wreck during the takeoff. Although not absolutely authentic, it has been reported that one of the Frenchmen said something along the lines of, "Instead of the radio, throw him out."

There was some discussion of turning back, but they had come so far that they could not bear to linger long on that contingency. With Schreiber in the cabin, it was possible to get the plane to fly at a normal attitude, but his extra weight took its toll in additional fuel consumption. Then during the night they encountered storms, which threw off their compasses, and they drifted to the south of the intended course. When morning came—June 14, 1929—their suspicions were confirmed by radio contact with several ships. Due to fatigue and the knowledge that, thanks to the extra load contributed by a contrite Arthur Schreiber, they would not have enough fuel to reach Paris, they agreed to land at the first possible sight of land, which, in the evening twilight, turned out to be Spain at Cape Finisterre. There being fuel remaining Assolant flew on for another 250 miles and then landed on the beach near Comillas, still over 100 miles from the French border and a long way from Paris.

It was still good to get down, despite their disappointment in failing to reach Paris. They had covered a distance of 3,560 miles in 28 hours, 52 minutes—and they were the first French airmen to cross the North Atlantic (Costes and Bellonte were the second French crew, although the first to make it between Paris and New York in the following year).

Everyone was so delighted that the *Yellow Bird* had actually made it safely that all was forgiven by the time the aircraft finally arrived at Le Bourget in the evening of June 16. The airmen even forgave Arthur Schreiber, who had climbed aboard on a dare, and the French Air Ministry forgave them in turn for their illegal flight; in fact, they were all awarded the Order of the Legion of Honor for their feat. Leaving Schreiber behind, the three new French air heroes took the *Yellow Bird* on a tour of France and then to various major cities of Europe.

As for Arthur Schreiber, he seems not to have pursued his interest in aviation after the single transatlantic flight (he *was* the first man to stowaway in a heavier-than-air craft). As an additional parenthetical note, it might be mentioned that shortly after the *Yellow Bird* finally got pulled off the sand of Old Orchard Beach, another plane, a Bellanca named *Green Flash* carrying Roger Q. Williams and Lewis A. Yancey, got under way. A wheel struck a soft spot in the sand, the landing gear snapped and that ended their try for Rome. They tried again in July in another Bellanca *(Pathfinder)* and made it across the Atlantic, but practically on the same course as the *Yellow Bird* had covered and ended up near the same beach in Spain, far short of their goal.

Another classic misadventure occurred in the late summer of 1931. A young (he was all of twenty-one) newly-wed who had inherited some money and who loved flying purchased a plane with some of that money and then romantically named it for his bride, Esa. He was Willy Rody, the plane was a Junkers W-33 (which had once been owned by Charles Levine, who had hoped, with Bert Acosta, to use it to fly from Europe to America). That became Rody's plan too, to fly from Berlin to New York, and he even began such a venture in August, 1931, but turned back because of a malfunctioning oil pressure gauge. Rody and his companion copilot, Christian Johannsen, returned to Tempelhof airport, discouraged but determined to try again.

The *Esa* was a low-wing all-metal monoplane with a fixed landing gear and because of a rather clunky configuration and corrugated "skin" looked too heavy to fly. It was, however, an advanced plane for its time and one of its type, the *Bremen*, had successfully made the first westward nonstop Atlantic crossing in 1928.

Rody and Johannsen switched their plans a bit, and set out again. They flew to Lisbon, intending to make Portugal their jumping-off spot, and they added a new crew member, Fernando Costa Viega, a Portuguese pilot. They took off from Juncal do Sol on September 13, 1931, headed out to sea, passed over the Azores to check their navigation and then proceeded on. Soon after trouble struck: a cylinder in the engine began missing; there being five others still operating all right, the problem did not trouble them enough to cause them to turn back or even to ditch in the water near a ship they spotted, the *Pennland*. Instead they pushed on.

That was the last seen of the *Esa*. There was no word on the fourteenth, nor the day after, or the day after that. It was obvious by that time that something had happened to the *Esa* and its crew.

What had happened was that because of the engine trouble, fuel was consumed much faster than normally (even with a slight margin to allow for the head winds and storms) and somewhere out at sea the Junkers sputtered and died. They were then about eighty miles from Cape Race, the southernmost tip of Newfoundland. The great metallic aircraft splashed into the water and began filling up, the water running through the fuselage carrying away the emergency rations the three men had carried. Of them all, only Viega was slightly injured in the ditching.

They estimated that, with luck—and with the empty fuel tanks—they would be able to float for a few hours. That the all-metal Junkers floated at all was a miracle. All they could hope for was a passing ship to find them before the *Esa* sank. But no ships came—and, incredibly, neither did the *Esa* sink. As one day merged into another they suffered miseries, subsisting on a little chocolate and water from the *Esa's* radiator, and were constantly wet. This torture went on for no less than seven days with the damaged, water-logged *Esa* keeping them afloat. On that seventh day, with the three men all but totally exhausted, a ship, the *Belmoira*, steamed into sight and spotted them perched atop the plane. After they had been taken off and made comfortable and headed homeward, the *Esa* continued drifting tail up, wings awash and with a smashed elevator. It was never seen again, but it had somehow, contrary to the rules of flotation, sustained Rody, Johannsen and Viega long enough—the longest week of their lives. (Their ordeal, the first of its kind, was duplicated the next year by Warsaw-bound Stanislaus Haussner, although in an aircraft that appeared to be more seaworthy than the *Esa*.)

The next year, too, was notable for the most senseless Atlantic attempt of the age. There being such flying families as the Lindberghs and Mollisons (though neither had yet flown the Atlantic), an idea dawned in the mind of one George Hutchinson, of Baltimore, Maryland: why not the Flying Hutchinsons? He was a flying enthusiast, apparently a creditable pilot with a curious sense of showmanship. He added something strikingly dramatic to the flying family idea—his whole family, wife and two daughters, one eight years old and the other six, and, to round it off, a dog. It was Hutchinson's idea to take his family on a pleasure jaunt to London by air. While he made this appear to be rather prosaic, Hutchinson obviously had a sharp eye on the publicity value of such a family jaunt; they could certainly count on a great future in vaudeville.

Hutchinson did not, however, leap into the project without some serious thought and planning. He acquired a Sikorsky twin-engined S-38 amphibian which was christened *City of Richmond*, in recognition of the source of some of the flight's backing. Hutchinson would, of course, serve as pilot; navigation would be in the expert hands of Peter Redpath; the engineer was Joseph Ruff, Gerald Altissish was radio operator and, last but not least, there was Norman Alley along to man the camera. Hutchinson was not missing a trick, nor was he leaving too much to chance—although sour noises were already being raised by the press about his carrying his wife and young daughters on such a flight, however well-planned and competently manned. There was still that one

unforeseen thing that could turn up. But Hutchinson remained stead-
fast.

On August 23, 1932, all eight members of the party (plus dog)
boarded the *City of Richmond* to take off from Floyd Bennett Field and,
following an uneventful flight of a little over 500 miles, landed in the
waters near St. John, New Brunswick. There the wheels were removed,
thus eliminating a certain amount of weight (for the eight people and
dog aboard was taxing the lifting capability of the S-38, what with the
load of fuel it would have to carry for the cross-ocean hop).

Hutchinson was in no hurry, but the next day did take off for and
land at Anticosti Island, in the Gulf of St. Lawrence. Weather held
them down there for nearly a week and then cleared, so that on August
30 they were away again for another short hop to Hopedale, on the east
coast of Labrador. It was at this point that certain problems began to
accumulate. Danish officials refused to grant Hutchinson permission to
land in, or fly over, Greenland, which lay across the more than 600-mile
watery stretch from Hopedale. The Danes wanted no part of a flight
involving a woman and children. Undaunted, on September 2, Hutchinson blithely lifted the *City of Richmond* off from the waters at Hopedale
and, with Redpath supplying him with fine navigational direction, soon
brought the Sikorsky down in the harbor at Godthaab, Greenland.

And into the arms of the law. Outraged officialdom descended on the
Flying Hutchinsons as soon as they set foot in Greenland and slapped an
Illegal Entry charge against the leader. For reasons known only to that
officialdom, and to Hutchinson, the whole matter was cleared up very
simply with a payment of a fine of a thousand *kroner* (about $180). From
then on, the officials cooperated with Hutchinson on the flight; perhaps
the fact that he had been able to make it that far without mishap was
justification of his airmanship and of Redpath's navigation.

Hutchinson continued to show good sense of a kind. He wished to
make his next stop Angmagssalik on the east coast of Greenland almost
directly opposite Godthaab on the east, but he did not want to attempt
flying directly over Greenland's icy surface in September. They would
thus make their way southward down Greenland's west coast to Julianehaab, then around Cape Farewell and north along the east coast to
Angmagssalik. From there they could jump off on their Atlantic crossing
proper, with Iceland and the Faroe Islands comfortably in between
Greenland and Great Britain.

On September 7 they covered the 310 miles between Godthaab and
Julianehaab; on the eleventh they set out for Angmagssalik. After
rounding Cape Farewell the Sikorsky was heading northwestward hug-
ging the coastline when a massive fog bank closed them off from the

land. The buffeting the plane had taken in its various landings and in the air may have contributed to their next problem: a leak in the fuel line which Ruff could not get at to fix. The last word that a by then rather agitated world heard from the *City of Richmond* was that they were forced to land in the sea. Once down their radio signals were little more than a jumble of static, thanks to Arctic atmospheric conditions.

Hutchinson chose to come down some miles offshore out of the fog bank and where the ice floes were not too thick; he estimated that they were about thirty miles short of their destination. He managed the difficult landing without mishap, but found that once down, it was impossible (once the fuel leak was fixed) to take off again—the seas were too rough and filled with floating ice. There was nothing else to do but head for land, which lay to the east under a blanket of fog.

For hours Hutchinson taxied through the waves and treacherous ice packs, with freezing water splashing over the hull and drenching everyone in the plane. It was touchy going, maneuvering a fragile craft through the ice without getting its hull bashed in; Hutchinson revealed a good command of seamanship as he sputtered landward through the frosty mist. But he had no idea what it was that he was taking his wife and children into. The shoreline of Greenland was not hospitable, being a rugged series of outcroppings and indentations of rock and ice. The question was, too, could he beach the Sikorsky on shore before it sank without its being battered to bits by the surf on the rocks?

Through the fog he spotted a small land mass and made for it, a tiny island of rock near one of the countless fiords that marked the coastline. It was a port in the storm and Hutchinson drove the prow of the Sikorsky up a slightly inclined rocky beach. The waves battered at them, the plane shuddered and pitched, and while Hutchinson held the hull against the rocks, the occupants of the plane scrambled out. Once the children and Mrs. Hutchinson were ashore, the men set to work salvaging as much as possible before the waves destroyed the Sikorsky. They did not get much, not even the radio, very little food and not enough warm clothing to protect them from the sweeping cold of the barren rock which had become their haven.

Their distress signal had been heard and rescue operations were immediately initiated by the Danish government. But the task was formidable, indeed, not only because of the weather and ice, but because the shoreline presented a myriad of possibilities of harbor or certain destruction. It could, literally, take forever before they might be found in the maze of ice and rock.

The Hutchinson party had gone down on September 11; the rescue parties were alerted and began searching soon after. By the twelfth, what with the cold, it appeared to be a vain hope. On the thirteenth it seemed a lost cause; not a sign of the Hutchinsons or the plane had been found as ships and boats cautiously skirted the shoreline, nosed into little inlets and harbors and generally fought the bitter wind. Not even an air search found anything.

One of the vessels participating in the search was a fish trawler, *Lord Talbot*, out of Aberdeen, Scotland, under the command of a Captain Watson. Discouraged and tired, and having lost two days of work, the crew of the *Lord Talbot* was certain by the evening of September 13 that they could not possibly find the Hutchinsons. Dark had come as the little trawler moved along the coast with Captain Watson, eyes peering through binoculars, facing the shore.

Suddenly and inexplicably a flicker of light broke the blackness of that utterly black Arctic night. Watson immediately ordered his radio operator to flash a Morse message, asking for a second show of lights (this in the eventuality that the flame had been made by Eskimos; no point in fighting one's way ashore only to find an Eskimo family instead of the Hutchinsons).

Practically the instant the message had been beamed at the source of light, another flash of flame came from the same point ashore. The *Lord Talbot* had found the Hutchinsons.

No little battle was required to get a small boat from the *Talbot* to the rocky island on which the Hutchinsons, suffering from exposure, had all but despaired at rescue. No one on the rock had seen the Morse message sent from the ship! By the merest accident Captain Watson had spotted a little flare of light (which he had taken for a campfire) that Hutchinson had made by lighting a length of film, hoping it might attract someone's attention (he had no idea that elaborate rescue operations had been under way, nor of the *Talbot*'s proximity). The second, confirming flame had not been an answer to the *Talbot*'s message, but only the lighting of a second strip of film.

Despite their ordeal lasting two days and nights, the Hutchinson party and dog were in remarkably good condition. Lack of food and the effects of exposure were not long lasting, and the entire party of eight was quickly back to normal and eventually taken to Britain for a celebration of their marvelous adventure.

There were, however, repercussions: transatlantic aviation was never quite the same after their ordeal and Hutchinson himself was rather taken aback to find himself *persona non grata* with various children's welfare societies (which eventually prevented him from making a vaudeville tour with his family), not to mention the canine lovers. The Danish government, also, took steps which all but cut off all transatlantic flights whose pilots hoped to fly over Greenland. In order to do this the pilot would have to deposit a bond of 10,000 *kroner* (about

LEFT The "Flying Hutchinsons" visiting the Sikorsky plant at Hartford, Connecticut. Perched on the prow, with dog, are daughters Blanche Kathryn (eight) and Janet Lee (six); below are F. W. Neilson, president of Sikorsky, George and Blanche Hutchinson and Igor Sikorsky. Their aircraft is a Sikorsky S-38 amphibian. (*Sikorsky Aircraft*)

BELOW The *City of Richmond* breaks up on the rocks of Greenland, ending the attempt of the Flying Hutchinsons to cross the Atlantic by air. (*Sikorsky Aircraft*)

$1,600, which put it beyond the financial reach of most individual pilots) against the expenses of any rescue operations, should they be required. This requirement was in force from 1932 until 1939, when flights of military aircraft from the United States over the Greenland-Iceland route became as common as they were safe.

As for the Flying Hutchinsons, they appear to have vanished from both aviation and show business after their venture in the *City of Richmond.*

The flight to end all Atlantic flights was the incongruous brainstorm of a Texas-born Californian, red-headed thirty-one-year old Douglas Corrigan. Despite his generally sunny disposition, Corrigan had had a hard life. Deserted by his father and left to support a younger brother and sister by the death of their mother when he was sixteen, young Corrigan struggled through a difficult youth, going from job to job, working hard but not actually finding himself.

But he had a way with a story, a fund of determination and a slightly askew view of life. For a time he worked as a carpenter and told of the day he was on a roof sawing a board when "my hand slipped and the saw went halfway through my thumb. Well, it hurt so much I dropped the saw and fell off the roof. Luckily the ground was soft. The foreman came running around the corner with a startled look on his face. Thinking he might be mad because I hadn't stayed up on the roof till it was finished I said quickly, 'It's all right, boss, I had to come down to get some more nails anyhow.' "

Obviously, a man with that kind of cheerful enterprise in the face of what might be called adversity could not be held down. Whether or not falling off the roof taught the dauntless Corrigan the lesson that he could not fly unaided, or whether it awakened in him the urge to fly, he never stated. But shortly after he did have his first look at an aircraft and his first flight in a Curtiss Jenny. After that he bent all his efforts toward taking flying lessons; he was then a youth of eighteen. He soon drifted away from carpentry and gave up all dreams of becoming an architect to concentrate on aviation.

Within a year he had made his first solo and earned a living as a mechanic around airports, eventually, by 1927, ending up at the Ryan company where he worked on the *Spirit of St. Louis.* Lindbergh supplanted Lincoln in Corrigan's estimation as "the greatest character in history." The great success of Lindbergh's flight was an even greater inspiration to the young, small, redhead who had to be content with various odd jobs and flying second-hand planes. For the next several years Douglas Corrigan covered a good deal of ground barnstorming the country, taking the curious up for flights and living the usual kind of doubtful existence of the gypsy pilot.

Eventually while in New York, hoping to return to California, Corrigan came across an old second-hand Curtiss Robin which, even with engine, the owner was willing to sell for $325. Corrigan and his younger brother Harry (who later became an aeronautical engineer) examined the Curtiss, found it more or less good—at least it was still flyable—and, depositing their belongings in the plane, climbed aboard and headed for California.

Corrigan's life in California was no great improvement over his unstable barnstorming existence. During one period of eight months he had three jobs (his brother was working as an aero-engineer) but he managed to keep his Curtiss Robin in good flying shape. With Harry's help he changed engines (an old OX-5 for a newer—1929— Wright J6-5), put new wheels on the plane, recovered it and generally patched it up.

Then in April, 1936, "I was pretty much disgusted with life in general, and my life in particular, and as I didn't have anything else to do nights, now that the plane was all overhauled, I started building the large gasoline and oil tanks I would need if I did get permission to make a long flight. If I didn't get permission I was going to punch holes in the tanks and throw them in the bay—with me and a big rock tied onto the tanks to make sure they wouldn't float."

Some months before it came to Corrigan that with a more powerful engine and additional tanks, which would make the total capacity 225 gallons, he just might pop off "and try to fly from Newfoundland to Ireland." For some reason, he did get a tentative OK from one of the chief inspectors for the Department of Commerce—although the department's engineering division frowned negatively upon the idea. Corrigan went ahead anyway, hoping that something would work out. Eventually with the large fuel tanks installed and the "new" engine ticking over nicely, he did get permission to make cross-country flights in the Robin.

In the summer of 1936 Corrigan filled the tanks and took off eastward and, although the engine gave him some trouble, he eventually arrived at Roosevelt Field, New York. Once there he began making inquiries about permission to fly from Newfoundland to Ireland. Officials looking upon the Curtiss Robin could not work up much enthusiasm for such a flight—also there was some problem about getting clearance for takeoff from Newfoundland. One official, however, did suggest that if Corrigan added more fuel tanks and learned instrument flying, he might just be able to take off from New York for Ireland.

Around this time Kurt Bjorkvall had decided to make his flight to Sweden unaccompanied by the Baroness Blixen-Finecke and had ended up in the Atlantic. Corrigan thought it would be best to give up asking for permissions till a better time. He returned to California and eventually applied for permission to fly from New York to London in 1937, but

this, too, had been ill-timed. Amelia Earhart had just been lost in the Pacific and the Department of Commerce was not encouraging flights over the oceans, especially not in an aged Curtiss Robin.

The Department of Commerce then went a step farther and refused to license the old plane, although Corrigan flew it anyway, even cross-country again, making certain to land at out-of-the-way clearings so that no one would notice the plane was not properly licensed. Thus did the old plane, which Corrigan had named *Sunshine*, confute all the experts by succeeding in making two round-trip flights across the country, two years running (not, however, without a number of forced landings).

Corrigan then went to work as a welder in an aircraft factory and when he did not get the 5¢ an hour raise that was coming to him, he quit in the summer of 1938. He worked on the plane a good deal and was finally able to get an X-license for it, placing it technically in the Experimental category, since it would not have passed in the regular classification. He also received official permission to attempt a nonstop flight from California to New York in the plane. If that worked out, he could return, also nonstop, and perhaps hold some record or other.

On Friday, July 8, 1938, Douglas Corrigan, with the *Sunshine*'s tanks full, took off from the Long Beach airport and did actually arrive at Roosevelt Field the next day, around sundown, with four gallons of fuel in his tanks (he had started out with 252 gallons). Although the story

LEFT Douglas Corrigan and the $325 second-hand Curtiss Robin, still capable of flying and which he names *Sunshine*. (*National Air & Space Museum, Smithsonian Institution*)

RIGHT Corrigan gassing up the *Sunshine*; for a small aircraft with limited performance capabilities, it has a large fuel capacity. Corrigan had added more fuel tanks, of course. (*U.S. Air Force*)

leaked out that a small redheaded Irish kid from California had just made a nonstop flight in an old plane, the flurry it might have generated was all but squashed in the news that Howard Hughes was about to set out on his round-the-world flight—which he did on July 10.

Corrigan did not seek publicity, feeling the less fuss the better, and spent a week working on the plane. He had found a leak in the fuel tank but decided it was not too bad, as fixing it would have required its removal, which would have taken a week of work. Now and then a reporter or a magazine writer would evidence a little interest in Corrigan and his plane. Ruth Nichols came around and after looking the plane over offered Corrigan the loan of her parachute. "I said thanks, but there wasn't room for a parachute, and anyway, that plane was all I had and if it fell to pieces, I'd go with it."

He was keeping an eye on the weather, and the word was out that he would make the attempt at a return trip, nonstop, to California. On Saturday, July 16, Corrigan took the *Sunshine* over to nearby Floyd Bennett Field from Roosevelt to "pack grease around the valve gear" and to attend to other small chores. He was not cleared for takeoff until early the next morning because the field manager expressed very little confidence in the plane.

Before taking off, according to his own account of the flight, Corrigan asked the manager which direction he should use for the takeoff.

LEFT Corrigan's *Sunshine* attracted attention when word leaked out he might try a long flight from New York to California. (Actually this photo was taken after the flight, when pilot and plane returned to the U.S.) (*U.S. Air Force*)

RIGHT Douglas Corrigan is greeted by some of his former co-workers at Ryan, where they had all worked on the *Spirit of St. Louis*. Among those present: Maj. H. A. Erickson (who took so many of the classic flight photos of Lindbergh's plane), second from left. (*Ryan Aeronautical Library*)

The answer was any direction "except don't head towards the buildings on the west side of the field."

"I'll take off east," Corrigan told him and noticed as he closed the cabin door a fire truck and an ambulance following him as he taxied down the runway. After a run of 3,000 feet the heavy plane lifted off and was soon fifty feet off the ground. Climbing slowly Corrigan found that by the time he was up 500 feet haze and fog obscured the ground. "During the first two hours I saw trees occasionally through holes in the fog and then saw a city I took to be Baltimore, Maryland, which I have since found out was Boston, of course."

Of course.

According to his story Corrigan read his compass wrong, and a likely story it is. He managed to read it wrong for 28 hours and 13 minutes, in itself quite a feat for so experienced a pilot. During most of the flight fog presented a problem but he managed to keep on the wrong course correctly by instrument. But the leaking fuel tank gave him concern, for eventually an inch-deep pool of gasoline filled the cockpit during the long night. With a screwdriver Corrigan poked a hole in the bottom of the cockpit (on the right side, for the hot exhaust pipe ran along the left) to let the excess fuel drain out. Then, he reasoned, "if I run the motor slow [which is generally done to conserve fuel on long flights] the gasoline will have more time to leak out, so I'll run the motor fast and use the gasoline up before it leaks out."

In the clouds he flew by instrument, but he also wished to avoid icing, so he descended lower to see what there was below and to his Irish surprise saw nothing but water, water everywhere. "This was strange, as I had only been flying twenty-six hours and shouldn't have come to the Pacific Ocean yet, so I started to figure out just what had happened. I looked down at the compass, and now that there was more light I noticed I had been following the wrong end of the magnetic needle on the whole flight. As the opposite of west is east, I realized that I was over the Atlantic Ocean somewhere."

Before long he spotted the inevitable little fishing boat on the surface of the water and dipped down, but saw no one. It reminded him that they were probably having lunch and that he had not eaten in hours. He had taken as provisions two boxes of fig newtons, two chocolate bars and a quart of water. As he munched land came in sight and he flew inland over what he "figured" must be Ireland. Eventually a little fighter plane of the Irish Air Force flew over to investigate, did—and then flew off before Corrigan could tag along to the nearest airport. He kept onward and saw a large city and a fine airport which was marked Baldonnel, and having "studied the map of Ireland two years before, I knew this was Dublin."

He circled to get the feel of the field and then set the *Sunshine* down on the Old Sod. Although there are several versions of what Corrigan's first words were when he stepped out of the plane, the most memorable and fitting generally attributed to him were, "Where am I?"

According to his own story, Corrigan's first words upon alighting were, "Is this the right field to land at?" Other versions have him announcing his name and then adding that he had left the morning before for California but that he had become "mixed up in the clouds and must have flown the wrong way." This comment, of course, inspired his nickname and he became known thereafter as "Wrong Way" Corrigan.

Although he had violated any number of international aviation laws, Corrigan immediately captivated the world with his ready smile, wry wit and simple manner. He always wore the slacks and leather flying jacket in which he had made the flight. He was small (about 5 feet 5 inches tall), jaunty without being cocky and absolutely incapable of guile. He was welcomed in Ireland with a ready hand and a warm smile. Once the various technical problems he had caused were solved (most of them by simply ignoring them), he was treated like a celebrity wherever he went. He met the Prime Minister of Ireland, Eamon De Valera, who immediately made it possible to ship the *Sunshine* home without formal complications, not to mention Corrigan himself. "He came into this country without papers of any kind," De Valera said. "Why, we'll just let him go back without any papers."

And he did, making a stopover in London, where he lunched with Ambassador Joseph Kennedy, and later made the rounds of various right places and was greeted wildly by people everywhere he went. Pictures of Corrigan's arrival were flown across the Atlantic in the Mercury, piloted by Donald Bennett, the upper component of the new pickaback Mayo Composite on its first flight.

Just as he was boarding a ship to return home Corrigan received official notification from the Department of Commerce which read in part, "Your pilot's license, number 4674, is hereby suspended until August 4." Since the *Manhattan* was due to arrive in New York on August 4, it meant that Corrigan would not be able to fly while coming home aboard the ship.

His reception was a gala one in New York—and continued so across the country. There were parades and motorcades (in one Corrigan sat in the car backward), gifts (in Abilene, Texas, he was presented with a watch which ran backward), luncheons and dinners, and Corrigan generally enjoyed himself and delighted everyone across the country. Most of the distance was covered in his Curtiss Robin as he worked his way homeward to California. Once the excitement died down, Corrigan in-

OVERLEAF Douglas Corrigan, airman extraordinary, who closed the great transatlantic aerial adventure with a practical joke. (*U.S. Air Force*)

telligently set out to exploit his venture: he appeared in a film of no great consequence, wrote up his own story of his early life and the flight to Ireland and then retired from the accomplishment of daring flying adventures and went into ranching.

The flight of the *Sunshine* had brought the Atlantic adventure full circle, had even helped to place such ventures in perspective. Corrigan had demonstrated that anyone, practically, could do such a thing even in an antique aircraft. At the same time he had shown that any such future attempts would be as risky and as pointless as his had been. Because his luck had held he had made it, but the day of luck and the kind of courage he had was over and a new day had dawned. That new day was proved by the various early commercial flights carried out immediately before and after Corrigan flew to Ireland. That the old day was finished was sadly demonstrated by the fatal flights, the following year, of Backman (who also attempted a "Corrigan" in the sense that he tried to get around regulations), Smith and Loeb and Decker. Corrigan's flight, then, truly closed the era of transatlantic aerial adventures that had opened with the pioneering crossings of the NC-4 and of Alcock and Brown, rose to a climax with Corrigan's idol, Charles Lindbergh, and then, the various aeronautical, technical and personal points having been made, closed with the light-hearted skylarking of Douglas Corrigan.

The time of the individual daredevil ended on a happy note; the new day of transatlantic aviation began, and it belonged to modern machines, crews of large numbers and various specialties, complex instruments and devices of amazing function. No more flying by the seat of the pants, no more derring-do: the Atlantic air belonged to the technician, the engineer and the scientist. At the same time, it also belonged to Everyman—anyone, indeed, could fly the Atlantic.

And that was, primarily, what all those who had gone before for varied reasons of their own had wanted to prove all along. Even those who had admitted that they only sought the fun of the adventure—and those who lost the gamble. They had all laid a foundation for an aerial highway that covers the earth and reaches for the moon.

Tabulation
of the Major
Transatlantic Flights:
1919–1939

The following table lists all transatlantic flights, both the successes and failures, attempted during the period covered in the main text of this book. Only flights that were planned as Atlantic crossings are included; such flights as those of Kingsford-Smith, Wiley Post, Howard Hughes *et al.* were only incidentally transatlantic attempts and are not included. They are mentioned in the main text, as is the U.S. Army's world flight of 1924, to place the several flights in the proper perspective in the aviation scene of the time. Likewise, certain historic airship crossings are listed, not regular scheduled crossings. Survey flights by commercial airlines, too, are included for completeness; these brought an end to individual exploits, the major subject of this book.

Note: An "x" in the TO column denotes an uncompleted flight; when word "Lost" appears in the REMARKS column it denotes total loss of plane and pilots.

1919

DATE	CREW	AIRCRAFT	FROM	TO	REMARKS
May 16–27	A. C. Read, W. Hinton, E. Stone, H. Rodd, E. Rhoads, J. Breese	Curtiss NC-4	Trepassey Bay, NFLand.	Lisbon via Azores then to Plymouth, England.	First crossing, in stages; NC-1 & NC-3 dropped out en route. No loss of life.
May 18	H. Hawker, K. Mackenzie-Grieve	Sopwith *Atlantic*	St. John's, NFLand.	x	First try at nonstop; forced down at sea; rescued by ship.
May 18	F. Raynham C. Morgan	Martinsyde *Raymor*	St. John's, NFLand.	x	Takeoff crash; no fatalities.
June 14–15	J. Alcock, A. Whitten Brown	Vickers Vimy	St. John's, NFLand.	Clifden, Ireland	First nonstop west-to-east crossing.
July 2–6	G. Scott & crew of 30	Airship R-34	East Fortune, Scotland	Mineola, L.I., N.Y.	First east-to-west crossing by airship; & first round-trip; returned Pulham, Norfolk, July 9–13.
July 4	M. Kerr, H. Brackley, T. Gran, F. Wyatt	Handley Page V/1500	Harbour Grace, NFLand.	x	Takeoff crash; no injuries.

1924

DATE	CREW	AIRCRAFT	FROM	TO	REMARKS
Aug. 9	A. Locatelli V. Crossio C. Marescalchi T. Rissilo	Dornier Wal	Brough, England	x	Forced down at sea; crew rescued.
Oct. 12–15	H. Eckener & crew	Airship LZ-126, later *Los Angeles*	Friedrichshafen, Germany	Lakehurst, N.J.	Delivery flight

1926

DATE	CREW	AIRCRAFT	FROM	TO	REMARKS
Jan. 23- Feb. 5	R. Franco, Druan, R. de Alda, Prata	Dornier Wal:*Plus Ultra*	Palos, Spain	Buenos Aires, Argentina	First crossing of South Atlan- tic in single plane, in stages.
Sept. 21	R. Fonck, L. Curtin J. Islamoff C. Clavier	Sikorsky S-35	New York	x	Takeoff crash; Islamoff, Clavier killed.

1927

DATE	CREW	AIRCRAFT	FROM	TO	REMARKS
Feb. 13- Feb. 24	F. de Pinedo C. del Prete & Zachetti	Savoia- Marchetti: *Santa Maria*	Sardinia, Italy	Pernam- buco, Brazil	South Atlantic; Also toured South America & U. S.
Apr. 26	N. Davis S. Wooster	Keystone Pathfinder: *American Legion*	Langley Field, Va.	x	Takeoff crash, both Davis & Wooster killed.
May 5	de Saint-Roman de Mounayres, Petit	Farman Goliath	St. Louis, Senegal, Africa	x	Plane lost, at- tempt at South Atlantic non- stop.
May 8	C. Nungesser F. Coli	Levasseur PL-8: *L'Oiseau blanc*	Le Bourget, Paris	x	Lost: first at- tempt at non- stop east-to- west.
May 20- May 21	C. Lindbergh	Ryan: *Spirit of St. Louis*	New York	Paris	First solo nonstop
May 23- June 11	F. de Pinedo C. del Prete & Zachetti	Savoia- Marchetti: *Santa Maria II*	Trepassey Bay, NFLand.	Lisbon, Portugal	Return flight with replace- ment aircraft.
June 4- June 6	C. Chamberlin C. Levine	Bellanca: *Columbia*	New York	Eisleben Germany	Distance re- cord: 3911 mi.

DATE	CREW	AIRCRAFT	FROM	TO	REMARKS
June 29– July 1	R. Byrd B. Acosta B. Balchen G. Noville	Fokker: *America*	New York	Ver-sur- Mer, France	Landed in sea, short of Paris.
Aug. 14	H. Koehl F. Loose G. von Huenefeld	Junkers: *Bremen*	Dessau, Germany	x	Returned
	J. Risticz C. Edzard H. Knicker- bocker	Junkers: *Europa*	Dessau, Germany	x	Returned
Aug. 31	A. Lowenstein- Wertheim F. Minchin, L. Hamilton	Fokker: *St.* *Raphael*	Upavon, England	x	Lost
Sept. 1	C. Schiller P. Wood	Stinson: *Royal* *Windsor*	Windsor, Canada	x	Canceled: weather
Sept. 2	L. Givon P. Corbu	Farman: *L'Oiseau* *bleu*	Le Bourget, Paris	x	Returned: flight abandoned
Sept. 3	F. Courtney F. Downer R. Little E. Hosmer	Dornier Wal	Calshot, England	x	Returned; flight abandoned in Spain: weather.
Sept. 6	L. Bertaud J. Hill P. Payne	Fokker: *Old Glory*	Old Orchard, Maine	x	Lost
Sept. 7	J. Medcalf T. Tully	Stinson: *Sir John* *Carling*	Harbour Grace, NFLand.	x	Lost
Sept. 16	J. Fitzmaurice R. McIntosh	Fokker: *Princess* *Xenia*	Baldonnel, Ireland	x	Returned: weather
Oct. 11	G. Haldeman R. Elder	Stinson: *American* *Girl*	New York	x	Down in sea; engine trouble; rescued.
Oct. 14	D. Costes J. Le Brix	Breguet: *Nungesser-* *Coli*	St. Louis, Senegal	Natal, Brazil	First nonstop South Atlantic.

DATE	CREW	AIRCRAFT	FROM	TO	REMARKS
Oct. 14	R. Starke F. Loose K. Loose L. Dillenz	Junkers	Lisbon, Portugal	x	Flight abandoned in Azores.
Nov. 4	H. Merz F. Rode W. Boch	Heinkel	Lisbon, Portugal	x	Abandoned in Azores after takeoff crash. No injuries.
Dec. 24	O. Omdahl B. Goldsborough F. Schroeder F. Grayson	Sikorsky: *Dawn*	New York	x	Lost

1928

DATE	CREW	AIRCRAFT	FROM	TO	REMARKS
Mar. 13	W. Hinchliffe E. Mackay	Stinson: *Endeavor*	Cranwell, England	x	Lost
Apr. 12– Apr. 13	H. Koehl J. Fitzmaurice G. von Huenefeld	Junkers: *Bremen*	Baldonnel, Ireland	Greenly Is., Labrador	First nonstop east-to-west crossing.
June 17– June 18	W. Stultz L. Gordon A. Earhart	Fokker: *Friendship*	Trepassey, NFLand	Burry Port, Wales	First crossing by woman.
June 28	F. Courtney H. Gilmour F. Pierce E. Hosmer	Dornier Wal	Lisbon, Portugal	x	Came down in sea because of fire; crew rescued.
June 28	T. Rasche U. Koenmann B. Zebora	Bellanca: *North Star*	Cap de la Madeleine, Quebec	x	Flight abandoned; could not get off ground.
July 5– July 6	A. Ferrarin C. del Prete	Savoia- Marchetti	Rome, Italy	Pt. Genipabu, Brazil	Nonstop South Atlantic flight; distance record: 4466 mi.
Aug. 5	J. Idzikowski C. Kabula	Amiot: *Marshal Pilsudski*	Le Bourget, Paris	x	Abandoned; engine trouble ditched in sea; rescued.

DATE	CREW	AIRCRAFT	FROM	TO	REMARKS
Aug. 8	M. Drouhin Gianoli Manuel Lanet	Couzinet: *Arc-en-Ciel*	Orly, Paris	x	Crashed & burned; Lanet & Drouhin killed.
Aug. 18	B. Hassell P. Cramer	Stinson: *Greater Rockford*	Cochrane, Canada	x	Forced down in Greenland; rescued after 2 weeks.
Aug. 25	Condouret Mailloux Mailly-Nesle	Bernard	Le Bourget, Paris	x	Abandoned; plane over-loaded.
Oct. 11– Oct. 15	H. Eckener, crew & passengers	Airship LZ-127: *Graf Zeppelin*	Friedrichshafen, Germany	Lakehurst, N.J.	First postwar German zeppelin; returned Oct. 29–Nov. 1. LZ-127 made 144 transatlantic flights.
Oct. 17	H. MacDonald	de Havilland Gypsy Moth	St. John's, NFLand	x	Lost

1929

DATE	CREW	AIRCRAFT	FROM	TO	REMARKS
Mar. 24– Mar. 26	F. Jiminez I. Inglesias	? *Jesús del Gran Poder*	Seville, Spain	Bahia, Brazil	South Atlantic
June 9	A. Ahrenberg A. Floden R. Ljunglund	Junkers: *Sverige*	Bergen, Norway	x	Flight abandoned Ivigut, Greenland, on Aug. 7.
June 13– June 14	J. Assolant A. Lotti R. Lefevre A. Schreiber (stowaway)	Bernard: *L'Oiseau Canari*	Old Orchard Beach, Maine	Santander, Spain	First French crew to cross Atlantic.
June 13	L. Yancey R. Williams	Bellanca: *Green Flash*	Old Orchard Beach, Maine	x	Takeoff crash; no injuries.

DATE	CREW	AIRCRAFT	FROM	TO	REMARKS
June 21	R. Franco R. de Alda R. Gallarza	Dornier Wal: *Numancia*	Los Alcazares, Spain	x	Ran out of fuel near Azores; crew rescued.
July 3	R. Gast P. Cramer R. Woods	Sikorsky: *"Untin"* *Bowler*	Chicago, Ill.	x	Abandoned; aircraft crushed by ice at Port Bur- well, Canada.
July 8– July 9	L. Yancey R. Williams	Bellanca: *Pathfinder*	Old Orchard Beach, Me.	Santan- der, Spain	Second try; Rome was goal.
July 13	J. Idzikowski C. Kabula	Amiot: *Marshal* *Pilsudski*	Le Bourget, Paris	x	Crashed: Horta, Azores; Idzikowski killed.
July 13	D. Costes M. Bellonte	Breguet: *Point* *d'Inter-* *rogation*	Le Bourget, Paris	x	Returned: bad weather.
July 22	L. Paris A. Marmot J. Cardion	CAMS-54: *La Frégate*	Brest, France	x	Abandoned, Azores; engine trouble
Aug. 19	O. Kaeser K. Luscher	Farman: *Jung* *Schweit-* *zerland*	Juncal, Portugal	x	Lost; first at- tempt by Swiss pilots.
Oct. 22	U. Diteman	Barling: *Golden* *Hind*	Harbour Grace, NFLand	x	Lost
Dec. 5	T. Larre- Borges L. Challe	Breguet	Cordova, Spain	Natal, Brazil	South Atlantic. Forced landing.

1930

DATE	CREW	AIRCRAFT	FROM	TO	REMARKS
May 12	J. Mermoz Dabry Gimié	Latécoère: *Comte de* *la Vaulx*	St. Louis, Africa	Natal, Brazil	First airmail crossing, South Atlantic.

DATE	CREW	AIRCRAFT	FROM	TO	REMARKS
July 6	C. Wynn-Eaton	de Havilland Puss Moth	Harbour Grace, NFLand	x	Takeoff crash; pilot injured, but recovered.
July 7	J. Mermoz Dabry Gimié	Latécoère: *Comte de la Vaulx*	Natal, Brazil	x	Forced down in sea; crew rescued.
July 31	W. Hirth O. Weller	Klemm	Brough, England	x	Flight abandoned in Iceland.
July 29–Aug. 1	R. Booth & crew	Airship R-100	Cardington, England	Montreal, Canada	Return flight Aug. 13–16.
Aug. 2	J. Brown H. Mears	Lockheed Vega: *City of New York*	Harbour Grace, NFLand	x	Takeoff crash tire blowout, no serious injuries.
Aug. 20–Aug. 26	W. von Gronau E. Zimmer F. Hack F. Albrecht	Dornier Wal: *Amundsen*	Warnemünde, Germany	New York	Flight made in stages.
Sept. 1–Sept. 2	D. Costes M. Bellonte	Breguet: *Point d'Interrogation*	Paris	New York	First nonstop Paris to N.Y.
Oct. 9–Oct. 10	J. Boyd H. Connor	Bellanca: *Maple Leaf*	Harbour Grace, NFLand	Tresco, Isles of Scilly, England	Original destination: Berlin; a/c formerly *Columbia*.

1931

DATE	CREW	AIRCRAFT	FROM	TO	REMARKS
Jan. 7	B. Hart W. MacLaren	Bellanca: *Tradewind*	Hampton Roads, Virginia	x	Lost; first try on Jan. 3.
June 22	R. Nichols	Lockheed Vega:*Akita*	New York	x	Crashed on landing at St. John, New Brunswick. Flight abandoned.

DATE	CREW	AIRCRAFT	FROM	TO	REMARKS
June 24– June 25	O. Hillig H. Hoiriis	Bellanca: *Liberty*	Harbour Grace, NFLand	Krefeld, Germany	Destination: Copenhagen.
July 15– July 16	A. Magyar G. Endres	Lockheed Sirius: *Justice for Hungary*	Harbour Grace, NFLand	Bicske, Hungary	Destination: Budapest
July 28– July 30	R. Boardman J. Polando	Bellanca: *Cape Cod*	New York	Istanbul, Turkey	Nonstop distance record: 5011 mi.
Aug. 2– Aug. 9	P. Cramer O. Paquette	Bellanca (w. Pack- ard Diesel eng.)	Detroit, Mich.	x	Lost; Cramer's 3rd attempt.
Aug. 8– Sept. 7	W. von Gronau E. Zimmer F. Albrecht F. Hack	Dornier Wal: *Gro- enlandwal*	Warne- münde, Germany	New York in stages	Crossed central Greenland east- to-west, a first.
Sept. 13	C. Johannsen W. Rody F. Viega	Junkers W-33: *Esa*	Juncal do Sol, Portugal	x	Down in sea off NFLand; crew resc. after 7 days
Nov. 26– Nov. 27	H. Hinkler	de Havil- land Puss Moth	Natal, Brazil	Bathurst, N. Africa	First solo west-to-east, S. Atlantic.

1932

DATE	CREW	AIRCRAFT	FROM	TO	REMARKS
May 13	L. Reichers	Lockheed Altair: *Liberty*	Harbour Grace, NFLand	x	Forced down eng. trouble ca. 50 mi. off Irish coast. Rescued.
May 20– May 21	A. Earhart	Lockheed Vega	Harbour Grace, NFLand	Culmore, N. Ireland	First solo crossing by a woman.
June 3	S. Haussner	Bellanca: *S. Rosa Maria*	Newark, N.J.	x	Second at- tempt; 1st on May 28. Down at sea off Portugal; rescued after a week afloat.

DATE	CREW	AIRCRAFT	FROM	TO	REMARKS
Aug. 18– Aug. 19	J. Mollison	de Havil- land Puss Moth: *The Heart's Content*	Portmarn- ock, Ireland	Pennfield Ridge, New Brunswick	First solo east to west.
Aug. 23	C. Petersen T. Solberg	Bellanca: *Enna Jettick*	New York	x	Crashed while landing: Darby's Harbour, NFLand. Crew OK.
Aug. 25	C. Lee J. Bochkon	Stinson: *Green Mountain Boy*	Harbour Grace, NFLand	x	Lost
Aug. 23– Sept. 11	G. Hutchinson B. Hutchinson J. Hutchinson K. Hutchinson P. Redpath J. Ruff G. Altissish	Sikorsky: *City of Richmond*	New York	x	Forced down at sea off Greenland; all rescued.
Sept. 13	W. Ulrich L. Pisculli E. Newcomber	Bellanca: *The Amer- ican Nurse*	New York	x	Lost off coast of Spain.

1933

DATE	CREW	AIRCRAFT	FROM	TO	REMARKS
Jan. 16	J. Mermoz & crew	Couzinet: *Arc-en- Ciel*	St. Louis, North Africa	Natal, Brazil	Record cross- ing of South Atlantic (14 hrs.) Return flight May 15.
June 10– June 11	N. Barberan J. Collar	Breguet: *Cuatro Vientos*	Seville, Spain	Camaguey, Cuba	First flight Spain to Cuba; lost in attempt to fly to Mexico City.
July 1– Aug. 23	I. Balbo & others	Savoia- Marchetti	Orbetello, Italy	Chicago, Ill.	Mass flight of 24 flying boats. Return Aug. 8–9.

DATE	CREW	AIRCRAFT	FROM	TO	REMARKS
July 15– July 16	S. Darius S. Girenas	Bellanca: *Lituanica*	New York	x	Crashed: Soldin, Germany; both killed.
July 22– July 23	J. Mollison A. Johnson Mollison	de Havil- land Dragon: *Seafarer*	Pendine Sands, Wales	Bridge- port, Conn.	Cracked up short of desti- nation: New York. Both OK.
Aug. 5– Aug. 7	P. Codos M. Rossi	Blériot- Zappata *Joseph Le Brix*	New York	Rayak, Syria	Distance record: 5657 mi.
Aug. 5	J. Grierson	de Havil- land Gypsy Moth: *Rouge et Noir*	Brough, England	x	Flight aban- doned Reykjavik, Iceland, after takeoff ac- cident.
Aug. 8	J. Adamowicz B. Adamowicz E. Bergin	Bellanca: *White Eagle*	New York	x	Crashed land- ing at Harbour Grace, NFLand. Destination had been War- saw, Poland.
Sept. 2	F. de Pinedo	Bellanca: *Santa Lucia*	New York	x	Takeoff crash: de Pinedo killed.

1934

DATE	CREW	AIRCRAFT	FROM	TO	REMARKS
May 14– May 15	G. Pond C. Sabelli	Bellanca: *Leonardo da Vinci*	New York	Lahinch, Ireland	Destination: Rome; forced to land with engine trouble.
May 27– May 28	P. Codos M. Rossi	Blériot- Zappata: *Joseph Le Brix*	Paris	New York	Destination: San Francisco; forced down with engine trouble.
June 28– June 30	B. Adamowicz J. Adamowicz H. Hoiriis	Bellanca: *City of Warsaw*	New York	St. André de Messel, France	Continued on to Warsaw.

DATE	CREW	AIRCRAFT	FROM	TO	REMARKS
July 21– Aug. 27	J. Grierson	de Havil- land Fox Moth: *Robert Bruce*	Rochester, England	New York	Flight made in stages: Green- land, Canada, U. S.
Aug. 8– Aug. 9	J. Ayling L. Reid	de Havil- land Dragon: *Trail of the Caribou*	Wasaga Beach, Ont.	Heston, England	Distance at- tempt; mech. trouble ex- hausted fuel; aircraft formerly be- longed to Mol- lisons as *Seafarer II.*
Aug. 27– Sept. 6	R. Light R. Wilson	Bellanca: *Asulinak*	Cart- wright, Labrador	Edinburgh, Scotland	Continued on to Manila, P.I.
Dec. 15– Dec. 20	P. Hondong H. van Balkom Z. van der Molen J. Stolk	Fokker F-7	Amster- dam, Holland	Parama- ribo, Dutch Guiana, South America	Survey flight for future air route.

1935

DATE	CREW	AIRCRAFT	FROM	TO	REMARKS
June 22	G. de Monteverde A. de Monteverde	Bellanca: *Magellan*	New York	x	Takeoff crash; no serious injuries.
July 28– Aug. 16	T. Solberg P. Oscanyan	Loening: *Leiv Eiriksson*	Cart- wright, Labrador	Bergen, Norway	In stages: Greenland, Iceland, Faroe Is.
Sept. 21– Sept. 22	F. Waitkus	Lockheed Vega: *Lituanica II*	New York	Ballin- robe, Ireland	Forced down by weather; destination Kevno, Lithuania.

1936

DATE	CREW	AIRCRAFT	FROM	TO	REMARKS
May 6– May 9	H. Eckener crew & pas- sengers	Airship LZ-129: *Hinden- burg*	Frankfurt, Germany	Lakehurst, N.J.	Ist trip of *Hindenburg*; destroyed by explosion a year later.
Sept. 3	H. Merrill H. Richman	Vultee: *Lady Peace*	Harbour Grace, NFLand	Llandilo, Wales	Forced down short of desti- nation: London
Sept. 4– Sept. 5	B. Markham	Percival Vega Gull: *Messenger*	Abingdon, England	Cape Breton I., Nova Scotia	First solo east to west by woman; desti- nation NY; forced down by lack of fuel.
Sept. 14	H. Merrill H. Richman	Vultee: *Lady Peace*	Birkdale, England	Musgrave Harbour, NFLand	Return flight; forced down by weather.
Oct. 6	K. Bjorkvall	Bellanca: Pacemaker	New York	x	Forced down at sea off Irish coast; rescued.
Oct. 29	J. Mollison	Bellanca Flash: *Dorothy*	Harbour Grace, NFLand	Croydon, England	First west to east flight. for Mollison.
Dec. 7	J. Mermoz & crew	Latécoère: *Croix du Sud*	Dakar, North Africa	x	South Atlantic survey flight. Lost.

1937

DATE	CREW	AIRCRAFT	FROM	TO	REMARKS
May 8– May 9	H. Merrill J. Lambie	Lockheed Electra	New York	North Weald, England	Round-trip flight; return: May 13–14.

DATE	CREW	AIRCRAFT	FROM	TO	REMARKS
July 4– July 9	A. Wilcockson & crew	Short S-23 *Caledonia*	Southampton, England	New York	Commercial survey flight east to west. Imperial Airways
July 5– July 6	H. Gray & crew	Sikorsky S-42: *Clipper III*	Botwood, NFLand	Foynes, Ireland	Commercial survey flight: west to east; Pan American Airways

1938

DATE	CREW	AIRCRAFT	FROM	TO	REMARKS
July 17– July 18	D. Corrigan	Curtiss Robin: *Sunshine*	New York	Baldonnel, Ireland	A miracle
July 20– July 21	D. Bennett A. Coster	Short Mercury	Foynes, Ireland	Montreal & New York	Upper section of Mayo Composite; deliver mail. Return: July 25–27
Aug. 10– Aug. 11	A. Henke & crew	Focke- Wulf Kondor: *Brandenburg*	Berlin	New York	Commercial survey flight. Return: Aug. 14–15. Lufthansa Airlines.
Aug. 23	H. Guillaumet & crew.	Latécoère: *Lieutenant de Vaisseau de Paris*	Bordeaux, France	New York	Commercial survey flight via Lisbon & Azores. Return: Aug. 23. Air France– Transatlantique.

1939

DATE	CREW	AIRCRAFT	FROM	TO	REMARKS
Apr. 28– Apr. 29	V. Kokkinaki M. Gordienko	ZKB 26: *Moskva*	Moscow, Russia	Miscou I., Canada	Forced down short of dest: New York; low on fuel.
May 16	C. Backman	Monocoupe 90-A	Gander, NFLand	x	Lost
May 20– May 21	L. LaPorte & crew	Boeing 314: *Yankee Clipper*	New York	Northamp- ton, Eng.	Commercial mail crossing via Azores, Lisbon, Marseilles. Pan American
May 28	T. Smith	Aeronca Chief: *Baby Clipper*	Old Orchard Beach, Me.	x	Lost
June 17– June 19	Culbertson & crew	Boeing 314: *Yankee Clipper*	New York	Southamp- ton, England	First com- mercial passenger flight. Scheduled flights begun June 28-via Azores, Lisbon, Marseilles. Pan American.
Aug. 5	J. Kelly- Rogers & crew	Short S-30 Caribou	Southamp- ton, England	New York	Mail service; in-flight re- fueling; inter- rupted by war. Imperial Air- ways.
Aug. 11	A. Loeb R. Decker	Ryan Brougham *Shalom*	Cape Breton Is., Nova Scotia	x	Lost

Bibliography

Alcock, John, and Brown, Arthur Whitten. *Our Transatlantic Flight*. London: William Kimber & Co., Ltd., 1969.

Allen, Richard S. *Revolution in the Sky*. Brattleboro, Vt.: Stephen Greene Press, 1964.

Briand, Jr., Paul L., *Daughter of the Sky*. New York: Duell, Sloan & Pearce, 1960.

Byrd, Richard E. *Skyward*. New York: G. P. Putnam's Sons, 1928.

Chamberlin, Clarence D. *Record Flights*. Philadelphia: Dorrance & Co., 1928.

Corrigan, Douglas. *That's My Story*. New York: E. P. Dutton & Co., 1938.

de la Croix, Robert. *They Flew the Atlantic*. London: Frederick Muller Ltd., 1958.

Delear, Frank J. *Igor Sikorsky*. New York: Dodd, Mead & Co., 1969.

Earhart, Amelia *20 HRS. 40 MIN*. New York: G. P. Putnam's Sons, 1928.

————. *The Fun of It*. New York: Brewer, Warren & Putnam, 1932.

Ellis, F. H. & E. M. *Atlantic Air Conquest*. London: William Kimber & Co., Ltd., 1963.

Fokker, Anthony H. G., and Gould, Bruce. *Flying Dutchman*. New York: Henry Holt & Co., 1931.

Lindbergh, Charles A. *We*. New York: G. P. Putnam's Sons, 1928.

————. *The Spirit of St. Louis*. New York: Charles Scribner's Sons, 1953.

McDonough, Kenneth. *Atlantic Wings*. Hemel Hempstead, Hertforshire, England: Model Aeronautical Press, Ltd., 1966.

Roseberry, C. R. *The Challenging Skies*. Garden City, N.Y.: Doubleday & Co., 1966.

Sikorsky, Igor I. *The Story of the Winged-S*. New York: Dodd, Mead & Co., 1938.

Steirman, Hy, and Kittler, Glenn D. *Triumph: The Incredible Saga of the First Transatlantic Flight*. New York: Harper & Brothers, 1961.

Toland, John. *Ships in the Sky*. London: Frederick Muller, Ltd., 1957.

Walton, Francis, ed. *The Airman's Almanac*. New York: Farrar & Rinehart, Inc., 1945.

Wykes, Alan. *Air Atlantic*. New York: David White, Inc., 1969 (?).

Acknowledgments

Many have willingly contributed to the making of this volume; in addition to the authors whose works are listed in the bibliography, I owe much to a number of people who gave of their time and expertise most gracefully. A special thanks must be given to Charles L. Betts, Jr., of Yardley, Pennsylvania, who presented me with his aviation scrapbook plus a collection of clippings— enough to fill another volume—from which it was possible to reconstruct some of the background of the flights narrated in my text directly from the materials of the period, before anyone realized they were making history. The hundreds of articles, clippings from magazines and newspapers, as well as photographs (many in nostalgia-inducing rotogravure), made possible the identification of aircraft, individuals, dating and other fact-finding that might otherwise have been wearying and time-consuming.

Others who helped to make the work lighter were: R. W. Bradford, Curator, Aviation and Space Division, National Museum of Science and Technology, Ottawa, Canada; William G. Bridgman, Photographic Services Librarian, University of Georgia; Alan Dashiell, an old friend and lighter-than-air enthusiast, of Trenton, New Jersey; C. F. de Jersey, The de Havilland Aircraft of Canada, Limited; E. G. Fielding, Vickers Limited, London; Harry M. Halstead, Bellanca Aircraft Corporation, Alexandria, Minnesota; Lt. Col. Gerald M. Holland, Chief, Magazine & Book Branch, Public Information Division, Department of the Air Force, Washington, D. C.; William Kavanagh, USM, Rockaway Park, New York; Karl H. Koepcke, Lufthansa, New York; Mrs. Frances L. Kohl, Ryan Aeronautical Company, San Diego, California; Althea Lister, Curator, Clipper Hall, Pan American Airways, New York; Commander William Martin, USN, who participated in a latter-day transatlantic aerial adventure (which began for him with a plunge into New York's East River); Frank A. McClung, Sikorsky Aircraft, Stratford, Connecticut; Claudia Oakes, National Air and Space Museum, Smithsonian Institution, Washington, D. C.; C. R. Roseberry, author of the classic *The Challenging Skies,* of Albany, New York; John E. Scott, Hawker Siddeley Aviation, Hatfield, England; Wanda and Jerry Simpson, Saginaw, Michigan; William Wagner, Ryan Aeronautical Library, San Diego, California; Paul White, National Archives, Washington, D. C.; and last, but far from least, Robert B. Wood, Chief, Information and Research Divisions, National Air and Space Museum, Smithsonian Institution, Washington, D. C.

Finally, a brief personal note: an expression of gratitude to my editor, Ray A. Roberts, whose kindness and patience during the research and writing of *The Great Transatlantic Aerial Adventure* (which took longer than either of us had imagined at the beginning) were helpful and steadying; I hope that some of his enthusiasm for the project has been revealed in my text.

My thanks, too, to Barbara Probst and Kathie Fried, who so meticulously copy edited the manuscript without once wounding the ego of the author and who more than once saved that author from himself. The work was gently authoritative but never obtrusive so that the author can only admit that if any error, factual twist or slip remain, the fault is all his. And a special thank you to Jack Meserole for the handsome design job.

Index